THE INCOMPARABLE CHRIST

The London Lectures in Contemporary Christianity

This is an annual series of lectures founded in 1974 to promote Christian thought about contemporary issues. Their aim is to expound an aspect of historical biblical Christianity and to relate it to a contemporary issue in the church in the world. They seek to be scholarly in content yet popular enough in appeal and style to attract the educated public; and to present each topic in such a way as to be of interest to the widest possible audience as well as to the Christian public.

Recent lectures:

1994 'Transforming Leadership: A Christian approach to managing organizations', *Richard Higginson*

1995 'The Spirit of the Age', *Roy McCloughry*

1996 'The Word on the Box: Christians in the media', *Justin Philips, Graham Mytton, Alan Rogers, Robert McLeish, Tim Dean*

1997 'Matters of Life and Death: Contemporary medical dilemmas in the light of the Christian faith', *Professor John Wyatt* (published by IVP in 1998 as *Matters of Life and Death: Today's healthcare dilemmas in the light of Christian faith*)

1998 'Endless Conflict or Empty Tolerance: The Christian response to a multi-faith world', *Dr Vinoth Ramachandra* (published by IVP in 1999 as *Faiths in Conflict: Christian integrity in a multicultural world*)

2000 'The Incomparable Christ: Celebrating his millennial birth', *John Stott*

2001 'Moral Leadership', *Bishop James Jones*

The London Lectures Trust

The London Lectures in Contemporary Christianity are organized by the London Lectures Trust, which was established as a charity in 1994. The committee represents several different evangelical organizations.

THE
INCOMPARABLE
CHRIST

JOHN STOTT

Based on the AD 2000 London Lectures
in Contemporary Christianity

Inter-Varsity Press

INTER-VARSITY PRESS
38 De Montfort Street, Leicester LE1 7GP, England
Email: ivp@uccf.org.uk
Website: www.ivpbooks.com

First published 2001

British Library Cataloguing in Publication Data
A catalogue record for this book is available from the British Library.

ISBN 0–85111–485–7

Set in Garamond
Typeset in Great Britain
Printed in Great Britain by Creative Print and Design (Wales), Ebbw Vale.

Inter-Varsity Press is the publishing division of the Universities and Colleges Christian Fellowship (formerly the Inter-Varsity Fellowship), a student movement linking Christian Unions in universities and colleges throughout Great Britain, and a member movement of the International Fellowship of Evangelical Students. For more information about local and national activities write to UCCF, 38 De Montfort Street, Leicester LE1 7GP, email us at email@uccf.org.uk, or visit the UCCF website at www.uccf.org.uk.

CONTENTS

PART II: THE ECCLESIASTICAL JESUS
(or how the church has presented him)

PART III: THE INFLUENTIAL JESUS
(or how he has inspired people)

PART IV: THE ETERNAL JESUS
(or how he challenges us today)

FOREWORD

I have no doubt, as Archbishop of Canterbury, that the greatest and most important task we have as Christians today, whatever our denomination, is to name the Name, and to do so not only with the greatest of courtesy for the beliefs of others, but also with a conviction that the person of Christ continues to meet the longings and hopes of every human heart.

Dr John Stott has made the subject of Jesus Christ the centre of his life's work and study. From his pen have flowed penetrating works that combine scholarship with years of passionate commitment to the pastoral and evangelistic work of the church. From his mouth have flowed powerful and convincing expositions of the relevance of Christ for today.

But while John is a brilliant and well-read scholar, he has never been an ivory-tower theologian. He falls into the classic Anglican tradition of the 'teaching pastor'. His classroom has been first the parish and second the world. He has not sought academic position or ecclesiastical preferment. And yet, according to no less an authority than David Edwards, 'With the exception of William Temple, John Stott is the most influential clergyman in the Church of England of the twentieth century.'

John, being the humble man of God he is, will shift uncomfortably at these words. But I too want to pay tribute to this remarkable ministry in the contemporary church.

The four main objectives of the London Lectures are: 'to expound some aspect of historic biblical Christianity; to relate it to a contemporary issue in the church or the world; to be scholarly in content, yet popular enough in appeal and style to attract the educated public; and to present each topic in such a way as to be of interest to the secular as well as the Christian public'.

These four objectives are, in my opinion, an exact outline of John's own ministry, from the earliest days when he was a curate here at All Souls, Langham Place, to his current role as an international ambassador for Jesus Christ. His biographer, Bishop Timothy Dudley-Smith, sums up his ministry with these words: 'no one can read John Stott's writings without being aware that his concern is to teach and expound a revealed faith, and to interpret the authoritative and timeless Scriptures for a contemporary world'. John, as pastor, preacher, scholar, writer, apologist, evangelist and brother Christian, we thank God for you, and your long and graced ministry.

The London Lectures in Contemporary Christianity, which John himself founded in 1974, have apparently never had the founder as a lecturer until now. It is most fitting, therefore, that in this millennium year he should be the one to deliver the series. It is also most fitting that in this millennium year the theme should be the one that has always been the centre of John's ministry: the incomparable Christ.

Dr George Carey
Archbishop of Canterbury

CHAIRMAN'S PREFACE

It seemed fitting to the London Lectures Management Committee that in the millennial year we should focus our attention on Jesus, and especially fitting that John Stott, whose vision and energy had given rise to the lecture series, should be invited to lecture.

Our hopes were not misplaced. A lively crowd attended the lectures, All Souls Church in London being nearly full on each of the four Thursdays. The last lecture was given in the presence of Her Royal Highness Princess Alexandra and was introduced by the Archbishop of Canterbury. The talks provided much to stimulate the mind and warm the heart. The scholarship and personal enthusiasm of the lecturer were clear, as he drew on a lifetime's work and study of great breadth and depth, whose focus and centre have always been Christ.

I am delighted to commend this thought-provoking and inspiring study of Jesus on behalf of the London Lectures Committee.

John Grayston
Chairman, London Lectures Committee

ACKNOWLEDGMENTS

I am deeply grateful to the London Lectures Committee both for inviting me to deliver the AD 2000 lectures and for proposing that the only appropriate topic would be Jesus himself, whose millennial birthday we were supposed to be celebrating. Having made those two decisions, the Committee left me free to develop the chosen theme at my discretion. But they offered me steady encouragement, with John Grayston an excellent chairman and Betty Baker a conscientious and efficient secretary.

I am also grateful to several friends who lent me books, gave me advice and helped me compile a bibliography. I am thinking, in particular, of Richard Bewes, Dick France, Timothy Dudley-Smith, Paul Barnett, Paul Blackham, John W. Yates III, René Padilla and Eunice Burton.

In addition, I am thankful to Inter-Varsity Press, the publishers, to Stephanie Heald, the editor, and to Steve Motyer and David Wright. They were appointed by IVP as the official readers of the manuscript and made a number of perceptive comments.

But my special thanks are due to Corey Widmer, my current study assistant, whose horizons were bounded by the lectures for about eighteen months. In a very personal way he has taken them to his heart. He has shown remarkable persistence in surfing the net, in tracking down references I could not find, in discovering books I needed to consult or read, and in making full use of the facilities of the recently opened British Library. As for the text of the lectures, he must have read it at least ten times at different stages. His suggestions have always been positive and helpful, and he also wrote the study guides which accompany the set of four video-tapes of the lectures. For all this I thank him very much indeed.

Then both of us have relied much on Frances Whitehead: her unique perseverance as my personal secretary for 45 years, her considerable computer skills, and her willingness to see the text through its three main stages – the original edition, its abbreviation for the spoken lectures, and its conversion into this book. When in April 2001 it was announced in a public meeting that the Archbishop of Canterbury had decided to honour her with a Lambeth MA degree, those present gave her an immediate and spontaneous standing ovation.

So I send the book on its way, with the hope and prayer that many readers will acknowledge Jesus Christ as the proper object of our worship, witness and hope, and as deserving the description 'incomparable'. For he has neither rivals nor peers.

John Stott
July 2001

INTRODUCTION

1. The centrality of Jesus

'Regardless of what anyone may personally think or believe about him, Jesus of Nazareth has been the dominant figure in the history of western culture for almost twenty centuries.' So wrote Jaroslav Pelikan at the beginning of his wide-ranging book *Jesus through the Centuries*.[1]

It seemed appropriate, therefore, that the millennial London Lectures in Contemporary Christianity should be concerned with Jesus Christ, since it is his birthday (whatever its precise date may have been) that we have been celebrating. Consider his dominance in three spheres.

First, Jesus is *the centre of history*. At least a large proportion of the human race continues to divide history into BC and AD by reference to his birth. In the year 2000 the world population reached 6,000 million, while the estimated number of Christians was 1,700 million or about 28%.[2] So nearly one third of the human race professes to follow him.

Secondly, Jesus is *the focus of Scripture*. The Bible is not a random collection of religious documents. As Jesus himself said, 'The Scriptures ... bear witness to me' (John 5:39, RSV). And Christian scholars have always recognized this. Jerome, for example, the great church father of the fourth and fifth centuries, wrote that 'ignorance of the Scriptures is ignorance of Christ'.[3]

In the sixteenth century, it is noteworthy that both Erasmus of the Renaissance and Luther of the Reformation emphasized the same centrality of Christ. The Bible 'will give Christ to you', wrote Erasmus, 'in an intimacy so close that he would be less visible to you if he stood before your eyes'.[4] Luther similarly, in his *Lectures on Romans*, was clear that Christ is the key to Scripture. In his gloss on Romans 1:5 he wrote: 'Here the door is thrown open wide for the understanding of Holy Scripture, that is, that everything must be understood in relation to Christ.' And later he wrote 'that the entire Scripture deals only with Christ everywhere'.[5]

Thirdly, Jesus is *the heart of mission*. Why is it that some Christians cross land and sea, continents and cultures, as missionaries? What on earth impels them? It is not in order to commend a civilization, an institution or an ideology, but rather a person, Jesus Christ, whom they believe to be unique. This is particularly clear in the Christian mission to the world of Islam. 'Our task', wrote scholarly missionary Bishop Stephen Neill, 'is to go on saying to the Muslim with infinite patience, "Sir, consider Jesus". We have no other message ... It is not the case that the Muslim has seen Jesus of Nazareth and has rejected him; he has never seen him ...'[6]

But those who do see Jesus and surrender to him, acknowledge him to be at the centre of their conversion experience. Take as an example Sadhu Sundar Singh. Born in 1889 into an affluent Sikh family in India, he grew up to hate Christianity as (in his view) a foreign religion. He even expressed his hostility at the age of fifteen, by publicly burning a Gospel. But three days afterwards he was converted through a vision of Christ, and later, though still in his teens, he determined to become a Sadhu, a wandering holy man and preacher.[7] On one occasion Sundar Singh visited a Hindu college and was accosted rather aggressively by a lecturer who asked him what he had found in Christianity that he did not have in his old religion. 'I have Christ', he replied. 'Yes, I know', continued the lecturer impatiently, 'but what particular principle or doctrine have you found that you did not have before?' 'The particular thing I have found', replied Sundar Singh, 'is Christ'.[8]

But which Jesus are we talking about? For the fact is that there are many Jesuses on the overcrowded shelves of the world's religious markets. Already before the end of the first Christian century the tendency had begun for teachers to create an image of Jesus according to their own whim and fancy. So Paul had to remind the Corinthian Christians that he had betrothed them 'to one husband, to Christ', in order that ultimately he might present them 'as a pure virgin to him'. But he was afraid, he added, lest their minds should be led astray from their 'sincere and pure devotion to Christ' (2 Cor. 11:2).

My plan, therefore, is to investigate (in Parts I and IV of this book) the Christ of the New Testament witness, and to consider in church history how some people have presented him (Part II) and how others have been influenced by him (Part III).

To elaborate this, my concern is to ask and answer four basic questions about Christ.

First, *how does the New Testament bear witness to him?* I hope to show that its testimony to Jesus, although admittedly rich in its diversity, is at the same time recognizedly a united witness. I am calling Part I 'The original Jesus'.

Secondly, *how has the church portrayed Jesus Christ down the centuries?* I am calling Part II 'The ecclesiastical Jesus', because I want to consider how the church at different times, now faithfully, now unfaithfully, has presented Christ to the world.

Thirdly, *what influence has Christ had in history?* This third part is complementary to the second, as we move on from the church's presentation of Christ to Christ's challenge to the church. Our perspective now, however, will not be the successive stages of church history, but rather the successive stages of Christ's career, and how each stage (with its different emphasis) has inspired different people. I am calling this part 'The influential Jesus'.

Fourthly, *what should Jesus Christ mean to us today?* In Part IV we will remind ourselves that Jesus Christ is not only historical (indeed, a figure of distant history) but eternal (in fact 'the same yesterday, today and for ever'), and therefore also our contemporary. He confronts every new generation, century and millennium in his roles of Saviour, Lord and Judge. The context for this fourth and final study will be the New Testament's last book, the book of Revelation, the Christian apocalypse. For in its very first verse it claims to be not primarily a prophecy but 'the revelation of Jesus Christ'. We will focus on the ten main visions of Christ in the book of Revelation.

This book, therefore, will be a blend of Scripture and history. We will consider the church's presentation of Christ and Christ's influence on the church, against the background of the New Testament in general and the book of Revelation in particular. In this way the biblical portrait of Christ is seen to be normative. He is the authentic Jesus by whom all the fallible human pictures of him must be judged. My hope is that these studies in the Bible and church history will be seen to justify my title, *The incomparable Christ*. There is nobody like him; there never has been, and there never will be.

2. History and theology

Many would advise us to begin our New Testament survey with the letters, not the gospels, since the letters came first. Paul's first letter to the Thessalonians was written from Corinth in or soon after AD 50, only twenty years after the death and resurrection of Jesus, whereas the gospels were published at least a decade or two later. Bishop Paul Barnett has mounted a sustained critique of this tendency to begin with the gospels. 'The flood of literature attempting to recover the "historical" Jesus has limited its field of enquiry to the Jesus of the gospels; the letters and the early church have generally been ignored.'[9]

And yet, in its wisdom the early church put the gospels first because, although published later, the events they record took place earlier. Moreover, if read first, we are immediately confronted by the historical figure of Jesus. But is his portrait in the gospels authentically historical?

The twentieth-century emphasis among theological scholars was on the quest of the historical Jesus. The so-called 'first' or 'original' quest is associated with Albert Schweitzer, whose book of this title was published in 1906.[10] It is a monumental survey of all the romantic nineteenth-century 'Lives of Jesus'. Schweitzer himself portrayed Jesus as an eschatological prophet, whose expectation of an imminent end was never fulfilled. This quest, initiated by Schweitzer, concluded with Bultmann, who belongs to the twentieth century and who claimed that to demonstrate the historicity of Jesus was neither possible nor (if it were) necessary for faith.

So after the Second World War, the new quest of the historical Jesus began. It is usually dated from an address given in 1953 by Ernst Käsemann, a former disciple of Bultmann, entitled 'The Problem of the Historical Jesus'. He expressed himself dissatisfied with Bultmann's extreme scepticism. He and other 'post-Bult-mannians' urged a more positive view of history and tended to regard Jesus as a teaching sage, a religious genius or a social revolutionary – constructions which present Jesus as too tame either to provoke his crucifixion or to launch the worldwide Christian movement.

And now, since the 1980s, some scholars have been heralding

the birth of the third quest of the historical Jesus.[11] One of its most significant features is that the Christian and Jewish scholars who are involved in it are stressing both the Jewishness of Jesus and his mission to vindicate and restore Israel. This third quest expresses a greater confidence in the reliability of the gospels' portrait of Jesus.

Such confidence is by no means universal, however, as is evident from 'The Jesus Seminar' in the United States. Jointly founded in 1985 by Robert W. Funk and John Dominic Crossan, its seventy-five or so 'fellows' have been meeting twice a year in order to assess the authenticity of all the sayings attributed to Jesus. They have used a colour-code, namely red for undoubtedly authentic sayings, pink for those which are probably so, grey for sayings which are not authentic but close, and black for those which are not authentic at all but a later tradition. Their book *The Five Gospels: what did Jesus really say?* (the fifth being the apocryphal Gospel of Thomas) concluded that in their view '82% of the words ascribed to Jesus in the Gospels were not actually spoken by him'. Now they have turned from an examination of the words of Jesus to his works. Their study is not likely to be any more profitable, however, as their criteria are largely subjective.[12]

Before looking at the gospels ourselves, we need to report a significant shift of emphasis among scholars from history to theology. Whereas 'form criticism' was preoccupied with the concerns of the early church, 'redaction criticism' is preoccupied rather with the concerns of the individual gospel authors. However strong our conviction may be that they are conscientious historians (as Luke claims in 1:1–4), it is also important to hold that they are evangelists, consciously proclaiming the gospel, and theologians, developing their own distinctive emphasis. This being so, it is clear that the process of divine inspiration did not smother the personality of the human authors. For this is the double authorship of Scripture, that God chose to speak his word through human words. The Holy Spirit selected, fashioned, prepared and equipped the human authors in order to communicate through each a message that is both appropriate and distinctive.

PART I

THE ORIGINAL JESUS

(or how the New Testament witnesses to him)

PART I: THE ORIGINAL JESUS
(or how the New Testament witnesses to him)

The four gospels

1. The Gospel of Matthew:
Christ the fulfilment of Scripture

How thankful we should be that in God's providence we have four gospels! For Jesus Christ is too great and glorious a person to be captured by one author or depicted from one perspective. The Jesus of the gospels is a portrait with four faces, a diamond with four facets.

What then is the major feature of Jesus according to Matthew? It can be stated in one word: *fulfilment*. Strongly Jewish in his origin and culture, Matthew portrays Jesus as the fulfilment of the Old Testament. For his Gospel serves as a bridge between the two testaments, between preparation and fulfilment. Consider these words of Jesus recorded in Matthew 13:16–17: 'Blessed are your eyes because they see, and your ears because they hear. For I tell you the truth, many prophets and righteous men longed to see what you see but did not see it, and to hear what you hear but did not hear it.'

In other words, the Old Testament prophets lived in the period of anticipation; the apostles were living in the time of fulfilment. Their eyes were actually seeing, and their ears actually hearing, what their predecessors had longed to see and hear. So Matthew does not portray Jesus so much as another prophet, one more seer in the succession of the centuries, but rather as the fulfilment of all prophecy. It was in and with the ministry of Jesus that the long-awaited kingdom of God had come.

First, then, Matthew's Christ was *the fulfilment of prophecy*. This is forced on our attention by the genealogy with which the Gospel begins (1:1–17). For Matthew traces Jesus' lineage back to Abraham, the father of the chosen people, through whom God promised to bless the world, and to David, the greatest of Israel's kings, who was the exemplar of the great king to come. Thus Matthew gives the genealogy of the royal line. His concern is to show that Jesus was 'the son of David' (a title he uses more often than the three other evangelists together), who had a right to David's throne.

Matthew's favourite formula is 'now this took place that it might be fulfilled which was written'. It occurs eleven times. His anxiety is to demonstrate that everything that happened had been predicted and that everything predicted had been fulfilled. In addition, Matthew sees in the story of Jesus a recapitulation of the story of Israel. As Israel had been oppressed in Egypt under the despotic Pharaoh, so the baby Jesus became a refugee in Egypt under the despotic Herod. As Israel passed through the waters of the Red Sea, in order to be tested in the wilderness for forty years, so Jesus passed through the waters of John's baptism at the River Jordan, in order to be tested in the wilderness of Judea for forty days. Again, as Moses from Mount Sinai gave Israel the law, so Jesus from the Mount of the Beatitudes gave his followers the true interpretation and amplification of the law.

The theme of fulfilment is most clearly displayed in Jesus' inauguration of the kingdom of God. All four evangelists write that he proclaimed the kingdom, but Matthew had his special emphasis. In deference to Jewish reluctance to pronounce the sacred name of God, Matthew uses instead the expression 'the kingdom of heaven' (about fifty times). He also grasps that the kingdom is both a present reality (for the kingdom had 'come upon' them, 12:28) and a future expectation (for at the end of history the King would sit on his glorious throne and judge the nations, 25:31–46). In all these ways – in the genealogy, in Matthew's favourite formula, in the recapitulation of the story of Israel and in his teaching about the kingdom – Matthew's Christ is the fulfilment of prophecy.

Secondly, Matthew's Christ is *the fulfilment of the law*. Jesus seemed to his contemporaries to be disrespectful to the law: for example, breaking the sabbath law, flouting the laws of ritual purification and neglecting the law of fasting. He seemed to be lax where they were strict. But Jesus insisted that he was loyal to the law. Some scholars think that Matthew deliberately portrayed Jesus as the new Moses. For, just as there are five books of Moses in the Pentateuch, so there are five collections of Jesus' teaching in Matthew's Gospel, which is a kind of Christian Pentateuch.

At all events, Matthew records these words of Jesus:

'Do not think that I have come to abolish the Law or the Prophets; I have not come to abolish them but to fulfil them. I tell you the truth, until heaven and earth disappear, not the smallest letter, not the least stroke of a pen, will by any means disappear from the Law until everything is accomplished … For I tell you that unless your righteousness surpasses that of the Pharisees and the teachers of the law, you will certainly not enter the kingdom of heaven' (Matt. 5:17–18, 20).

The disciples must have been dumbfounded by these words of Jesus, for the Pharisees were the most righteous people in the world. How, then, could the followers of Jesus be more righteous than the most righteous people on earth? The Master must be joking! But Christian righteousness is greater than Pharisaic righteousness because it is deeper. It is a righteousness of the heart, a righteousness not of words and deeds only, but especially of thoughts and motives (see Matt. 5:21–30). It is in this sense that Jesus was the fulfilment of the law. He took it to its logical conclusion. He looked beyond a superficial understanding of it to its radical demand for heart-righteousness.

Thirdly, Matthew's Christ is *the fulfilment of Israel.* This is the most subtle of the three fulfilments. It is possible to read Matthew and miss it. Matthew sees Jesus confronting Israel with a final summons to repent. So Jesus told the apostles that he had been sent 'only to the lost sheep of Israel' (15:24) and that they were to go only 'to the lost sheep of Israel' (10:6). Later, of course, Jesus' great commission would open the apostles' horizons to the Gentile world; now, however, during his earthly ministry, Israel was to be given one more chance. But they persisted in their rebellion. So Jesus wept over the city, expressed his longing to have gathered her citizens under the shelter of his wings, and warned her that his judgment would fall on that very generation, which happened of course in AD 70 (Matt. 23:36–39).

Thus Jesus saw himself as the sole surviving representative of authentic Israel. He alone remained faithful; otherwise the whole nation had become apostate. At the same time, he was the beginning of a new Israel. So he deliberately chose twelve apostles as equivalent to the twelve tribes and as the nucleus of the new Israel. To them the kingdom of God would be transferred (21:43). Moreover, he called this people his 'church', a counter-cultural community characterized by the values and standards of his kingdom, as described in the Sermon on the Mount.

Jesus also made it clear that this new Israel would be interracial and international, and salt and light to the world. It is especially remarkable that Matthew, the most Jewish of the four evangelists, nevertheless portrays near the beginning of his Gospel the visit of those mysterious Magi, representatives of the Gentile nations, and at its end the commission of the risen Lord to go and disciple the nations. Thus his kingdom community would grow like a mustard seed from tiny, unpropitious beginnings until it fills the earth: 'I say to you that many will come from the east and the west, and will take their places at the feast with Abraham, Isaac and Jacob in the kingdom of heaven' (Matt. 8:11).

2. The Gospel of Mark: Christ the Suffering Servant

If Matthew presents Jesus as the Christ of Scripture, Mark presents him as the Suffering Servant of the Lord, who dies for his people's sins. The cross is at the centre of Mark's understanding of Jesus.

Mark's Gospel, like the other three, is strictly anonymous. Its author does not disclose his identity, but a very ancient tradition attributes the second gospel to Mark. At the same time, there is known to have been a close association between Mark and the apostle Peter. Papias, Bishop of Hierapolis at the beginning of the second century, called Mark Peter's 'interpreter', who recorded Peter's memoirs and sermons. Certainly there are more references to Peter in Mark's Gospel than in the others, and Mark tells more fully and vividly than the other evangelists the follies, foibles and denials of Peter. Some have suggested that this gave Mark a fellow-feeling with Peter, because Mark too had been a failure. If the young man who fled naked in the garden of Gethsemane was Mark (14:51–52), then he also ran away. And during Paul's first missionary journey he ran away a second time (Acts 13:13; 15:37–

38). But if, like Peter, Mark had denied Jesus, like Peter he had also been restored. For in later New Testament letters we find Mark giving loyal service to both Peter and Paul. For example, 'Mark ... is helpful to me in my ministry', wrote Paul (2 Tim. 4:11).

Consider now a crucial passage from Mark's Gospel, which brings together three of his favourite themes, namely who Jesus was, what he had come to do, and what he requires of his followers. This text is a turning point in the Gospel because it was a turning point in the ministry of Jesus. Before this incident Jesus had been fêted as a popular teacher and healer; from now on he warned his disciples of the coming cross.

> Jesus and his disciples went on to the villages around Caesarea Philippi. On the way he asked them, 'Who do people say I am?'
>
> They replied, 'Some say John the Baptist; others say Elijah; and still others, one of the prophets.'
>
> 'But what about you?' he asked. 'Who do you say I am?' Peter answered, 'You are the Christ.'
>
> Jesus warned them not to tell anyone about him.
>
> He then began to teach them that the Son of Man must suffer many things and be rejected by the elders, chief priests and teachers of the law, and that he must be killed and after three days rise again. He spoke plainly about this, and Peter took him aside and began to rebuke him.
>
> But when Jesus turned and looked at his disciples, he rebuked Peter. 'Out of my sight, Satan!' he said. 'You do not have in mind the things of God, but the things of men.'
>
> Then he called the crowd to him along with his disciples and said, 'If anyone would come after me, he must deny himself and take up his cross and follow me. For whoever wants to save his life will lose it, but whoever loses his life for me and for the gospel will save it. What good is it for a man to gain the whole world, yet forfeit his soul? Or what can a man give in exchange for his soul? If anyone is ashamed of me and my words in this adulterous and sinful generation, the Son of Man will be ashamed of him when he comes in his Father's glory with the holy angels' (Mark 8:27–38).

First, *consider who Jesus was.* He knew there was a difference between the people's public perceptions of his identity and the apostles' private dawning conviction. According to public opinion he was John the Baptist, Elijah or another prophet; according to the Twelve he was not another prophet, but 'the Christ', the fulfilment of all prophecy. Matthew adds 'the Son of God', probably meaning not that he was the eternal Son, but (as in Psalm 2:7–8) the Messiah.

Immediately after the disciples had made this confession of faith, 'Jesus warned them not to tell anyone about him' (8:30), but to remain silent and keep his identity a secret. This command to silence and secrecy has puzzled many readers. But it is not hard to understand, for Mark has already given two examples of the command to silence. After curing a leprosy sufferer, Jesus said to him 'See that you don't tell this to anyone' (1:44). And after a deaf-mute had been healed, Jesus 'commanded them not to tell anyone' (7:36). But why were they to keep their mouths shut? The reason is that the public had false political notions of the Messiah. For more than 700 years Israel had been oppressed by a foreign yoke, except for a brief and intoxicating period of freedom under the Maccabees. But now the people were dreaming that Yahweh was going to intervene again, that his enemies would be destroyed, that his people would be liberated, and that the Messianic age would dawn. Galilee was a hotbed of such nationalistic expectations.

Jesus was evidently afraid that the people would cast him in this revolutionary role, and he had good reasons for this fear. After the feeding of the 5,000, according to John, the crowd 'intended to come and make him king by force' (John 6:15). But he had not come to be a political Messiah. He had come rather to die, and through death to secure a spiritual liberation for his people. So (8:31) once the disciples had recognized him as the Messiah, 'he then began to teach them that the Son of Man must suffer many things and be rejected by the elders, chief priests and teachers of the law, and that he must be killed and after three days rise again'. Further, he spoke 'plainly about this' (v. 32), that is, openly and publicly; there was to be no secret about the kind of Messiah he had come to be.

Secondly, *consider what Jesus came to do.* Mark explains that, once the Twelve had grasped his identity, he laid all his emphasis on the cross. On three more separate occasions Jesus plainly predicted his sufferings and death (9:31; 10:33, 45). Indeed one third of Mark's whole Gospel is devoted to the story of the cross.

Three phrases in Jesus' predictions are worthy of special note. First, 'the Son of man *must* suffer many things and ... be killed' (8:31, my emphasis). This note of compulsion is introduced. Why *must* he suffer and die? Answer: because the Scriptures must be fulfilled. Hearing Jesus' prediction of the cross, Peter was brash enough to rebuke him, so that Jesus turned and rebuked Peter (vv. 32–33). Nothing must be allowed to undermine the necessity of the cross.

The second phrase of note is that it is 'the *Son of Man*' who must suffer. Although 'son of man' is the regular Hebrew expression for a human being, and is often used thus in Scripture, it seems clear that Jesus adopted it as a self-designation in reference to the vision of Daniel 7. Here 'one like a son of man' (that is, a human figure) came with the clouds of heaven, approached the Ancient of Days (Almighty God) on his throne, and was given authority, glory and sovereign power, so that in consequence all peoples, nations and men of every language worshipped him. His dominion, Daniel adds, is an everlasting dominion that will not pass away, and his kingdom is one that will never be destroyed (Dan. 7:13–14). But now Jesus makes the astonishing declaration that the son of man must suffer. It means that Jesus adopted the title but changed his role. According to Daniel, all nations will serve him. According to Jesus, he would not be served, but serve. Thus Jesus did what nobody else had ever done. He fused the two Old Testament images – the servant who would suffer (Is. 53) and the son of man who would reign (Dan. 7). Oscar Cullmann writes:

> 'Son of man' represents the highest conceivable declaration of exaltation in Judaism; *ebed Yahweh* (the servant of the Lord) is the expression of deepest humiliation ... This is the unheard-of new act of Jesus, that he united these two apparently contradictory tasks in his self-consciousness, and that he expressed that union in his life and teaching.[1]

The third expression Jesus used in reference to his death is that 'even the Son of Man did not come to be served, but to serve, and *to give his life as a ransom for many*' (Mark. 10:45, my emphasis). A 'ransom' is a price paid for the release of captives. So Jesus taught that human beings are in captivity (especially to sin, guilt and judgment), and that we cannot save ourselves. So he would give himself as a ransom instead of the many. The cross would be the means of our liberation. Only because he died in our place can we be set free. All this is part of Jesus Christ's understanding of the cross, according to Mark.

Thirdly, *consider what Jesus asks of us*. After speaking of his coming death, Jesus called the crowd to him and said: 'If anyone would come after me, he must deny himself and take up his cross and follow me' (8:34). That is, Jesus moved at once from his cross to ours, and portrayed Christian discipleship in terms of self-denial and even death. For we can understand the significance of cross-bearing only against the cultural background of Roman-occupied Palestine. The Romans reserved crucifixion for the worst criminals and compelled those condemned to death by crucifixion to carry their own cross to the place of execution. So if we are following Christ and bearing a cross, there is only one place to which we can be going, and that is the scaffold.

Christian discipleship is much more radical than an amalgam of beliefs, good works and religious practices. No imagery can do it justice but death and resurrection. For when we lose ourselves we find ourselves, and when we die we live (8:35).

Here are three fundamental Marcan themes. Who is Jesus? The Christ. What did he come to do? To serve, to suffer and to die. What does he ask of his disciples? To take up our cross and follow him through the death of self-denial into the glory of resurrection.

All down church history the crucial questions have been christological. They concern the identity, the mission and the demands of Jesus. In seeking to discover these things, we should beware both of public opinion ('Who do people say I am?') and of idiosyncratic church leaders (who like Peter are impertinent enough to contradict Jesus). Instead, we should listen to him in his own self-testimony, especially as Mark records his emphasis on the cross. There is no authentic Christian faith or life unless the cross is at the centre.

3. Luke's Gospel and the Acts: Christ the Saviour of the world

There is a fundamental correspondence between who the evangelists are and how they present Jesus Christ. For divine inspiration shaped but did not obliterate the human personality of the writers. The best New Testament example of this principle is Luke. He is the only Gentile contributor to the New Testament. So it is entirely appropriate that he should present Jesus neither as the Christ of Scripture (as Matthew does), nor as the Suffering Servant (as Mark does), but as the Saviour of the world, irrespective of race or nationality, rank, sex, need or age.

First, Luke was *a doctor* (Col. 4:14). Consequently he was well educated, a man of culture (writing polished Greek) and a compassionate human being (who presumably will have sworn the Hippocratic Oath).

Secondly, Luke was *a Gentile*, for Paul distinguished him from 'the only Jews among my fellow-workers' (Col. 4:11). So he belonged to the extensive world of the Roman Empire. During at least three periods (the 'we' sections of the Acts) Luke accompanied Paul on his travels. He was a man of wide horizons and broad sympathies. Whereas the other three evangelists refer to the Sea of Galilee, only Luke calls it a lake. In comparison with the Great Sea, the Mediterranean, on which he had sailed, Galilee was not much more than a pond.

Thirdly, Luke was *a historian*. We must take at full value what he writes about his method in his preface to his Gospel. He has written neither myth nor midrash; he claims to have written historical truth. For the events surrounding the birth, ministry, death and resurrection of Jesus had been handed down by eyewitnesses. Luke had himself investigated them, and he was now writing them down, so that his readers might know the certainty of what they had been taught and had believed.

When did Luke undertake his own investigations? He was not one of the Twelve, nor was he himself an eyewitness. Later, however, beginning about AD 57, he enjoyed a two-year residence in Palestine. He had arrived by ship with Paul, who soon after was arrested and imprisoned. Then, while Paul was in prison in Caesarea for two years, Luke was a free man (Acts 21:17 and

24:27). How did he occupy himself during this period? We do not know, but it is a reasonable conjecture that he spent the time travelling the length and breadth of the country, visiting the sacred sites associated with Jesus, familiarizing himself with Jewish customs, and interviewing eyewitnesses. These will probably have included the Virgin Mary, now an elderly lady. For Luke tells Mary's story, and the intimate details of Jesus' birth and infancy, which Luke shares with his readers, must go back ultimately to her.

This, then, was Luke – doctor, Gentile and historian, well qualified to write his two-volume work on the origins of Christianity, which occupies more than a quarter of the New Testament and which we may approach with confidence in its reliability.

What then is Luke's message? It is encapsulated in the *Nunc Dimittis* or Song of Simeon, who claimed:

> My eyes have seen your salvation ...
> a light for revelation to the Gentiles
> and for glory to your people Israel.
>
> (2:30–32)

This reference to salvation for the Gentiles is repeated in Luke 3:6: 'all mankind will see God's salvation'. All four evangelists refer to the ministry of John the Baptist and quote from Isaiah 40 about 'a voice of one calling in the desert', but only Luke continues the quotation to include the statement that 'all mankind will see God's salvation' (3:6).

First, then, Luke's message is *good news of salvation*. 'Salvation' is a key word in Luke's Gospel. He was clear that it included two components. Negatively, it is the removal of guilt (bringing forgiveness). Positively, it is the bestowal of the Holy Spirit (conveying new birth). Both feature prominently in Luke's two-volume story.

Take forgiveness. Only Luke records Zechariah's prophecy that his son John would 'give his people the knowledge of salvation through the forgiveness of their sins' (1:77). Only Luke tells how Jesus gave forgiveness to the woman who had anointed his feet with ointment and wet them with her tears (7:48). Only Luke tells the incomparable parable of the prodigal son, who repented and returned home, and was welcomed with hugs, kisses and a celebration party (15:11–32). Only Luke records the great commission in the terms that 'repentance and forgiveness of sins' would be proclaimed to all nations (24:47). And only Luke describes how Paul in Pisidian Antioch proclaimed 'through Jesus the forgiveness of sins' (Acts 13:38).

The complementary aspect of salvation is the bestowal of the Holy Spirit to bring new birth and new life. Of all the evangelists Luke shows the greatest interest in the work of the Spirit. He portrays Jesus as having been anointed by the Spirit and as exercising his ministry in the power of the Spirit (3:22; 4:1, 14, 18). And it is only Luke who describes the coming of the Spirit on the Day of Pentecost, and the subsequent development of the Christian mission (Acts 2:1–12; 13:2, etc.).

So these are the two components of salvation. Forgiveness eradicates our past, and the Spirit transforms our future. Peter sums it up at the conclusion of his sermon on the Day of Pentecost, for, to those who repent, believe and are baptized, he promises both forgiveness of their sins and the gift of the Holy Spirit (Acts 2:38). Moreover, this great salvation brings great joy. Luke begins his Gospel with the announcement of 'good news of great joy' (2:10) and ends it with the statement that the apostles 'returned to Jerusalem with great joy' (24:52). Indeed, throughout both of Luke's volumes, joy accompanies the gift of salvation, since there is great joy in heaven over even one sinner who repents (15:7, 10, cf. Acts 8:8, 39).

Secondly, Luke's message is good news of salvation *through Christ*. This truth is clear in the story of Simeon, for he took the baby Jesus in his arms and spoke of what he had seen. What he actually saw was a baby; what he said he had seen was God's salvation (2:28, 30), for that is what Jesus was. So Luke tells in his own elegant way the matchless story of Jesus Christ: how he was born of the Virgin Mary in the city of David, to be our Saviour; how he told Zacchaeus that salvation had come to his house that day, adding that the Son of Man had come 'to seek and to save what was lost' (19:9–10); how he prayed for the forgiveness of his executioners and promised the penitent criminal on the cross a place in paradise that same day (23:34, 43); and how, having been exalted to the place of supreme authority at God's right hand, he sent the Holy Spirit and still bestows salvation today (Acts 2:33).

Further, because Jesus is unique in his birth, death, resurrection and exaltation, his salvation is also unique. Since in no other person has God become human, died, been raised from death, and been exalted to heaven, there is no other saviour, since no-one else possesses his qualifications. Luke preserves the affirmation of the apostle Peter that 'salvation is found in no-one else, for there is no other name under heaven given to men by which we must be saved' (Acts 4:12).

Thirdly, Luke's message is good news of salvation through Christ *for the whole world*. Luke deliberately places at the beginning of each of his two volumes a statement of universality: on the one hand 'all mankind will see God's salvation' (3:6) and on the other 'I will pour out my Spirit on all people' (Acts 2:17). Both verses contain the same expression *pasa sarx*, meaning 'all flesh' or 'all people'. They act as signposts pointing to the story which follows, for Luke depicts Jesus as going out of his way to honour those whom the world despised, to befriend the friendless and to include the excluded.

First, *the sick and the suffering*. Of course, all four evangelists describe the healing ministry of Jesus, but Dr Luke shows a special interest in it. In 1882 W. K. Hobart's book *The Medical Language of St Luke* was published. He listed more than 400 words shared by Luke and the Greek medical writers of the times. Although his case was exaggerated, some evidence remains. As William Barclay has written, 'instinctively Luke uses medical words'.[2] He took a doctor's interest in symptoms, diagnosis and remedy. It is amusing that, although Mark says that the woman with a haemorrhage had suffered a great deal under many doctors and had spent all her money, yet instead of getting better she grew worse, Luke seems keen to preserve the reputation of his profession and is content to write simply that 'no-one could heal her' (8:43).

Secondly, *women and children*. In the ancient world women were generally despised and oppressed, and unwanted children were abandoned or killed. But Luke emphasizes that Jesus loved and respected both. Only he tells the stories of Elizabeth and Mary, of Mary and Martha, of the widow of Nain who lost her only son (7:11–17), of the women who supported Jesus out of their own resources (8:3), and of the women who watched at the foot of the cross and came early the following morning to the tomb (23:49,

55–56; 24:1). As for children, Matthew and Mark both record Jesus' invitation 'Let the little children come to me', but Luke refers to them as 'babies', and adds that Jesus 'took a little child and had him stand beside him' (9:47; 18:15–17).

Thirdly, *the poor and the oppressed.* Luke is more interested than the other evangelists in questions of wealth and poverty. He is concerned for economic equality and affirms that Jesus had been anointed 'to preach good news to the poor' (4:18). He tells three parables about money, and portrays the generosity of the early Jerusalem church in sharing their goods with the needy.

Fourthly, *publicans and sinners.* Both groups were social outcasts: 'publicans' (tax collectors) because they were employed by the hated Romans, and 'sinners' because they were ignorant of Jewish laws and traditions. But Luke tells us that publicans and sinners gathered round him (15:1), that in spite of criticism Jesus ate with them (5:30; 15:2), and that he was nicknamed their friend (7:34). It was a vivid anticipation of the Messianic banquet.

Fifthly, *the Samaritans and Gentiles.* Because the Samaritans were a hybrid people, half Jew, half Gentile, descended from the mixed population of the eighth century BC, Jews did not associate with them. But Jesus rebuked James and John for wanting, like Elijah, to call fire down from heaven to destroy a Samaritan village (9:54–55); he told the memorable parable of the good Samaritan, in which a Samaritan did for a Jew what no Jew would ever do for a Samaritan (10:25–34); and he commissioned his people to be his witnesses after Pentecost in widening circles, including Samaria (Acts 1:8). As for Gentiles, Luke was of course one himself. So he traced the genealogy of Jesus back to Adam, and in the Acts he followed the spread of the gospel from Jerusalem the capital of Jewry, to Rome the capital of the world. The chief human actor in this exciting drama was Paul, who was the apostle to the Gentiles and Luke's hero.

So Luke chronicles the main events of Paul's three missionary journeys, first evangelizing the Galatian cities, next reaching Europe, and thirdly spending about five years in Ephesus and Corinth. His arrest in Jerusalem, subsequent trials and the dangerous voyage to Rome culminated in his detention there, where he told Jewish leaders 'that God's salvation has been sent to the Gentiles', and for two whole years 'boldly and without hindrance he preached the kingdom of God and taught about the Lord Jesus Christ' (Acts 28:28–31).

The justification for adding the Acts to Luke's Gospel in this section is threefold. First, Luke was the author of both books. Secondly, he himself affirmed a fundamental continuity between them, his former work (the Gospel) containing all that Jesus 'began' to do and to teach during his earthly ministry (Acts 1:1), and his later work (the Acts) evidently containing all that Jesus continued to do and to teach through his appointed apostles. Thirdly, both books focus on the same message, namely God's salvation to the whole world through Christ (Luke 2:30–32; Acts 28:28).

These, then, are the parameters of Luke's two-volume story: salvation (comprising forgiveness and the Spirit), Christ (who by his birth, death and resurrection was uniquely competent to save) and the world he came to save, irrespective of ethnicity, class, sex, age or need. God's love in Christ encompasses everybody, and specially those who are pushed to the margins of society. He reaches out to touch those whom others regard as untouchable. Luke's Christ is the Saviour of the world.

4. The Gospel and letters of John: Christ the Word made flesh

Each of the four gospels has a different beginning. Matthew opens with Jesus' genealogy, tracing his family tree back to Abraham, and Luke with Jesus' conception, birth and infancy. Mark starts with the ministry of John the Baptist, while John goes right back to the beginning of time: 'In the beginning was the Word, and the Word was with God, and the Word was God' (1:1). This personal and eternal Word was also the agent of creation, who had never left the world he had made, and who is the light and life of all human beings.

It was this Word of God, the perfect expression of the Father's being, who one day 'became flesh and lived for a while among us' (1:14). To him John bore witness. It was not a visitation, but an incarnation. He became a human being in Jesus of Nazareth. The paradox is amazing. The Creator assumed the human frailty of his creatures. The eternal one entered time. The all-powerful made himself vulnerable. The all-holy exposed himself to temptation. And in the end the immortal died.

What was John's purpose in writing his Gospel? He tells us: 'Jesus did many other miraculous signs in the presence of his disciples, which are not recorded in this book. But these are written that you may believe that Jesus is the Christ, the Son of God, and that by believing you may have life in his name' (20:30–31).

Three clear stages are laid down: (1) John selected and recorded certain 'signs', (2) in order that his readers might believe in Jesus, and (3) in order that by believing they might receive life through him. Thus testimony would lead to faith, and faith to life.

Indeed, John seems to see his Gospel in terms of testimony to Christ. It is almost as if it is a kind of court scene, in which Jesus is on trial, and a succession of witnesses is called, beginning with John the Baptist who 'came as a witness to testify concerning that light' (1:6–7). What was his witness? It was both 'Look, the Lamb of God, who takes away the sin of the world' (1:29) and 'he ... will baptize with the Holy Spirit' (1:33). But other witnesses followed, both human and divine. For the Father himself bore witness to his Son through a combination of his words and works (5:31–40, 8:12, 14). His words interpreted his works, and his works dramatized his words. And after his death the Spirit of truth would also bear witness to him (15:26–27).

Many scholars believe that John deliberately assembled seven witnesses in the form of seven major miracles. These miracles are defined both as 'powers' (*dunameis*), because they were expressions of the creative power of God, and as 'wonders' (*terata*), because they evoked astonishment. But John's favourite word for them was 'signs' (*sēmeia*), because more important than the material phenomena was their spiritual significance. Jesus' miracles were acted parables, visibly dramatizing his claims through which his glory was revealed (2:11). Each sign contributed to the witnesses John was assembling, to the portrait he was painting.

Miracle 1: Jesus turned water into wine, as a sign of his claim to have inaugurated a new order. The six huge stone water jars, used for ceremonial washing, were seen at the Cana wedding as symbols of the old order, of Judaism. But Jesus turned the water into wine as a sign that in and with his arrival the kingdom of God had come. The same basic truth was elaborated when he cleansed the temple (2:13ff.), when he told Nicodemus of the necessity of the new birth (3:1ff.), and when he offered the Samaritan woman living water (4:1ff). Jesus had introduced a new beginning.

Miracles 2 and 3: Jesus performed two healing miracles, as signs of his claim to give new life. First he healed the son of a royal official in Capernaum (4:43, 54). This was his second sign. Then, at the Pool of Bethesda in Jerusalem, he healed a man who had been an invalid for thirty-eight years (5:1ff.). Following these signs, John records another of Jesus' discourses in which he claimed that the Father had given him authority to bestow life and to execute judgment. Both judging and life-giving are divine prerogatives (5:24–27).

Miracle 4: Jesus miraculously fed 5,000 people with five barley loaves and two fish, as a sign that he claimed to be the bread of life. The feeding of the 5,000 is the only miracle recorded by all four evangelists, but only John adds the discourse which followed, in which Jesus claimed: 'I am the bread of life. He who comes to me will never go hungry, and he who believes in me will never be thirsty' (6:35). There is a hunger in the human heart which none but Christ can satisfy, a thirst which none but he can quench. The feeding of the crowd was an acted parable of this claim.

Miracle 5: Jesus walked on water as a sign of his claim that the powers of nature were subject to his kingdom authority. When Jesus went up a mountainside to pray, and the Twelve got into a boat to cross the lake, they were overwhelmed by a violent storm. They felt alone and abandoned. But then, in the darkness and the squall, Jesus came to them, walking on the water. They were terrified, but he said to them: 'It is I; don't be afraid.' Even the wind and the water obeyed him (6:16–21).

Miracle 6: Jesus gave sight to a man born blind, as a sign of his claim to be the light of the world. 'I am the light of the world', he said. 'Whoever follows me will never walk in darkness, but will have the light of life' (8:12). As John relates this story, he draws a contrast between the Pharisees and the man born blind. The Pharisees had their sight, but were spiritually blind, whereas the man born blind had his sight restored to him and at the same time believed.

Miracle 7: Jesus raised Lazarus who had been dead for four days, as a sign of his claim to be the resurrection and the life. In this story the strong emotions of the Word made flesh are revealed. For he both 'snorted' with anger and indignation in the face of death (11:33, literally; 'was deeply moved' NIV), and 'wept' in compassion for the bereaved sisters, Mary and Martha (11:35). He then said: 'I am the resurrection and the life. He who believes in me will live, even though he dies; and whoever lives and believes in me will never die' (11:25–26). In other words, Jesus is the life of the living and will be the resurrection of the dead. For those who live will never die, and those who die will live again.

So here are the seven signs which John selected, each dramatizing one of his claims. This is the Jesus to whom John bears witness, and in whom we have come to believe. He has inaugurated the new order. He is both life-giver and judge. He controls the powers of nature. He is the bread of life, the light of the world, and the resurrection and the life.

Yet there is another side to John's witness to Jesus. The seven signs are signs of power and authority, and are all recorded in the first half of the Gospel. In the second half John records signs of humility and of weakness. He begins in the upper room when Jesus took off his outer clothing, wrapped a towel round him, and, kneeling, washed the feet of the Twelve. Above all there was the cross. According to John, although Jesus revealed his glory in signs of power (2:11), the chief means of his glorification was the cross. '*The hour* has come', he said, 'for the Son of Man to be glorified' (12:23).

If John's purpose in his Gospel is so to witness to Christ that his readers will believe in him and receive life (20:31), his purpose in his letters, to which a brief reference may conveniently be made here, is to take his readers a step further. He writes, 'to you who believe in the name of the Son of God so that you may know that you have eternal life' (1 John 5:13). For it is one thing to receive life; it is another to know that we have received it. So having assembled the seven signs which witness to Christ, John now develops three tests which undermine the false assurance of counterfeit Christians and confirm the true assurance of genuine Christians. He does not mince his words. He identifies three liars. First, whoever denies that Jesus is the Christ come in the flesh is a liar (1 John 2:22). This is *the doctrinal test*. Secondly, whoever claims to enjoy fellowship with God while walking in darkness lies (1 John 1:6). This is *the moral test*. Thirdly, whoever says he loves God but hates his brother is a liar (1 John 4:20). This is *the social test*. Conversely, (1) we know the Spirit of God, because he acknowledges Christ (1 John 4:2; cf. 2 John 9); (2) we know that we know him, because we obey his commandments (1 John. 2:3); and (3) we know that we have passed out of death into life, because we love our Christian brothers and sisters (1 John 3:14). John even assembles three verbs which characterize God's people: they believe in Christ, they love one another, and they obey his commands (1 John 3:23–24).

5. The fourfold gospel

So far we have gazed at the four faces of Christ, each with a different facial expression. Now we need to affirm that they are not incompatible with one another. As Bishop Stephen Neill wrote, 'the central message of the gospels is not the teaching of Jesus but Jesus himself'.[3] Speaking personally, I find it helpful to detect in the four evangelists four dimensions of the saving purpose of God: its length, depth, breadth and height. Matthew reveals its length, for he depicts the Christ of Scripture, who looks back over long centuries of expectation. Mark emphasizes its depth, for he depicts the Suffering Servant who looks down to the depths of the humiliation he endured. In Luke it is the breadth of God's purpose which emerges, for he depicts the Saviour of the world who looks round in mercy to the broadest possible spectrum of human beings. Then John reveals its height, for he depicts the Word made flesh who looks up to the heights from which he came and to which he intends to raise us.

No wonder Paul prayed that with all God's people we might be able to 'grasp how wide and long and high and deep is the love of Christ' (Eph. 3:18) – the dimensions which some of the early church fathers saw symbolized in the shape of the cross.

Several attempts have been made throughout the history of the church to compose a harmony of the gospels. The first seems to have been Tatian, who was converted to Christ when visiting Rome in the middle of the second century, and became a disciple of

Justin Martyr. His harmony came to be known as *Diatessaron*, which was originally a musical term for a four-part harmony. It was a remarkably skilful weaving together of the four gospels, without any editorial additions of his own.[4]

The next serious attempt to harmonize the four gospels was made by Augustine. His concern was to vindicate them against the slanderous criticisms of pagan philosophers. He systematically compared the evangelists' accounts of the words and works of Jesus, arguing that there is a genuine 'harmony' or 'consistency' between them and an absence of 'discrepancy' or 'contradiction'.[5]

The tension between the one and only authentic Jesus and his four faces as portrayed in the gospels is the theme of a fascinating book entitled *Four gospels, One Jesus?* by Dr Richard Burridge, Dean of King's College, London University. Dr Burridge has a vivid imagination, a sincere faith and a devout spirit. He takes up the four 'living creatures' of Ezekiel 1:10 and Revelation 4:7, whose faces are said to resemble those of a man, a lion, an ox and an eagle, which are respectively the king of all creatures (the human being), of wild beasts (the lion), of domestic animals (the ox) and of birds (the eagle). The church fathers applied these symbols to the four evangelists, to their gospels, and so to the Christ they portray. They are very common in Christian art. Thus Mark's Jesus is like a bounding lion ('rushing around and roaring enigmatically, and dying terribly alone'). Matthew's Christ has a human face (because he is a new Moses, the supreme teacher of Israel who nevertheless rejected his teaching, thus making way for the Gentiles). Luke's Jesus resembles an ox (because he is the strong, patient bearer of the burdens of the poor, the needy and the outcasts). Finally John's Jesus is a 'high-flying, far-seeing, all-knowing eagle' (because he comes from the heights of heaven to dwell with us on earth and then to carry us with him to glory).

What, then, is the relationship 'between the four gospels and the one Jesus?' Dr Burridge answers that we must allow each evangelist to paint his own portrait and tell his own story. We have no liberty either to turn the four into one by ironing out the individuality of each, or to turn the one into four by exaggerating the individuality of each, and so making a composite picture impossible. No, 'there are four gospels, with four pictures, telling four versions of the one story of Jesus'. And this one story in its four versions remains normative; it is the criterion by which to judge the authenticity of all attempts to reconstruct other Jesuses.[6]

6. Jesus and Paul

As we move on from the gospels to the epistles, and so from Jesus to Paul, an immediate problem confronts us. Is Paul related to Jesus by continuity or by discontinuity? Beginning in the middle of the nineteenth century, a number of scholars have described Paul as 'the second', and even 'the real', founder of Christianity. He is seen as having corrupted the simple, unsophisticated religion of Jesus into the complicated theologizing we tend to associate him with. Paul called down an anathema on anybody who perverts the gospel of Christ (Gal. 1:6–9); was he guilty of perverting it himself? Albert Schweitzer declared that he saw no discernible continuity between Christ and Paul.[7] He called Paul a 'morbid crank' who falsified the true gospel by his dogmas. Similarly, in our own day A. N. Wilson has written: 'If there is any single individual who can be labelled the "originator" of Christianity … it would be Paul.'[8] In consequence, a 'back from Paul to Jesus' movement developed at the beginning of the twentieth century, and still rumbles on today.

It is of course true that Paul quoted Jesus on only four occasions (1 Cor. 7:10; 9:14; 11:23ff. and 1 Thess. 4:15). It is also true that Paul's letters contain some surprising omissions. For example, they do not refer directly to Jesus' baptism or transfiguration, his parables or miracles. Nevertheless, there is abundant evidence, often by allusion rather than quotation, that Paul was familiar with the teaching and the story of Jesus. Jesus proclaimed the kingdom of God as both present reality and future expectation, with the implication that we are living in between times, between the 'already' and the 'not yet' of salvation. Paul taught the same double perspective. Jesus also claimed to enjoy a unique relationship with God as 'Abba, Father', which Paul confirmed by calling him God's Son (Rom. 1:3–4).

Above all, Jesus stressed the necessity of his sufferings and death, in fulfilment of Scripture, as a ransom for sinners, to be followed by the resurrection. And the cross and resurrection lie at the centre of Paul's gospel. Because of them, sinners may be justified by faith alone without works, as Paul emphasized and as Jesus also insisted in his parable of the Pharisee and the publican. Jesus also delineated the lifestyle appropriate to his disciples, as he told them to beware of hypocrisy and covetousness, and stressed the priority of love, which does not retaliate, fulfils the law and expresses itself in lowly service. All this is paralleled in the ethical teaching of Paul. W. D. Davies could go so far as to say that 'Paul is steeped in the mind and words of his Lord.'[9] This is hardly surprising, since 'Christ is the whole subject of Paul's thought and gospel.'[10]

If one turns from the teaching of Jesus to his whole life and ministry, his 'story', it is evident that Paul was neither ignorant of, nor indifferent to, Jesus' earthly career. For Paul refers in his letters to Jesus' birth (Gal. 4:4), his descent from Abraham and David (Rom. 9:5; 1:3), and his human family (1 Cor. 9:5; Gal. 1:19). Paul knew that Jesus was 'without sin' (2 Cor. 5:21), gentle (2 Cor. 10:1), humble and obedient (Phil. 2:8), and above all, willing to sacrifice himself for others (2 Cor. 8:9). If Paul knew about Jesus' life, he particularly knew and stressed his death, preceded by the supper he instituted (1 Cor. 10:16; 11:23ff.), and followed by his burial, resurrection, exaltation and gift of the Spirit. Next, he sent out his apostles to evangelize the Jews first, then the Gentiles, and to gather his people together out of every race (Gal. 3:28). Their mission would fill the gap between his first and second comings. Then he would come like a thief, as both Jesus and Paul taught, to bring his salvation and judgment to completion.

Dr David Wenham has written a comprehensive study of Paul's use of the sayings and the story of Jesus, entitled *Paul: Follower of Jesus or Founder of Christianity?*[11] His conclusion, after a very thorough survey of the field, was that 'there is massive overlap' between Jesus and Paul.[12] At the same time there are differences of theological focus which, however, 'do not represent any fundamental divergence of outlook'.[13] Almost all of them reflect the change of situation which had taken place. On the one hand Jesus taught Jewish people in Palestine about his death and resurrection, which lay still in the future. On the other hand, Paul wrote to largely Gentile congregations in the Graeco-Roman world about the cross and resurrection, which had already taken place.

Thus David Wenham has successfully demonstrated 'that Paul

is much better described as "follower of Jesus" than as "founder of Christianity"'.[14] As between the four gospels, so between Jesus and Paul, what we find is unity in diversity.

The thirteen letters of Paul

Our argument moves on now from the relationship between Paul and Jesus to a consideration of Paul himself. He shows an extraordinary versatility in his letters, which together account for a quarter of the New Testament. Thirteen letters are attributed to him (excluding Hebrews), only seven of which are generally regarded as indisputably Pauline, namely Galatians, Romans, 1 and 2 Corinthians, Philippians, Philemon and 1 Thessalonians. The most widely questioned are the pastoral letters, although in the twentieth century a vigorous defence of their authenticity has been mounted by a significant number of New Testament scholars. I have attempted to summarize the case for and against Pauline authorship myself, and believe that the variations of style and vocabulary in the pastorals are best accounted for by Paul's constructive use of a personal amanuensis.[15]

So for my purpose (which is to survey the whole New Testament) I am going to assume the Pauline authorship of all thirteen letters which are attributed to him. It is not easy to do justice to his witness to Jesus Christ, but once again I hope to show that it is a combination of unity and diversity. I propose to group his letters according to their dating during a period of twenty years, beginning with the first missionary journey (c. 48–49) and ending with his martyrdom in Rome, which may have taken place as late as AD 68. In each of the five groupings Christ is portrayed in a somewhat different light. (This may be tabulated as shown on page 45.)

7. A polemical letter (Galatians): Christ the liberator

I am numbered among those who believe that Galatians was the first letter Paul wrote. My main reason is that it contains no

Approx. date	Period	Group	Letters	Presentation of Christ
48–49	End of 1st missionary journey	A polemical letter	Galatians	Christ the liberator
50–52	During 2nd missionary journey	The early letters	1 & 2 Thessalonians	Christ the coming judge
53–57	During 3rd missionary journey	The major letters	Romans, 1 & 2 Corinthians	Christ the Saviour
60–62	During 1st imprisonment in Rome	The prison letters	Colossians, Philemon, Ephesians & Philippians	Christ the supreme Lord
62–67	During release and 2nd imprisonment	The pastoral letters	1 Timothy and Titus, 2 Timothy	Christ the head of the church

Table 1: The thirteen letters of Paul

reference to the epoch-making Jerusalem Council and its decrees which declared that Gentile converts did not need to be circumcised or to observe the ceremonial law. Although the argument from silence is always precarious, Paul's failure to mention these decrees in Galatians must mean that they had not yet been promulgated. This would date Galatians in AD 49 between the first and second missionary journeys.

Galatians has aptly been named a 'polemical' letter, for one senses throughout it Paul's hot indignation in relation to the false teachers who were troubling the church by perverting the gospel (1:7). Paul pronounces an anathema upon such. Whether they are humans or angels or even the apostle himself, those preaching a gospel different from the original apostolic gospel of grace deserved to fall under the judgment of God (1:8–9). So keenly did Paul feel this need to be loyal to 'the truth of the gospel' that he was prepared even to have an embarrassing public confrontation with his fellow-apostle Peter over it (2:11–14).

Probably the key text of Galatians is 5:1 where Paul writes: 'It is for freedom that Christ has set us free. Stand firm, then, and do not let yourselves be burdened again by a yoke of slavery.' Paul thus portrays Christ as the supreme liberator, and salvation in terms of freedom. What is this freedom?

First, Christian freedom is *freedom from the law*. Paul writes of 'the curse of the law', meaning by this expression not the law itself but the judgment which the law pronounces on those who disobey it. For all those who rely for salvation on observing the law are under God's judgment (3:10). But Christ has redeemed us from this judgment by becoming a curse for us (3:13). He took our place, bore our curse and died our death. But the Galatians ('You foolish Galatians!' the apostle dubs them, 3:1), instead of putting their trust in Christ crucified, were trusting in themselves that they were righteous and were thus setting themselves against the cross. 'For if righteousness [i.e. justification] could be gained through the law, Christ died for nothing!' (2:21). No wonder Paul was determined to boast in nothing except the cross (6:14).

Freedom from the law and its curse, however, does not give us freedom to disobey the moral law or to indulge our sinful nature (5:13). On the contrary, Christian freedom is freedom to serve, not freedom to sin (5:13). In fact, 'the entire law is summed up in a single command: "Love your neighbour as yourself"' (5:14, cf. 6:2).

Secondly, Christian freedom is *freedom from the flesh* (*sarx*), from our fallen, self-indulgent nature. Paul writes in Galatians that even those who have been justified by grace through faith in Christ are involved in an unrelenting conflict between the flesh (our fallen nature) and the Spirit (the indwelling Holy Spirit). The deeds of our sinful nature include immorality, idolatry, hatred, jealousy and selfish ambition (5:19–21). 'But the fruit of the Spirit is love, joy, peace, patience, kindness, goodness, faithfulness, gentleness and self-control' (5:22–23). The winner in this internal conflict depends on the attitude we adopt to each. On the one hand, if we belong to Christ, we have 'crucified' (that is, radically repudiated) our 'sinful nature with its passions and desires' (5:24). On the other hand, we are to 'live by the Spirit' and 'keep in step with the Spirit' (5:16, 25), that is, follow the Spirit's promptings, for then the flesh will be subdued to the Spirit, and the fruit of the Spirit will ripen in our character.

Paul's witness to Christ the liberator in Galatians is that by his cross we can be redeemed from the law's curse, and that by his Spirit we can be delivered from the power of our fallen nature. As a result, we are no longer slaves, but Abraham's children and the sons and daughters of God (3:29; 4:7).

8. The early letters (1 & 2 Thessalonians): Christ the coming judge

Paul and his companions visited Thessalonica during his second missionary journey, and his first letter to them was evidently written and dispatched within months, even weeks, of his visit. And his second letter followed soon afterwards. So both letters were addressed to some very new converts. Only recently had they 'turned to God from idols to serve the living and true God' (1 Thess. 1:9). Paul's immediate purpose in the first letter was to defend himself against the slander of those who were saying that he had run away from their city and did not care about the young Thessalonian believers.

His second purpose was pastoral. He loved them as fathers and mothers love their children (1 Thess. 2:7, 11), and was anxious to help those who were in special need. Although he urged them to be 'patient with everyone', he singled out three particular categories. They were to 'warn those who are idle, encourage the timid, help the weak' (1 Thess. 5:14). It seems plausible, as some commentators have suggested, that 'the weak' are the sexually weak whom he has exhorted to self-control in 4:1–8; that 'the idle' (*ataktoi*), who were playing truant from work, needed to be admonished, to mind their own business and work with their own hands (4:9–12); and that 'the timid' were the bereaved who were overcome with excessive grief (4:13–18).

But the chief emphasis of the Thessalonian letters relates to the coming of Christ to save and to judge. Each of the eight chapters into which 1 and 2 Thessalonians have been divided contains a reference to the parousia (the return of Christ).[16] Expectation for the future is an essential ingredient of Christian discipleship, which is characterized not only by faith and love, but also by 'hope' (1 Thess. 1:3). And having turned to God from idols, we both serve the living God and 'wait for his Son from heaven' (1 Thess. 1:10).

As always, Paul is addressing pastoral problems which he knows only sound doctrine can solve. The Thessalonian letters contain four main eschatological passages, each of which is addressed to a particular group of people.

First, some were *grieving in bereavement* (1 Thess. 4:13–18). They feared that their dead friends or relatives would stand at a disadvantage when Christ comes, and even forfeit the blessings he will bring. Paul's answer is to supply a simple eschatological creed, 'We believe that ... and so we believe that ... and we tell you that ...' (vv. 14–15): (1) the Lord Jesus himself will come from heaven; (2) the Christian dead will be the first to rise from the dead; (3) God will bring them with Christ; (4) then the Christian living, far from preceding the Christian dead, will be reunited with them and with the Lord; and (5) so we will all be with the Lord for ever. This does not answer all our questions, but it gives us basic information about the return, the resurrection, the rapture and the reunion.

Secondly, some were *curious about chronology* (1 Thess. 5:1–11). They were evidently apprehensive as to whether they would be ready to stand before Christ at his coming, and they thought the best way to prepare would be to know the date. But this was the wrong solution to their problem. For they knew that the Lord's coming would be sudden and unexpected (like a burglar in the night), and sudden and unavoidable (like labour at the end of pregnancy). Instead, the right way to prepare is to remember that we are already children of light. Since we belong to the day, we need to keep awake, not to go to sleep. Then we will not be taken by surprise.

Thirdly, some were *experiencing severe persecutions* (2 Thess. 1:4–10). Their perseverance and faith in the midst of their trials, however, were evidence of God's righteous judgment. For those who share in Christ's sufferings will also share in his glory. More than that, God is just and will one day vindicate his people publicly. At the same time he will punish those who wilfully reject the truth, 'those who refuse to acknowledge God and ... will not obey the gospel' (v. 8, NEB). The alternative destinies of heaven and hell are presented in vivid imagery. On the one hand, the Lord Jesus will be glorified in his people (v. 10). On the other hand, those who have rejected him will be excluded from 'the presence of the Lord and the glory of his might' (v. 9, RSV).

Fourthly, some were *confused by a rumour* that the day of the Lord had already come. Paul refutes this error by unfolding a Christian philosophy of history (2 Thess. 2:1–12). The parousia (the coming of Christ) cannot take place, he explains, until the rebellion (the coming of Antichrist) occurs, and this rebellion will not happen until what is holding it back has been removed. The identity of the restraining influence (v. 6), which is personalized in verse 7, has long occupied the ingenuity of students. But the most probable reconstruction is that it refers to Rome and the power of the state. For 'what obstacle is there,' asked Tertullian, 'but the Roman state?'[17] Indeed, every state, being the official guardian of law and order, public peace and justice, is intended by God to restrain evil.

Meanwhile, even during the period of restraint, and before the lawless one (Antichrist) is revealed, 'the secret power of lawlessness is already at work' (v. 7a). His anti-social, anti-law, anti-God movement is at present largely underground. We detect its subversive influence in atheism, totalitarianism, materialism, moral relativism and social permissiveness. But one day secret subversion will become open rebellion, when the lawless one is revealed. Then we can expect a period (mercifully short) of political, social and moral chaos in which both God and law are impudently flouted, until suddenly the Lord Jesus will come and overthrow him.

Here then are the three acts in the eschatological drama. Now is the time of *restraint*, in which lawlessness is being held in check. Next will come the time of *rebellion*, in which the control of law will be removed and the lawless one will be revealed. Finally will come the time of *retribution*, in which the Lord Christ will defeat and destroy the Antichrist. This is God's programme. Meanwhile, the Thessalonians were to stand firm in the teaching they had previously received from the apostle. Whatever their troubles, Paul points them to the coming Christ.

9. The major letters (Romans, 1 & 2 Corinthians): Christ the Saviour

During Paul's so-called third missionary journey, he spent two years in Corinth and three in Ephesus. In both cities he began in the synagogue, and only when the Jews rejected the gospel did he move to a secular venue: in Corinth to the house of Titius Justus and in Ephesus to the lecture hall of Tyrannus.

Busy though these five years were in the exacting ministries of evangelism, apologetics and instruction, at least Paul was not travelling. So he seems to have had time for writing. It was in this period that he wrote his letter to the Romans (whose material he may have tried out in the hall of Tyrannus) and his two surviving letters to Corinth.

The contents of these three 'major letters' is full and varied, since each was written in response to particular needs and issues. Nevertheless, it would not be unfair, I think, to identify 'salvation' as their dominant theme. Here, for example, are some key texts:

Romans 1:16: 'I am not ashamed of the gospel, because it is the power of God for the salvation of everyone who believes: first for the Jew, then for the Gentile.'

1 Corinthians 1:21: 'For since in the wisdom of God the world through its wisdom did not know him, God was pleased through the foolishness of what was preached to save those who believe.'

1 Corinthians 15:1–2: '... I want to remind you of the gospel I preached to you, which you received ... By this gospel you are saved ...'

2 Corinthians 6:2: 'I tell you, now is the time of God's favour, now is the day of salvation.'

Romans

In Romans, after a brief introduction which focuses on Christ (1:1 – 5), the universal need for salvation is set forth powerfully. First depraved pagans, next critical moralizers, and then self-confident Jews are arraigned, until the whole human race is found guilty and inexcusable (1:18 – 3:20). 'But now', Paul continues, with a mighty adversative, 'a righteousness from God' (that is, God's righteous way of 'righteousing' the unrighteous) has been revealed in the gospel (3:21–31), to be received by faith alone, as is plain in the case of Abraham (ch. 4). In consequence, having been justified by faith, we enjoy peace with God, we are standing in grace and we rejoice in the prospect of sharing God's glory (5:1–11).

Two humanities have now been portrayed, one characterized by sin and guilt, the other by grace and faith. The head of the old humanity is Adam, the head of the new is Christ. With almost mathematical precision Paul compares and contrasts them (5:12–21).

Next, Paul responds to two criticisms. In Romans 6 he refutes the slander that the gospel encourages sin. Having been united with Christ (through baptism) in his death and resurrection, although it is not impossible that we go on sinning, yet it is inconceivable that we should. How can we live in what we have died to?

In Romans 7 Paul answers a second criticism, namely that the law is to blame for sin. Instead, Paul blames our 'flesh', our fallen human nature. Romans 7 is full of the power of indwelling sin, but Romans 8 is concerned with the indwelling Spirit, through whom alone we can 'put to death the misdeeds of the body' and so live (8:13). The apostle also looks forward to the redemption of the created universe (8:18–27) and expresses his unbreakable conviction of our ultimate salvation, since nothing can separate us from God's love (8:28–39).

Romans 9 – 11 are emphatically not the parenthesis which some readers suppose, but an integral part of Paul's argument. Throughout the first half of his letter he has forgotten neither the ethnic mix of the church in Rome ('first for the Jew, then for the Gentile', 1:16; 2:9–10), nor the tensions that kept surfacing between the Jewish Christian minority and the Gentile Christian majority. Now the time has come for him to address head-on the underlying theological problem. How is it that the Jewish people as a whole have rejected their Messiah? And how did the inclusion of the Gentiles fit in with God's plan? At the beginning of each chapter Paul makes an emotional statement of his longing for their salvation and of his own continuing Jewishness (9:1–6; 10:1; 11:1).

In chapter 9 Paul defends God's covenant loyalty on the ground that his promises were not made to all Jacob's descendants, but to Israel within Israel, the elect remnant. In chapter 10, however, the unbelief of Israel is attributed not to God's purpose of election (as in chapter 9) but to her pride, ignorance and stubbornness. Then, in chapter 11, Paul looks into the future. He declares that Israel's sin is neither total (since there is a believing remnant) nor final (since there will be a recovery). His vision is that the 'fulness' of both Jews and Gentiles will ultimately be gathered in (11:12, 25). No wonder this prospect leads him to break out into a doxology in which he praises God for the depth of both his riches and his wisdom (vv. 33–36).

With Romans 12 Paul turns from doctrine to ethics. On the ground of God's mercies, which he has been expounding, he calls for the consecration of our bodies and the renewal of our minds. The choice is between conforming to the fashions of the world and being transformed according to the will of God.

Further, the will of God concerns our relationships – all of which are changed radically by the gospel. Paul treats seven of them: firstly, our relationship to God (12:1–2), then to ourselves in the evaluation of our gifts (12:3–8), and thirdly to one another (12:9–16) in a love which binds the Christian family. Fourthly, there is our relationship to our enemies and to evildoers, which echoes the call of Jesus to non-retaliation (12:17–21) and fifthly to the State in recognition of its God-given authority and ministry (13:1–7). In verses 8–10 Paul reverts to love, emphasizing that love to our neighbour is both an unpaid debt and the fulfilment of the law. This sixth relationship is the more urgent as the last day approaches (13:11–14).

The seventh and final relationship, which Paul treats at considerable length, concerns our behaviour towards 'the weak', whose over-scrupulous conscience is not to be trampled on (14:1 – 15:13). Instead, they are to be welcomed into the family as Christ has accepted us.

The most notable feature of Paul's practical instructions about the weak is that he grounds them on his Christology, and in particular on the death, resurrection and parousia of Jesus. The weak are brothers and sisters for whom Christ died. Christ rose in order to be their Lord, and we have no liberty to interfere with his servants. He is also coming to be our judge; we should not play the role of judge ourselves.

Paul ends this section with a beautiful vision of Jewish and Gentile believers, who are bound by such a 'spirit of unity' that 'with one heart and mouth' they glorify God together (15:14–22).

The epistle concludes with news of Paul's travel plans, personal greetings to and from a number of named individuals, a warning against false teachers and a final doxology similar to the letter's introduction, which alludes to the gospel of Christ, the commission of God, the outreach to the nations and the summons to the obedience of faith (16:1–27).

Romans is the New Testament's most thorough exposition of salvation, describing its need, its nature and its means, indicating its radical implications in the new multi-racial community, and celebrating Jesus Christ crucified, risen, reigning and coming as the only Saviour.

1 Corinthians

Paul's first letter to the Corinthians is about the same length as his letter to the Romans, but its contents are very different. Romans is an orderly, carefully constructed exposition of the gospel, whereas 1 Corinthians handles an assortment of as many as twenty diverse themes, in which Paul is responding either to pastoral needs he has perceived in Corinth or to questions which the Corinthians have put to him. Each topic is treated with care, however, so that the letter contains some extremely valuable instruction on doctrinal, ethical and social subjects, which local churches still need to ponder today.

Paul begins with an acknowledgment of the ambiguity of the church. He describes it as being simultaneously holy and called to be holy, united ('the church of God', v. 1) and divided, complete and incomplete. In particular the apostle is horrified by the factions in the church, and by the personality cult which lies behind them. It leads him to develop the theme of 'power through weakness' which is so much needed in our contemporary power-hungry world. Paul saw it at work in the gospel of the cross (1:18–25), in the Corinthian converts (1:26–31) and in himself as a preacher (2:1–5), as he brought a weak message in his own personal weakness, but trusting in the power of the Spirit.

Parallel to 'power through weakness' is the principle of 'wisdom through folly'. Although 'the message of the cross is foolishness to those who are perishing' (1:18), it is nevertheless the power and the wisdom of God. And Paul goes on to write about the true wisdom which has been revealed by God through the inspiration of the Holy Spirit (2:6–16).

The apostle sees clearly that the Corinthian factions were ultimately due to their mistaken views of both the church and the pastoral ministry. When we have a humble view of the church, we will have a humble view of Christian leadership. So in chapter three Paul gives us a trinitarian understanding of the church as 'God's field' in which God is the farmer, as 'God's building' in which Christ is the foundation, and as 'God's temple' indwelt by the Holy Spirit. If chapter three gives us a picture of the church, chapter four gives us a picture of the pastor (indeed of the apostle first, but in a secondary sense of Christian leaders today). They are ministers of Christ, stewards of God's revelation, the scum of the earth (v. 13) and the fathers of the church family. Each model is a humbling one.

In the next chapters Paul gives apostolic instruction about disciplining, and even excommunicating, a serious offender (ch. 5); about *not* taking our Christian brothers and sisters to court (6:1–6); about sexual immorality and the Christian view of the human body (6:7–20); and about marriage, singleness and divorce (ch. 7). The teaching is hard-hitting and straight from the shoulder. Paul makes no concessions to contemporary culture, for he knows that the church is called to be a counter-culture. We are summoned not to feeble-minded conformity, but to radical non-conformity to the world around us.

In chapters 8 and 9 Paul broaches the sensitive issue of our rights and their renunciation. His first example concerns idol-meats. That is, should Christians buy and eat meat which, previous to its sale in the butcher's shop, had been used in a pagan sacrificial ritual? Would not such meat have been contaminated? As a knowlegable believer Paul was able to declare strongly that there is only one God, that idols are nothing, and that therefore there is no reason for not eating idol-meats. But how should we behave towards a fellow-Christian, probably a recent convert, who does not share this knowledge and therefore has a weak or over-scrupulous conscience? If he sees us eating, he may be emboldened to follow our example against his conscience and so wound it, and even sin against Christ. If my eating will cause my brother to fall into sin, Paul added with characteristic hyperbole, 'I will never eat meat again' (8:13). The principle then is plain: knowledge brings freedom, but love limits it, for love is greater than knowledge (8:1; 13:2, cf. 10:23–33).

Paul's second example is more personal to him, and is opened up in chapter 9. He is an apostle, for he has seen the risen Lord (one of the conditions of apostleship). As such he has a right to marry and to receive support. After all, soldiers, farmers and shepherds do not work for nothing. And the Old Testament law says that oxen might eat the grain they are treading out and that priests in the temple might share in the sacrifices. And as a third argument the Lord Jesus himself commanded that 'those who preach the gospel should receive their living from the gospel' (v. 14). So there is no doubt about the principle. But, Paul continues (v. 12b and 15), he has not used his right, nor was he asking for it now. He would rather die than be deprived of his boast that he preached for nothing. Besides, it was not a boast, but a compulsion. 'Woe to me if I do not preach the gospel!' (v. 16). He makes himself a slave to everyone, in order to win as many as possible (v. 19).

Both examples illustrate the same fundamental principle: although we may have rights, there may be sound reasons for waiving them.

In chapters 10 – 14 the apostle addresses himself to important questions about the life and worship of the church. He begins with a warning from the history of Israel that the visible and professing church may not be the genuine people of God. For all the Israelites had been baptized in the Red Sea, and all had partaken of the same food and drink. In other words, they were all baptized communicant members of the visible church. Nevertheless, God was not pleased with most of them, and his judgment fell upon them in the desert (10:1–13). After making this vital distinction between the nominal and the real church (which still needs to be made today), the apostle moves on to various aspects of public worship.

First, they must flee from idolatry, as Israel should have done, since participation in the body and blood of Christ is incompatible with pagan idol-feasts and sacrifices. 'You cannot drink the cup of the Lord', Paul states, 'and the cup of demons too' (10:21).

Next, Paul gives instructions about the public worship of the

Corinthians, which was being marred by inappropriate behaviour. The first related to gender. The difficulty we have in interpreting Paul's teaching is that he combines theological and cultural issues in the same passage. Most of us will agree that questions of length of hair and wearing veils are cultural, in that they may vary in different places and at different times. But Paul's teaching about 'headship' (God–Christ–man–woman) is profoundly theological. Moreover, as between God and Christ, so between man and woman, 'headship' is not incompatible with equality.

The second situation Paul addresses is the Lord's Supper. He is deeply grieved that the Corinthian factions were manifesting themselves even at the Lord's table, and that class distinctions also appeared, so that some worshippers went hungry while others got drunk. So Paul reminds his readers of the institution of the Eucharist during the Last Supper (11:23–26). He therefore emphasizes the seriousness of eating and drinking in an unworthy manner, and urges the need for self-examination before coming to the table, lest they experience more of the judgment of God.

Next, in chapters 12 – 14 Paul responds to their questions about *charismata*, spiritual gifts. This passage is an outstanding further example of our theme of diversity in unity. Four times Paul insists on their fundamental unity, as the background against which their diversity can be appreciated. First, they had all received the Holy Spirit, because 'no-one can say, "Jesus is Lord", except by the Holy Spirit' (12:3). Secondly, they had had the same experience of the Trinity, for behind their different gifts and ministries is 'the same Spirit', 'the same Lord' and 'the same God' (12:4–6). Thirdly, after listing nine gifts (others occur in other lists), Paul concludes: 'All these are the work of one and the same Spirit ...' (12:7–11). And fourthly, Paul resorts to his favourite metaphor of the human body, which is 'a unit, though it is made up of many parts ... So it is with Christ. For we were all baptized (by Christ) by (or with) one Spirit into one body' (my parentheses) and, changing the metaphor, 'we were all given the one Spirit to drink' (12:12–13).

For the rest of chapter 12 the apostle develops the model of 'one body, many parts'. All members of the body are useful in different ways. So we must neither despise our own gifts, nor depreciate those of others. The arrogance which says 'I don't need you' and the false modesty which says 'you don't need me' are both destructive attitudes. They undermine the body's unity-in-diversity. They need to hear the affirmation, 'Now you are the body of Christ, and each one of you is a part of it' (12:27).

After considering the danger that diversity may lead to disunity, Paul shows the Corinthians what he calls 'the most excellent way'. His hymn to love is unparalleled in the literature of the world. Love is greater than tongues and prophecy, greater than knowledge and faith, greater than philanthropy and heroism (13:1–3). It is the greatest thing in the world. Love is patient and kind; it is therefore neither jealous nor boastful, neither proud nor rude, neither self-seeking nor irritable. It rejoices not in evil but in truth. It always protects, trusts, hopes and perseveres (13:4–7). And love lasts for ever (13:8–13). Such love welcomes the diversity of Christ's body. It is neither resentful nor conceited. It is the essential atmosphere within which spiritual gifts can operate.

In chapter 14 Paul reverts to spiritual gifts and in particular to prophecy, which he declares to be more profitable than tongues because it is intelligible and brings people strength, encouragement and comfort (14:3). This is in keeping with the apostle's principle: 'try to excel in gifts that build up the church' (14:12).

This letter began with the factions which were tearing the Corinthian church apart. By contrast, chapter 15 (its last main chapter, apart from the personal messages of chapter 16) is a magnificent exposition of the gospel which, more than anything else, is calculated to unify the church.

Paul says he wants to remind the Corinthians of the gospel, which he assumes is a universally recognizable message. He had himself proclaimed it to them, and they had received it. More, they had taken their stand on it. And they were being saved by it, so long as they were holding firm to it, since otherwise they would have believed in vain. What was this gospel? It was the apostolic tradition which he had received and passed on. Of first importance in this gospel were four events, namely the death, burial, resurrection and appearances of the Lord Jesus.

Perhaps it would make for clarity, however, if we made explicit what is already surely implicit, namely that these four events are not of equal importance. Of supreme importance, as we know from repeated references in the New Testament, are the death and resurrection of Jesus; the importance of the burial and the appearances is in relation to these. Thus, Christ died for our sins according to the Scriptures, and then was buried to demonstrate the reality of his death. Next, Christ was raised on the third day according to the Scriptures, and then appeared and was seen, to demonstrate the reality of his resurrection.

Paul goes on to list the main resurrection appearances, official and personal, to groups and to individuals, putting himself at the end of the list. Several things need to be said about the Damascus Road experience.

First, it was a genuine resurrection appearance, and not some kind of vision or apparition. We know this because Paul includes it with the others he lists, and because what was 'raised' was what had been 'buried', namely his body. In addition, Paul moves directly from 'he appeared to me also' to 'I am the least of the apostles', for a resurrection appearance was an indispensable qualification for apostleship (see Acts 1:21–22, 25; 1 Cor. 9:1).

Secondly, although it was a genuine resurrection appearance, nevertheless it was atypical because it did not take place during the forty days (like all the others) but after the ascension.

Thirdly, it was the final appearance, having taken place 'last of all'. Whatever visions of Jesus some people have claimed since then, we should not think of them as resurrection appearances.

Having given his list of appearances, Paul now concludes with an important statement about the gospel (15:11): 'Whether, then, it was I or they, this is what we preach, and this is what you believed.'

The four pronouns are extremely significant: I, they, we and you. 'I' is the apostle Paul and 'they' the Jerusalem apostles. 'We' is all the apostles together, who preach the same gospel, and 'you' is the members of the church of Corinth who have all received it. It is a claim to the unity both of the apostles' proclamation and of the church's faith, alongside their diversity of gifts.

The rest of 1 Corinthians 15 is a closely reasoned statement about different aspects of the resurrection: the dire consequences if Christ has not been raised (vv. 12–19); the fact that Christ has risen, setting in motion the eschatological programme (vv. 20–28); more questions about the situation if there is no resurrection (vv. 29–34); instruction about the nature of the resurrection body, combining both continuity with our earthly body and discontinuity (vv. 35–49); an assurance that those who die will be raised and that those who survive till Christ's coming will be changed, so that death will be swallowed up in victory (vv. 50–57); and a final exhortation to his readers to stand firm and work hard, knowing that, in the light of the resurrection, their labours will not be in vain (v. 58).

2 Corinthians

The apostle's relations with the Corinthian church (both his visits and his letters) are complicated and need not concern us here. But we note that 2 Corinthians is arguably the most personal of all Paul's letters, since he needs to defend himself against the many criticisms of those who regarded themselves as 'super-apostles' (11:5), although in reality they were 'false apostles' (11:13). In contrast to them, Paul delineates the essentials of an authentic Christian ministry.

He begins with a reference to his troubles and hardships. In and through Christ, he declares, he has been experiencing comfort in suffering and even resurrection-life through death (1:3–11). In response to criticism, he now defends his alteration of plans. He had not been guilty of vacillating, of changing his mind in a frivolous or worldly manner, or of saying 'yes and no' in the same breath. Such behaviour would have been incompatible with the faithfulness of God and with the truth that all God's promises find their 'yes' in Christ (1:12–22).

This leads Paul on to a general defence of himself and his colleagues as 'ministers of a new covenant' (3:6). To be sure, the ministry of the old covenant was attended by a degree of glory; but the ministry of the new covenant is 'much more glorious' (3:9), since it is a ministry of the Spirit (not of death), a justifying ministry (not a condemning one), and permanent (not fading away) (3:1–18).

Because we have received this glorious ministry, 'we do not lose heart' (4:1, 6), but rather 'we are always confident' (5:6, 8). Mind you, there are good reasons why we might lose courage. The first is 'the veil', which lies over the mind of unbelievers to keep them from seeing the light of the gospel of Christ's glory (3:12–18; 4:3–4). The second is 'the body', our fragile and mortal body that is like a clay jar in which the gospel treasure is housed (4:7). It is utterly impossible for us to solve either of these two problems by ourselves. Only God can remove the veil by causing light to shine into human darkness (4:6). Only God can cause 'the life of Jesus' to be revealed in our mortal bodies now (4:10–11) and on the last day 'raise us with Jesus' (4:14 – 5:10). No wonder we are of good courage, and refuse to lose heart!

The ministry of the new covenant is also a ministry of reconciliation, and 5:18–21 is one of the most sublime passages in the New Testament on the subject of reconciliation. First, God is its *author* ('all this is from God ... God was in Christ reconciling ...' vv. 18–19); there can never be any suggestion that Christ took the initiative to wrest reconciliation from a reluctant God. Secondly, Christ is the *agent* of the reconciliation. In two of Paul's daring expressions, God refused to count the sins of human beings against them (v. 19), but instead made the sinless Christ to be sin for us (v. 21). Thirdly, we are the *ambassadors* of the reconciliation, for both the ministry and the message of reconciliation have been committed to us (vv. 18–19), and God is now making his appeal through us, imploring people on behalf of Christ to be reconciled to God (v. 20; cf. 6:1–2).

Paul continues his appeal at the beginning of chapter 6, and then goes on to describe his ministry. On the one hand, he is determined to put no stumbling block in anyone's path, so that his ministry is not discredited. On the other hand, he is equally determined to commend his ministry in every possible way, by endurance in all his afflictions and by moral qualities such as purity and love. The paradoxes of verses 8 to 10 (e.g. 'sorrowful, yet always rejoicing' and 'poor, yet making many rich') set over against each other appearance and reality, what he is in the opinion of humans and of God.

Chapters 8 and 9 are devoted to the collection that Paul was organizing among the affluent churches of Greece on behalf of the impoverished churches of Judea. He deploys every possible argument with which to persuade the Greek churches to contribute generously. But the greatest of them all is 'the grace of our Lord Jesus Christ'. What is that? It is 'that though he was rich, yet for your sakes he became poor, so that you through his poverty might become rich' (8:9). Paul never forgets Christ; he keeps returning to him, even in the middle of his financial appeal.

In the rest of his letter (chs. 10 – 13), the apostle returns to the defence of his own ministry against the false apostles. He is unsure how heavy-handed he could or should be. Because he is a genuine apostle of Christ, authenticated by his miracles and by his pioneer evangelization of Corinth (10:8; 12:12), part of him wants to assert his apostolic authority. But another part of him is extremely hesitant. He knows that it is much more appropriate to appeal to them 'by the meekness and gentleness of Christ' (10:1). At all events his motives are pure. He is jealous for them 'with a godly jealousy'. He had promised them to one husband, to Christ, but he is afraid that they are being led astray from their 'sincere and pure devotion to Christ' (11:1–3).

He feels a fool, for he knows that in his self-confident boasting he is 'not talking as the Lord would' (11:17). Yet his opponents are forcing him into it (11:18). So he goes ahead. He lists his Jewish pedigree, and his loyalty to Christ in spite of floggings and imprisonments, not to mention all the dangers he has risked in sea and river, from bandits and enemies, in city and country, in hunger and thirst, nakedness and sleeplessness. And, besides everything else, he has experienced the pressure of his concern for the churches (11:21–33). And then there were his 'visions and revelations from the Lord' (12:1). To keep him from becoming conceited because of these, he continues, 'there was given me a thorn in my flesh, a messenger of Satan, to torment me' (12:7). It was evidently a physical infirmity of some kind. Although he pleaded three times for its removal, the Lord Jesus told him instead that his grace was sufficient for him, for his power was perfected in weakness. So he learned to rejoice in his weakness, for when he was weak, then he was strong (12:7–10). He has returned to the paradox of 'power through weakness'. It is one of the main themes of Paul's Corinthian correspondence. It was true in Christ and in Paul; it is true also in us.

10. The prison letters (Colossians, Philemon, Ephesians and Philippians): Christ the supreme Lord

That Paul was several times incarcerated as 'a prisoner for the Lord' (Eph. 4:1, cf. 2 Cor. 11:23) is well known. 'I am in chains for Christ', he wrote (Phil. 1:13, 17). Again, 'remember my chains' (Col. 4:18; Philem. 10, 13). But not all scholars are agreed either when or where these imprisonments took place. I shall follow the traditional view that he suffered two main periods of detention in Rome, with several years' freedom between them (Acts 28:30–31).

What it seems reasonable to conjecture is that while in prison, delivered from the feverish activity of his missionary lifestyle, he had extra time in which to meditate. He declared that on one occasion during his first defence no human being came to his support, for everybody deserted him. Nevertheless, he added, 'the Lord stood at my side and gave me strength' (2 Tim. 4:16–17). Luke tells us that something similar had taken place before, both after his arrest in Jerusalem (Acts 23:11) and while he was on his voyage to Rome (Acts 27:23). So there is no reason why it should not have happened at other times too. Prison bars could confine his body, but not his soul. It seems that during those years, although he could neither evangelize more cities nor visit the churches, his mind soared into heaven.

Ephesians and Colossians are closely related to one another. Their texts and topics run parallel at several important points. In particular, both express a wonderfully exalted Christology.

In Ephesians 1:15–23 Paul prays that the eyes of his readers' heart may be enlightened to comprehend God's incomparably great power which he displayed when he resurrected Christ and set him at his right hand in the place of supreme honour, far above all conceivable rivals. Indeed, 'God placed all things under his feet and appointed him to be head over everything for the church, which is his body, the fulness of him who fills everything in every way' (v. 23).

Colossians contains a similar passage on the absolute pre-eminence of the cosmic Christ, except that it begins with the creation and includes the cross. Identifying Jesus as the visible image of the invisible God, Paul goes on (in opposition to all forms of gnostic dualism) to call him the firstborn over all creation, the agent through whom all things were created and now cohere, and the heir for whom all things were made. He is thus 'before all things' in both time and rank. He is head of the body – the church, and the firstborn from among the dead, 'so that in everything he might have the supremacy'. For God was pleased to have all his fullness both to dwell in Christ and through Christ to reconcile all things to himself by making peace through his blood shed on the cross (1:15–20).

The perspective is almost overwhelming, as Jesus is seen to be the supreme head of both creations, of the universe and of the church.

But there is something more. The death and resurrection of Jesus Christ are not only objective, saving events; God's purpose is also that we should participate personally in their reality. Paul affirms this in both Ephesians and Colossians. He writes in Ephesians that God has 'made us alive with Christ ... and ... raised us up with Christ and seated us with him in the heavenly realms in Christ Jesus' (2:5–6).

This union of believers with Christ is even more strikingly expressed in Colossians, where four times the adverb *sun* (meaning 'with') is used: 'you died with Christ ... you have been raised with Christ ... your life is now hidden with Christ ... you will appear with him in glory' (2:20; 3:1, 3, 4).

Ephesians and Colossians do not depict the Christian life only on this exalted level, however, as participating in Christ 'in the heavenly realms'. Both epistles are also known for their down-to-earth exhortations relating on the one hand to the church, God's new society, whose unity, truth and holiness Paul describes, and on the other to the family or household in which our new life demands new relationships. This is beautifully illustrated in the little letter to Philemon.

The letter to the Philippians also combines great heights of Christological faith with the good works of Christian behaviour. It is widely accepted that the so-called *carmen Christi* ('Song of Christ') in chapter 2 is an early Christian hymn which Paul has borrowed. Whether composed or borrowed does not, however, matter greatly since in either case it enjoys Paul's apostolic endorsement. In keeping with Jesus' epigram that 'whoever humbles himself shall be exalted', the hymn describes both the depths of humiliation to which the incarnation and atonement took him ('he humbled himself and became obedient to death, even death on a cross') and the heights of exaltation to which in consequence the Father raised him, giving him 'the name that is above every name', that is, the rank beyond all others, as implied in the title 'Lord', so that every knee should bow to him and every tongue confess him Lord (2:9–11).

As with Ephesians and Colossians, so with Philippians, the supreme lordship of Jesus is not limited to ivory-tower theology. Paul also writes of his own personal commitment to Christ. He draws up a kind of profit-and-loss account. On one side of the ledger he puts everything which could be considered 'profitable' – his ancestry, parentage and education, his Hebrew culture, his religious zeal and legalistic righteousness. In the other column he puts 'Christ'. Then he makes a careful calculation and concludes: 'I count everything sheer loss, far outweighed by the gain of knowing Christ Jesus my Lord' (3:7–8, REB). Moreover this lordship of Christ worked itself out in his everyday living – in joy and gentleness, in freedom from anxiety and inner peace, in a disciplined thought-life and in contentment in all circumstances (4:4–13). Why? Because 'the Lord is near' (4:5).

Conviction about the Lord Jesus, highly exalted yet simultaneously near, dominates the prison letters.

11. The pastoral letters (1 Timothy, Titus and 2 Timothy): Christ the head of the church

The authenticity of the pastoral letters to Timothy and Titus has regularly been called into question since F. C. Baur of Tübingen rejected them in 1835. At the same time, during the second half of the twentieth century a considerable number of scholars have rallied to the defence of their Pauline authorship. Those who still reject their genuineness are often quite rude in their evaluation of the letters' theology, or rather (in their opinion) lack of it. A. T. Hanson, for example, declared that 'there is a complete absence of unifying theme in them', even 'an impression of relative incoherence'.[18]

Others, however, have a decidedly different opinion. Paul's overriding preoccupation in all three pastoral letters is with the church. For Christ died 'to purify for himself a people ...' (Titus 2:14). Consequently, Paul is concerned with the life of the local church and particularly with the church's responsibility to guard and teach the truth. For he defines the church as 'the pillar and foundation of the truth' (1 Tim. 3:15); its foundation to hold it firm and its pillar to thrust it high.

In 1 Timothy Paul gives instruction about sound doctrine, public worship, pastoral oversight, local leadership, social responsibilities and material possessions – all of which are of vital importance to the local church. In his letter to Titus Paul directs him how to select and appoint pastors, and how to relate duty and doctrine in the home and in public life. The second letter to Timothy seems to have been written from prison shortly before Paul was executed. It is probably the most intimate and affectionate of all Paul's letters. Knowing that his death is approaching, Paul exhorts Timothy not to be ashamed of Christ, but to be conscientious in his life and ministry, to cling in difficult times both to the Old Testament Scriptures and to the apostle's teaching, and to preach the Word.

Perhaps the text which best sums up the main message of all three pastorals is 2 Timothy 2:2, 'the things you have heard me say in the presence of many witnesses entrust to reliable men who will also be qualified to teach others'. Here are four stages in the handing on of the truth.

First, there is Paul himself, 'an apostle of Christ Jesus', whose self-conscious apostolic authority is apparent in his letters. He refers again and again to what he calls indiscriminately 'the truth', 'the faith', 'the sound doctrine', 'the teaching' or 'the deposit'. The clear implication is that a body of apostolic doctrine existed, which he taught.

Secondly, there are Timothy and Titus. They stand between the apostle and the church, in the sense that they represent him and relay his teaching to the church. During the apostle's personal absence his authority is mediated through his letters. As many as ten times in 1 Timothy and Titus Paul writes 'teach these things', 'command and teach these things' or 'give the people these instructions'. They were to pass on faithfully to others the precious truths the apostle had taught them.

Thirdly, there are the true and trustworthy pastors whom Timothy and Titus were to appoint. In both 1 Timothy and Titus Paul lays down the conditions of eligibility they must fulfil. Apart from a consistent character and home life, they must be loyal to the apostles' teaching and have a gift for teaching it (Titus 1:9; 1 Tim. 3:2).

Fourthly, these pastors 'will also be qualified to teach others'. This is the true apostolic succession – the transmission of the apostles' teaching from generation to generation through the New Testament.

In our post-modern era the self-confidence of the Enlightenment has gone, the very concept of objective 'truth' is rejected, and all that remains are purely personal and subjective opinions. So it is a relief to listen to the apostle Paul. Not only does he call himself an apostle 'for the ... knowledge of the truth that leads to godliness' (Titus 1:1), and define the church in relation to the truth, but he describes the false teachers as people who 'have wandered away from the truth' (2 Tim. 2:18) and even 'oppose the truth' (2 Tim. 3:8). Nothing is more necessary for the life, health and growth of the church than the faithful teaching of the truth.

This rapid overview of Paul's letters demonstrates conclusively the Christ-centredness of his faith, life and ministry. 'To me, to live is Christ', he could say (Phil. 1:21) and again 'whatever was to my profit I now consider loss for the sake of Christ' (Phil. 3:7). Each letter or cluster of letters, responding to different situations, contributes to a composite picture of Christ – the liberator, the judge, the Saviour, the supreme Lord and the head of the church. Paul does not contradict himself. A rich variety of colourful strands is woven into his tapestry of Christ.

Three more Jewish authors

Having considered the thirteen letters attributed to Paul, we turn to the remaining letters of the New Testament: the letter of James, the letter to the Hebrews, and the two letters of Peter (including Jude which has great similarities to 2 Peter). Paul was the acknowledged apostle to the Gentiles (e.g. Rom. 15:16; Gal.1:16;

2:7), whereas the three letters, whose testimony to Christ we are now to look at (James, Hebrews and 1 Peter), were intended in differing degrees for a Jewish readership. I take James's letter first because of the alleged disagreement between him and Paul.

12. The letter of James: Christ the moral teacher

This James was one of the Lord's brothers who, though unbelieving during Jesus' lifetime, seems to have come to faith through a resurrection appearance (Mark 6:3; John 7:5; 1 Cor. 15:7). He later became the acknowledged leader of the Jerusalem church and of Jewish Christians (Acts 12:17; Gal. 1:18–19). He chaired the Jerusalem Council (Acts 15:13–21), and continued to maintain that, although circumcision was not necessary for Gentile converts, Jewish believers should continue to show great respect for the Mosaic ceremonial law (e.g. Acts 21:17–26).

James became known as 'James the Just' because of his personal righteousness and godliness. Hegesippus, towards the end of the second century, is quoted as having said: 'He was in the habit of entering alone into the temple, and was frequently found upon his knees begging forgiveness for the people, so that his knees became hard like those of a camel, in consequence of his constantly bending them in his worship of God.'[19]

It is not surprising, therefore, because of the holiness of James the Just, that his letter (which is really a tract or treatise), addressed to 'the twelve tribes scattered among the nations' (1:1), should focus on living a life that is pleasing to God. What sort of witness, then, does James bear to Jesus? 'Very little', some will reply. And it is true that Jesus is named only twice, once in the first verse in which James identifies himself as 'a servant ... of the Lord Jesus Christ', and on the other occasion when his readers are called 'believers in our glorious Lord Jesus Christ' (2:1). They are also referred to as bearing 'the noble name' (2:7), and on the eight or more times when 'the Lord' occurs, more often than not it means Jesus (1:7; 4:10, 15; 5:7, 8, 10, 11, 15). But indirectly James witnesses to Jesus throughout. For one of the most interesting features of his letter is the number of times he alludes in a clear way to the recorded teaching of Jesus and specifically to his Sermon on the Mount, as if he had been present and heard it – which is not impossible. There are at least twenty echoes, like inheriting the promised kingdom; the blessedness of peacemakers, of those who suffer for righteousness, and of those who show mercy; questions of wealth and poverty; not speaking evil of others or judging them; and being patient until the Lord comes. It is indisputable, there-fore, that James presents Jesus as essentially a moral teacher.

This emphasis leads naturally to the apparent contradiction between him and Paul. Paul taught that Abraham was justified not by works but by faith (Rom. 4:2–3). But James asks here: 'Was not Abraham our father justified by works?' (2:21, RSV). The discrepancy looks obvious and led Luther to reject James's letter as made of 'straw'. But the New Testament presents the two leaders as respecting one another. James had welcomed Paul's mission to the Gentiles (Gal. 2:9), and Paul had accepted James's concern for Jewish feelings (Acts 15:12–30; 21:17–26).

A natural harmony between them emerges when we note that they were responding to different situations, needing different theological emphases. Paul was writing against Judaizers, who taught justification by works of the law; James against intellectualizers who taught justification by 'faith' in the sense of barren orthodoxy. Both groups were mistaken. In opposition to Judaizers Paul emphasized justification by faith alone without works; in opposition to intellectualizers James emphasized justifi-cation not by the faith of barren orthodoxy (which the demons share and shudder! Jas. 2:19) but by a living faith which is fruitful in good works. Thus both apostles taught the same way of salvation, namely justification by faith unto good works. Paul wrote of 'faith expressing itself through love' (Gal. 5:6), and James wrote 'I will show you my faith by what I do' (2:18). But Paul stressed the faith that issues in works, while James stressed the works that issue from faith.

The best summary of James's concerns may be found in 1:26–27, where 'pure and faultless religion' is said to have three characteristics: (1) to bridle the tongue, (2) to look after orphans and widows in their distress, and (3) to keep ourselves from being polluted by the world. Here is our threefold ethical duty, namely to ourselves, to our neighbour and to our God. Tongue-control is an index of self-control. The care of widows and orphans is an example of neighbour-love. To keep oneself unstained by the world is the negative counterpart to giving God the worship due to his name. The rest of James's letter contains challenging variations on this threefold theme.

13. The letter to the Hebrews: Christ our great high priest

The letter to the Hebrews is anonymous, and debate continues about its authorship. Nevertheless, although the author's identity is uncertain, his purpose is not. He is writing his letter or treatise to a local church of Hebrew Christians, perhaps in or near Jerusalem, in order to stop them from apostatizing. Owing partly to their persecutions (10:32–39), but more specifically to their theological confusion, they are in evident danger of relapsing into Judaism. The author hopes to establish them in Christ by demonstrating his finality.

That the author is well qualified to accomplish his task is evident from his comprehensive knowledge of both the Old Testament and the story of Jesus. He makes something like seventy Old Testament allusions and about twenty-five to the New Testament story. Knowing both intimately, he is well placed to argue the superiority of the New Covenant to the Old and so to show that the new wine has burst the old bottles. His argument is threefold, namely that Christ's priesthood, sacrifice and covenant are perfect and cannot be superseded.

Before developing this theme, our author introduces it with a brief but magnificent Christological statement. The same God, he declares, who spoke to the fathers through the prophets in many parts and many ways, has in these last days spoken to us in his Son, who is the agent, the upholder and the heir of the creation. As for his person, he is both 'the radiance of God's glory' (ensuring his community of nature with the Father) and 'the exact representation of God's being' (ensuring the distinctness of his person). And this unique Jesus Christ, who has not yet been named, having made purification for sin, sat down at the Father's right hand. In these ways he, who is superior to the prophets, is superior to the angels as well. It is this exalted Son, unrivalled in the dignity of his person and work, in whom God's final revelation has been given.

After this introduction the author moves towards his first great theme, which is the superiority of the priesthood of Christ. He affirms that Jesus is superior to both Moses and Aaron. In fact his priesthood is not Aaronic (because he was not descended from Levi) but 'in the order of Melchizedek'. Melchizedek was a shadowy Old Testament figure who blessed Abraham and whose eternal priesthood is mentioned in Psalm 110:4. The old Levitical priests had to be continuously replaced, because death prevented them from continuing in office, but Jesus holds his priesthood permanently because he lives for ever.

Having established the final supremacy of the priesthood of Jesus, the author comes to the achievement of his sacrifice. For a priest must have something to offer. What, then, did Jesus have to offer? The answer is 'his own blood', that is, himself laid down in violent death. So he was the victim as well as the priest, and the author explains the superiority of his sacrifice. Only the high priest might enter the holy of holies; but Jesus has secured access into God's presence for all his people. Only once a year (on the Day of Atonement) might the high priest enter; but Jesus has secured for us continuous access. Only with the blood of animal sacrifice might the high priest enter; but Jesus entered with his own blood. Only cleansing from ceremonial defilement was secured by the Old Testament sacrifices; but Jesus secured the forgiveness of our sins. Only by regular sacrifices could the people remain clean; but Jesus died once and for all. Point by point our author has shown the fulfilment in Christ of the imperfect foreshadowing of Old Testament ritual.

The writer now introduces his principal theme. It is that this unique priest through his unique sacrifice has established a unique covenant. This new covenant is a 'better' covenant (7:22) because it is enacted on 'better promises' (8:6). These were foretold by God through Jeremiah (Jer. 31:31–34), and our author quotes them twice. God promises (1) to write his laws on our hearts, (2) to reveal himself to each of us personally, and (3) to forgive our sins, remembering them no longer. These promises of inward holiness, individual knowledge and full forgiveness have been fulfilled through Christ.

Once we have grasped the finality of Christ's priesthood, sacrifice and covenant, we cannot contemplate any alternative. There can be no question of other sacrificing priests, since through our great high priest we enjoy direct access to God. There can be no question of other sacrifices for sin, for our salvation has been achieved by Christ's unique sacrifice; our sacrifices are sacrifices of praise and thanksgiving. There can be no question of another covenant, for the new covenant is the last covenant, and the better covenant is the best. It will never be superseded. The eternity of our final and perfect salvation fills the writer's mind. Christ is a priest 'for ever', who has made 'one sacrifice for sins for ever', and thus established an 'eternal covenant', which brings to God's people an 'eternal salvation' (5:9), an 'eternal redemption' (9:12) and an 'eternal inheritance' (9:15).

Those Hebrew Christians were in danger of backsliding. Exposed to vicious persecution and specious argument, they were wavering in their Christian faith and contemplating apostasy to Judaism. If only they could grasp the absolute finality of Jesus Christ, it is inconceivable that they should drift back.

Having concluded his exposition of the unique person, work and covenant of Christ, our author continues with an exhortation.

Therefore, brothers, since we have confidence to enter the Most Holy Place [i.e. God's immediate presence] by the blood of Jesus ... and since we have a great priest over the house of God, let us draw near to God with a sincere heart in full assurance of *faith*, having our hearts sprinkled to cleanse us from a guilty conscience and having our bodies washed with pure water. Let us hold unswervingly to the *hope* we profess ... And let us consider how we may spur one another on towards *love* and good deeds ... (10:19–24, my emphasis).

It would be difficult to miss the author's reference to the famous Christian triad of faith, hope and love. And the rest of the letter seems to elaborate it. Certainly chapter 11 focuses on faith, first defining it and then parading before us some of the great Old Testament heroes of faith. But they were people of hope as well as of faith because 'faith is being sure of what we hope for' (11:1). Some promises were inherited during their lifetime, yet in another sense 'none of them received what had been promised' (11:39), because there are depths to the promises of God which cannot be inherited until the next world. Hence the need for hope, and for the acceptance of divine discipline, as we wait patiently for the fulfilment of the promises.

Chapter 13 touches briefly on aspects of reciprocal love in the Christian family, how we are to be hospitable to strangers, to remember prisoners, to honour marriage, to prefer contentment to covetousness, to respect our Christian leaders, and to go to Jesus 'outside the camp, bearing the disgrace he bore' (13:13).

These Christian privileges and obligations, namely access to God by faith, endurance through hope, and brotherly love in the church family, all issue from the great fact which our author has been at pains to emphasize, namely the absolute uniqueness and finality of our Lord Jesus Christ.

14. The letters of Peter: Christ the exemplary sufferer

It may come as a surprise that I should place Peter under the heading of 'Jewish authors', since it was through him that Cornelius, the first Gentile, was converted (Acts 10). But Peter 'had been given the task of preaching the gospel to the Jews' (Gal. 2:7), and it seems clear that in his first letter he has Jewish readers principally (though not exclusively) in mind. He refers to them as belonging to the 'diaspora' in five provinces of Asia Minor, and he alludes to 'Gentiles' as a separate group (2:12; 4:3). His vocabulary is similarly suggestive as he refers, for example, to our 'inheritance' (1:4), the call to be holy (1:6–7), and the blood of Christ as of a lamb without blemish (1:2, 19). His many quotations from the Pentateuch, Psalms, Proverbs and Prophets also indicate that he is very familiar with the Old Testament.

Peter's opening doxology praises God that he has given us a new birth into a living hope through the resurrection of Jesus Christ (1:3). And this living hope sustains us, however fierce the opposition to Christians may be. Although Peter handles many other topics in his first letter, his main emphasis is on Christian behaviour in the face of persecution. The words 'suffer' and 'suffering' occur seven times in relation to Christ and nine times in relation to Christians.

So far as we know, there had as yet been no official edict proscribing Christianity and Christians. Nevertheless, the opposition Peter's readers were experiencing was severe (4:12) and widespread (5:9). It seems that the storm-clouds of more serious and systematic persecution were darkening the horizon. Local outbursts had begun. How should Christians behave in these circumstances? What is the Christian attitude to undeserved suffering? Christians were not to retaliate; that much was clear. But Peter went further than that. His first letter contains six passages on suffering: each expresses a different admonition, and each points his readers to Christ.

1 Peter 1:6–7: As they endure all kinds of trial, they must remember that *suffering tests, strengthens and purifies their faith*, as fire does gold. This will result in glory to God when Jesus Christ is revealed.

1 Peter 2:18–25: This paragraph relates particularly to Christian slaves whose masters are not considerate but harsh. They must bear unjust suffering. Why? Because *suffering is part of the Christian calling*. Christ had left them an example of non-retaliation, so that they might follow in his steps.

1 Peter 3:8–18: When suffering for what is right, Christians must not be frightened, but rather set Christ apart as Lord in their hearts, and always be ready to give an answer to everyone who asks them to give a reason for their Christian hope. *Suffering gives opportunities for witness.*

1 Peter 4:1–6: Peter here emphasizes the physical nature of persecution. It is suffering 'in the body'. It was for Jesus; it may be for us. Then let us remember that 'he who has suffered in his body is done with sin'. Since *suffering has a sanctifying influence on us*, we should welcome it more readily.

1 Peter 4:12–19: We are not to be surprised by painful trials, as if something strange were happening, but rather to rejoice that *suffering gives us the privilege of sharing in the sufferings of Christ* and so of participating in his glory (4:13; cf. 1:11; 5:1; and Luke 24:25–26).

1 Peter 5:10–11: We must remember that we have been called to God's eternal glory in Christ, but that to suffer a little is

necessary first, for *suffering is the path to glory*, as death is the path to life.

The coming glory is one of the leading themes of Peter's second letter, whose authenticity is still defended by some scholars. In chapter 2 he describes false teachers in vivid terms and warns that God's judgment will fall on them. In chapter 3 Peter argues with scoffers the certainty of Christ's return (vv. 3–7) and then attributes its delay to God's mercy (vv. 8–10). But the day of the Lord will come and will usher in a new heaven and new earth.

So what kind of people should we be, as we prepare (v. 11)? We should make every effort to be found 'spotless, blameless and at peace with him' (v. 14), on our guard against false teachers (v. 17), and growing 'in the grace and knowledge of our Lord and Saviour Jesus Christ' (v. 18).

Conclusion: Diversity in unity

Even this brief survey of the New Testament literature (except for the book of Revelation which we will consider in Part IV) has been enough to reveal its variety. It is diverse in its writers (at least nine were involved), in its literary forms (gospel, chronicle, letter, treatise and apocalypse), in the topics addressed according to local needs, in its theological emphases and in its presentation of Jesus.

Yet this same New Testament lays claim to a unity of message. The same gospel of Christ, according to Paul, was proclaimed by all the apostles and believed by all the church (1 Cor. 15:11). Again 'there is one body and one Spirit ... one hope ... one Lord, one faith, one baptism; one God and Father of all' (Eph. 4:4–6). And the so-called 'biblical theology movement', which held sway in Europe during and after the Second World War, laid emphasis on this. A. M. Hunter in Britain, for example, could write that 'there is a growing recognition of the essential unity of the New Testament and of the need for synthesis',[20] 'a unity that transcended and dominated all diversities'.[21]

Another influential book from that era was *The Riddle of the New Testament* by Edwyn Hoskyns and Noel Davey. The 'riddle' concerned was the relation 'between the historical figure of Jesus and the exuberant faith of the church'.[22] After carefully weighing up the evidence, Hoskyns and Davey concluded that 'all the varied New Testament material concentrates upon, and has its origin in one, single, isolated historical event', namely 'the life and death of Jesus'.[23]

But during the last years of the twentieth century the pendulum swung in the opposite direction, towards an emphasis on diversity. It was partly a reaction against artificial harmonizations, although it also revealed that some New Testament scholars take what Oscar Cullmann called 'an almost sadistic pleasure' in finding apparent discrepancies![24] We were told that now there was no such thing as 'biblical theology'; there were only a number of mutually incompatible 'biblical theologies'. The apostles' names were turned into adjectives, and scholars wrote about a 'Lucan' or 'Pauline' view of some doctrine, or a 'Petrine' or 'Johannine' position, as if they were mutually exclusive. One of the most outspoken critics of attempts to unify the New Testament witness is Professor James Dunn of Durham University. In his book *Unity and Diversity in the New Testament: An enquiry into the character of Earliest Christianity*, he wrote that there is no uniform concept of orthodoxy in early Christianity. There is not one gospel, he continues: there are at least four – one of John, another of the Synoptic gospels, and two more in the Acts and Paul. 'Any attempt to find a single, once-for-all, unifying *kerygma* is bound to fail.'[25] At the same time, Professor Dunn does concede that there is a 'unifying element' in the New Testament, namely 'the unity between the historical Jesus and the exalted Christ'.[26] But in the light of his whole book this is a minimal and rather grudging concession.

How should we respond? We must emphatically agree that we have no liberty to manipulate biblical texts into an artificial harmony; that we may not iron out apparent discrepancies; and that we must allow each New Testament author to say what he does say. And when we do this, tensions will remain. But we have also seen from our survey that the four gospels complement each other; they do not contradict each other. Nor do Jesus and Paul. Nor are Paul's thirteen letters self-contradictory. Nor do the more distinctively Jewish books (James, Hebrews and 1 Peter) strike a discordant note. Even Paul and James do not preach a different gospel. All the New Testament authors find their unity, as Professor Charlie Moule has written, in 'devotion to the person of Jesus

Christ – the historical Jesus acknowledged as continuous with the one now acknowledged as the transcendent Lord'.[27]

Bishop Stephen Neill, as updated by Dr N. T. Wright, in *The Interpretation of the New Testament 1861–1986*, brought together its unity and diversity: 'The event of Jesus Christ is far too great to be caught and held in one interpretation and one only.' So the church gathered together into the New Testament canon 'many different streams of tradition and interpretation ... The startling thing about all these traditions is their unity; they all relate to one event, which must have been staggeringly great, and to one Person, who must have been unlike any other person who has ever lived.'[28]

And again: 'It is the view of many competent scholars today that all the fragments of Christian tradition which we possess in the New Testament bear witness with singular unanimity to one single historical figure, unlike any other that has ever walked among the sons of men ...'[29] 'The principle of unity is there, in the towering originality and spiritual force of Jesus of Nazareth.'[30]

We in our generation can do no more than endorse from our conviction and experience the witness of the New Testament to Christ. This witness is both united and immensely variegated. But this is exactly what we would expect to find if we believe in the double authorship of Scripture, namely that it is the Word of God spoken through human words. Its unity is due to the one divine mind from which it comes, and its variety to the many human minds through which it was spoken. We pay our tribute to the original Jesus, the Jesus of the New Testament witness, who is the incomparable Christ.

PART II

THE ECCLESIASTICAL JESUS

(or how the church has presented him)

PART II: THE ECCLESIASTICAL JESUS
(or how the church has presented him)

Introduction: 'Another Jesus'

The idea of an 'ecclesiastical' Jesus at first hearing sounds preposterous. Was Jesus a 'churchy' person? Does the church have some
kind of monopoly on him? No. What I am concerned with in this
second part is rather the ways in which the church has presented
him down the ages, and with the sad fact that it has often
imprisoned him in its own prejudices and traditions.

Consider the rebuke which Paul administered to the
compromising Corinthian Christians: 'I am afraid that your
thoughts may be corrupted and you may lose your single-hearted
devotion to Christ. For if someone comes who proclaims another
Jesus, not the Jesus whom we proclaimed ... you manage to put up
with that well enough' (2 Cor. 11:3–4, NEB).

'Another Jesus'. The very expression is provocative and unacceptable. For there is only one authentic Jesus, and that is the Jesus of
the apostolic witness in the New Testament. There is no other.
Similarly, there is only 'one Lord', as there is only 'one faith', 'one
hope' and 'one baptism' (Eph. 4:5). Again, although there are
many so-called 'gods' and many so-called 'lords' claiming people's
allegiance, 'yet for us there is but one God, the Father, from whom
all things came and for whom we live; and there is but one Lord,
Jesus Christ, through whom all things came and through whom we
live' (1 Cor. 8:5–6).

Yet the fact is that down the centuries of the Christian era
hundreds of different Jesuses have been on offer in the world's
religious supermarkets. Some resonate with contemporary culture,
but only by manipulating Scripture. Others are biblically faithful
but culturally alien. Yet others in differing degrees succeed in
relating to both Scripture and culture. In contrast to the 'one Lord'
of the diverse yet united witness of the New Testament, the church
has displayed a remarkable ingenuity in adapting, shaping and
presenting its own images of Christ.

As in Part I of this work I attempted a survey of the New

Testament in its variegated testimony to the one Jesus, so, in Part II, I will attempt a survey of church history in its amazingly versatile witness to him.

Mind you, church history is not as amenable to survey treatment as is the New Testament. For the story of the church over two millennia has included too vast a variety of people and movements to encompass them all. All I have been able to do is choose twelve examples of how Jesus has been presented by churches and church leaders down the ages.

Readers may well ask on what basis I have made my selection, since it will seem arbitrary to some. My answer is that, because a comprehensive survey is impossible, I have tried to assemble some of the main movements of thought in the church, and their representatives.

We begin in the second century AD, in the immediate post-apostolic period. One of the firm convictions of the early church at that time was that with Jesus something wonderfully new had begun. He had inaugurated the kingdom of God. He had ushered in the new age. His first recorded words when he began his public ministry were: 'The time has come; the kingdom of God is upon you' (Mark 1:15, NEB). Similarly, Paul wrote: 'When the time had fully come, God sent his Son …' (Gal. 4:4). And yet in another sense the new beginning was not new, because it had been predicted and promised for centuries. What had happened was the fulfilment of promise. So there was a vital continuity between the so-called Old and New Testaments.

1. Christ the complete fulfilment: Justin Martyr

The prophets and the philosophers

The church father who expressed this sense of fulfilment most forcefully was probably Justin Martyr (c. 100 – c. 165). Justin was born of pagan parents in Samaria. Intellectually precocious, his search for the truth began during his youth. He delved successively into the philosophies of the Stoics, Aristotle, Pythagoras and Plato. But he found neither truth nor peace. Then one day, in God's good providence, near the sea at Ephesus he met an old man, who introduced him to the Old Testament prophets, and so to Christ.

After his conversion he continued to wear the philosopher's robe, travelled on foot to a number of leading cities to teach, and founded a Christian school in Rome.

Justin became the greatest Christian apologist of the second century. He resolved to reconcile faith and reason, to harmonize Hebrew scripture and Greek philosophy, and to defend Christianity against misrepresentation and slander. His *First Apology* was addressed to Emperor Antoninus Pius, and to his adopted son and his successor, Marcus Aurelius. His *Second Apology,* addressed to the Roman senate, is a short appendix to the First, and was prompted by the unjust persecution of Christians. Justin's third and longest work is his *Dialogue with Trypho a Jew*, who was a learned Rabbi. It has been described as 'the first elaborate exposition of the reasons for regarding Christ as the Messiah of the Old Testament, and the first systematic attempt to exhibit the false position of the Jews in regard to Christianity'.[1] With courtesy and patience Justin witnessed to Christ in all the Scriptures (though resorting sometimes to fanciful allegory), proclaiming the gospel of Christ crucified and risen. He concluded with a moving appeal to Trypho and his friends to believe in Christ: 'Say no evil thing, my brothers, against him that was crucified ... Assent, therefore, and pour no ridicule on the Son of God.'[2]

In about AD 165 Justin was denounced as a Christian, he refused to offer sacrifice to the gods, and went to a martyr's death with calm and courage.

'Jesus Christ the complete fulfilment' is the phrase I am suggesting as a summary of Justin's theology. In his *First Apology* he marshalled many Old Testament prophecies (with a particular fondness for Moses, the Psalms and Isaiah) which pointed to Christ. His knowledge of the Old Testament was phenomenal. But he also believed that at least to some extent Christianity is the embodiment of all that is best in Greek philosophy. So at his conversion, although he renounced paganism, he did not renounce philosophy. How is it, then, that the philosophers came to know the truths they knew? It was partly that (so he claimed) Plato borrowed from Moses and the prophets. But it was also that the divine Logos, who had been in the world from the beginning and became fully incarnate in Jesus Christ, was distributed by the divine Sower everywhere. Thus 'there seem to be seeds of truth among all men'.[3] For example, the Stoics' moral teaching was admirable 'on account of the *logos spermatikos* (rational seed or seed of reason) implanted in every race of men'.[4] This applies to all the philosophers. 'For all the writers were able to see realities darkly through the sowing of the implanted seed that was in them.'[5] In consequence, 'those who lived in accordance with reason are Christians, even though they were declared godless [in relation to the pagan gods], such as among the Greeks Socrates ... and among the barbarians [i.e. non-Greeks] Abraham ... Elijah ... and many others'. For 'those who lived by reason, and those who so live now, are Christians ...',[6] that is, Christians before Christ.

Thus the prophets and the philosophers, though in differing degrees, bore witness to Christ, and what they wrote finds its fulfilment in Christ. One is filled with admiration for the breadth of Justin's vision, for his determination to claim for Christ everything that is true, wherever it might be found, and for his gracious and generous spirit.

Perhaps then it is ungenerous and ungracious of me to add that I wish he had developed a more obviously biblical basis for his theme. His references to *logos* ('word' or 'reason') could well have led him to the Prologue to John's Gospel. For John 1:9 seems to summarize Justin's conviction: 'The true light that gives light to every man was coming into the world.' That is, before he 'came' in the incarnation, he 'was coming', and is coming still, giving light to everybody. It is not saving light (as Justin knew), yet it is light, so that everything beautiful, good and true, wherever found, originates in the Logos, 'the true light', Jesus Christ.

2. Christ the unique God-man: the early councils

The importance of Christology

Justin Martyr emphasized that the New Testament was continuous with the Old, and that therefore the gospel was not a novelty. On the contrary, Jesus was the fulfilment of both Scripture and philosophy.

But still Jesus of Nazareth needed to be understood. So for a century and a half during the fourth and fifth centuries church leaders were engaged in serious Christological debate.

Progress towards agreement was charted by what came to be acknowledged as the first four ecumenical councils. They are perhaps best seen in two pairs. Thus the Council of Nicea (325) secured the truth that Jesus is truly God, while the Council of Constantinople (381) secured that Jesus is truly human. Next the Council of Ephesus (431) secured that, although both God and man, Jesus is only one person, while the Council of Chalcedon (451) secured that, although one person, he had two natures, divine and human.

It was a complex development, often marred by unseemly displays of anger, jealousy, malice and political intrigue. Yet at the same time one can detect the patient work of the Holy Spirit, who was enabling the church to get its mind clear on its Christology.

First came the Council of Nicea (325). What made it necessary was the teaching of the presbyter Arius. He was saying that Jesus was not God, although the first and finest of all God's creatures. He was not eternal, since he had a beginning ('once he was not') and even came into being out of nothing. So the Emperor Constantine called a council in order to promote unity and peace. More than two hundred bishops attended, mostly from the east, and many were maimed and scarred from the recent persecutions. The Council condemned Arius, and issued the creed of Nicea (not to be confused with the Nicene Creed), which affirmed that our Lord Jesus Christ was 'begotten not made', 'of the same substance (*homoousios*) with the Father'. Although some bishops expressed hesitation over this term, since it was not biblical, most accepted it, and the Council won a memorable victory for the full deity of Jesus.

Secondly, the Council of Constantinople (381) was convened by the Emperor Theodosius. The background to this council was the teaching of Apollinarius, who denied that Jesus had a human mind or soul. So now, having reaffirmed against Arius that Jesus was fully God, the Council also affirmed against Apollinarius that he was fully human. But how, in this case, could he be one person? This was the next question.

Thirdly, the Council of Ephesus (431) was called to consider the teaching of Bishop Nestorius of Constantinople. Nestorius was accused of dividing Christ into two persons, namely God the Word and Jesus the man, and of declaring that the man was indwelt by the Word. He was opposed by Cyril of Alexandria who insisted on the incarnation (in distinction to an indwelling). The Word actually became flesh, uniting himself fully with human nature.

Fourthly came the Council of Chalcedon (451), attended by some five hundred bishops, and called to deal with the teaching of Eutyches who fused the humanity and deity of Jesus, so that he had only one nature, the divine. These were the Monophysites ('one nature' people); they continue as members of the Coptic Orthodox and Ethiopian Orthodox Churches today. They were opposed by Pope Leo the Great, who was Bishop of Rome 440–461. His famous *Tome* refuted Eutyches, and was read and approved by the Council. The Council produced the so-called 'Chalcedonian Definition', which emphasized that, although one person, Jesus has two distinct natures. It included the following:

> We confess with one voice that the one and only Son, our Lord Jesus Christ, is perfect in Godhead and perfect in humanity, truly God and truly human ... He is of one substance (*homoousios*) with the Father as God, and also of one substance (*homoousios*) with us as man ... He was begotten of his Father before the ages as God, but in these last days and for our salvation, he was born of Mary the virgin ... This one and the same Christ ... is made known in two natures without confusion, without change, without division, without separation ...

Some Christians today are impatient with what seems to them an argument over words. But several points may be made in response.

First, the church fathers, uncontaminated by our post-modern culture, were profoundly concerned about God's truth, and saw the need to combat false teachers like Arius, Apollinarius and Eutyches. Would that we had the same zeal for the truth today as they had!

Secondly, they saw that debate about Christology was debate about salvation, for only a Saviour who is fully divine and fully human could represent both sides and reconcile us to God.

Thirdly, they did their work so well that it has lasted. The sixteenth-century Reformers, for example, who engaged in controversy with the Church of Rome over the supremacy and sufficiency of Scripture, and over justification by faith alone, saw no need to alter the Christological statements of the early centuries. Instead, they endorsed them. Thus the second Anglican Article (1563) reads:

> The Son, who is the Word of the Father, begotten from everlasting of the Father, the very and eternal God, and of one substance with the Father, took man's nature in the womb of the blessed Virgin, of her substance, so that two whole and perfect natures, that is to say, the Godhead and the manhood, were joined together in one person, never to be divided, whereof is one Christ, very God and very man ...

Fourthly, the reason why the Reformers were able to endorse this teaching is that they recognized its strong biblical basis. As B. B. Warfield of Princeton wrote: 'The Chalcedonian Christology ... is only a very perfect synthesis of the biblical data.'[7]

Fifthly, although we admire the careful balance of the church fathers in the work of definition, we also acknowledge that we ourselves are finite and fallen, that God in his infinite perfection is altogether beyond us, and that the incarnation is a mystery we shall no doubt continue to explore throughout eternity.

Sixthly, it is both wise and humble to accept the ultimate antinomy without supposing that we can resolve it. Pope Leo wrote in his *Tome*: 'Christ is God and Christ is man. The two natures co-exist. Neither nature diminishes anything or adds anything to the properties of the other.'

Nobody has put it better than the great Charles Simeon of Cambridge, who was vicar of Holy Trinity Church for fifty-four years at the beginning of the nineteenth century, and profoundly influenced generations of students. This is what he insisted on: 'The truth is not in the middle, nor in one extreme; but in both extremes.'[8] Simeon was speaking about divine sovereignty and human accountability. But his principle is equally applicable to the person of Jesus Christ. He was neither God pretending to be human, nor a human being with divine faculties, nor semi-divine and semi-human, but fully human and fully divine, the unique God-man.

3. Christ the perfect monk:
St Benedict

Two questions about monasticism

Mark 8:34 has always seemed to Christians a fundamental and
defining text. It is Jesus' message to would-be disciples: 'If anyone
would come after me, he must deny himself and take up his cross
and follow me.' Moreover, it is plain that 'denying self' and
'following Christ' are complementary aspects of the same relationship. In order to follow Christ, we must deny ourselves. But what
does this self-denial entail? Does it inevitably involve a monastic
life?

The monastic ideal did not originate with Christianity. Hindu
ashrams date from before the Christian era, and there were Jewish
communities too. It was not surprising, therefore, that some
Christians, determined to take Jesus' teaching seriously, should have
experimented with different styles of living as hermits and monks.

It was not until the sixth century, however, that the Christian
monastic lifestyle was regularized by St Benedict of Nursia in
central Italy (480–550). Sent to Rome to study as a teenager, he
was horrified by the degenerate morals of the city, and in reaction
withdrew into a cave at Subiaco. Later he founded twelve monastic
communities, each with twelve monks and a prior, and ultimately
established his own monastery at Monte Cassino between Rome
and Naples, where he remained until his death. Here he developed,
out of the embryonic rules of other groups, his full-scale 'Rule of
St Benedict', which won him the epithet 'patriarch of western
monasticism' and which has been called 'one of the most
influential documents of western civilization'.[9]

One is immediately struck by two qualities possessed by the
author of the Rule. First, he had an extremely tidy mind, for the
Rule is divided into seventy-three short chapters, each on a
different topic, and contains an additional seventy-three one-
sentence Christian duties.

Secondly, the author knows his Bible very well, for the Rule is
saturated with Scripture.

Its contents cover a wide variety of practical matters, including
instructions for the abbot as well as the monks. The abbot is

responsible for the discipline of the community, 'mingling gentleness with severity' (chapter 2). As for the monks, the emphasis is on humility and obedience. The 'vice of private ownership' (chapter 55) is totally rejected, and the monks' necessary food and clothing are assigned to them by the abbot. The Rule prescribes a not-too-rigorous schedule of worship and silence, reading library books, and manual labour in kitchen or cellar, laundry, garden or bakery. Other duties range from the development of their artistic gifts, the practice of hospitality to strangers, the education of the young, and the care of the sick, the elderly and the poor.

The basic conditions of a monastic life have always been the three vows of poverty, chastity (meaning celibacy) and obedience (to the abbot). And all three, it is claimed, are modelled on Christ who may be regarded as the perfect monk. He lived in poverty, having 'no place to lay his head' (Matt. 8:20); he never married; and he said he had come not to do his own will, but to do (i.e. obey) the will of his Father who had sent him (John 6:38).

There is no doubt that we owe a large debt to the monastic tradition. First, it was a radical protest against a wicked world and a corrupt church. It was an expression of the Christian hunger for holiness and of the Christian commitment to self-denial.

Secondly, it kept alive the Christian vision of scholarship, and preserved through its valuable libraries, even in times of barbarism, a distinctively Christian culture.

Thirdly, the medieval monks were missionaries, committed to both evangelism and social concern for the poor. Some of the finest missionaries, like Francis Xavier, were monks. In these respects they maintained a necessary witness. Father Zossima, in Dostoyevsky's *The Brothers Karamazov*, was right to say that the monks of the Russian Orthodox Church in their solitude 'keep the image of Christ fair and undefiled'.[10]

At the same time, having expressed a genuine appreciation of the gains of monasticism, I feel obliged to ask some questions. Is it either accurate or helpful to depict the Lord Jesus as the model monk? Is it correct to paint the Christian ideal in monastic terms? Because one admires the commitment, zeal and self-denial of Christian monks, one is hesitant to criticize them. Yet we must do so, if we are to be true to the New Testament picture of Jesus.

First, monasticism glorifies withdrawal from the world. Of course, just as Jesus withdrew from his busy public ministry into the mountains to rest and to pray, so his disciples must also, and still do. It is healthy for all Christians to maintain the rhythm of involvement and withdrawal. But a temporary withdrawal from the world, with a view to returning to it, is one thing; a lifestyle of seclusion is another. The essence of the incarnation is that the Son of God entered our world, refusing to remain aloof from it. He also made it clear that he wanted his followers similarly to identify with the world. 'My prayer', he said to his Father, 'is not that you take them out of the world but that you protect them from the evil one' (John 17:15). Then he said further: 'As you sent me into the world, I have sent them into the world' (John 17:18). So we must not glorify retreat from the world, except temporarily; it could be a denial of the incarnation.

Secondly, monasticism sets up a double standard. It implies that there are two kinds of Christian, first class and second class, or two moral standards, one good and the other better. A supposed biblical basis for this is Matthew's version of what Jesus said to the rich young ruler: 'If you want to be perfect, go, sell your possessions and give to the poor ...' (Matt. 19:21). From this saying was developed the distinction between 'commandments' (which are binding on all Christians) and 'counsels of perfection' (which are binding on monks). But what the New Testament sets before us is not two standards, one higher or better than the other, but a variety of vocations and ministries, equally good, but different from one another. Some Christians are still called to total voluntary poverty, like the rich young ruler in the Gospel, and like the late Mother Teresa and her sisters today. But the majority of Christians are called to be conscientious and generous stewards of their possessions. As the apostle Peter said to Ananias about his property: 'Didn't it belong to you before it was sold? And after it was sold, wasn't the money at your disposal?' (Acts 5:4). Neither of these vocations (poverty and stewardship) is higher than the other.

Or take celibacy. Without doubt, a minority of Christians are called to singleness. Jesus said so (Matt. 19:11–12). So did Paul (1 Cor. 7:1–7). It is not that singleness is superior to marriage, however, or that marriage is superior to singleness. Both are *charismata*, gifts of God's grace (1 Cor. 7:7), but some are called to the one, some to the other. This verse 7 is the key to understanding the whole chapter.

To sum up, the Christian paradox applies to all Christians. Only if we serve, will we experience freedom. Only if we lose ourselves in loving, will we find ourselves. Only if we die to our own self-centredness, will we begin to live.

4. Christ the feudal debtor: Anselm

Medieval atonement theology

For several centuries, since Origen in the third century and the Cappadocian Fathers in the fourth, the 'ransom' theory of the atonement held sway, namely that sin had put the human race into bondage to the devil, and that Christ has redeemed us by the payment of a ransom-price to the devil. This unacceptable theory was not seriously challenged until Anselm's great book *Cur Deus Homo* ('Why God became Man'). He argued that the debt was payable to God, not the devil.

Anselm was born in Italy in about the year 1033, sojourned for many years in Normandy, came to England after the Norman Conquest in 1066, and succeeded Lanfranc as Archbishop of Canterbury in 1093. He was a man of profound learning, clear thinking and personal piety. *Cur Deus Homo*, his book on the cross, was one of the most influential books about the atonement during the Middle Ages; it changed the church's thinking. James Denney went so far as to say that it is 'the truest and greatest book on the Atonement that has ever been written'.[11]

Anselm began his thinking with the human condition. Sin is 'not rendering to God what is his due'.[12] It is therefore to 'take away from God what is his own' and so to dishonour him. But why should God not simply forgive us, without the necessity of the cross? As the nineteenth-century cynic Heine put it, '*Le bon Dieu me pardonnera; c'est son métier.*'[13] 'After all', an objector might continue, 'we are required to forgive one another. Why can't God practise what he preaches and be equally generous?' Anselm's reply was straightforward: 'you have not yet considered the seriousness of sin'.[14] Nor, we might add, have we yet considered the majesty of God. When we have seen God in his holiness, however, and ourselves in our rebellion against him, the appropriate question to ask is not why God finds it *difficult* to forgive us, but how he finds it *possible*.

Anselm rejected the patristic ransom-theory on the ground that 'God owed nothing to the devil but punishment'.[15] Instead, man owed something to God, and this is the debt which had to be repaid. Yet we cannot pay it. The first book ends: 'Man the sinner owes to God, on account of sin, what he cannot repay, and unless he repays it, he cannot be saved.'[16] So there is only one way out of the dilemma: 'There is no-one ... who *can* make this satisfaction except God himself ... But no-one *ought* to make it except man; otherwise man does not make satisfaction.' Therefore 'it is necessary that one who is *God-man* should make it'.[17] 'It is needful that the very same Person who is to make this satisfaction be perfect God and perfect man, since no-one *can* do it except one who is truly God, and no-one *ought* to do it except one who is truly man.'[18] Hence the incarnation of God in Christ, who gave himself up to death freely for the honour of God. He is the only Saviour, since in him alone were the '*man should*' and the '*God could*' united.

The great merits of Anselm's *Cur Deus Homo* are his strong emphases (1) on the seriousness of sin as inexcusable disobedience to God; (2) on the impossibility of self-salvation; and (3) on the necessity of the incarnation, since no-one *ought* to make satisfaction except man (who has defaulted) and no-one *can* except God.

Understandably, however, Anselm has also had his critics. First, he was a medieval scholastic, attempting to reconcile philosophy and theology. Although he was anxious to be submissive to Scripture, his over-riding concern was that his teaching should be 'agreeable to reason'.[19] Sometimes, therefore, he indulged in speculation, and always he seems to have been governed by cold logic. One misses the fire which Peter Abelard kindled in the twelfth century when he contemplated the love of God in the cross of Christ.

Secondly, Anselm reflects throughout his treatise the feudal culture of his day. Feudalism was a medieval social system of land tenure and personal relationships which involved balancing rights and obligations on the part of both the lord and his vassals. The lord invested the vassal with his fief (land or fee) and undertook to protect him. In return, the vassal did homage to his lord and undertook specific services. A breach of duty by a vassal was regarded as such a heinous offence as to be a felony, and satisfaction would have to be done to his lord's offended honour. Is it appropriate, however, to portray God as a feudal overlord who demands honour, and Christ as a feudal debtor who makes satisfaction in our place?

If only we could add Abelard's passion to Anselm's logic! If only we could transform Anselm's image of God from being a feudal overlord, satisfying his personal honour as if he felt offended, into the Holy One who is resolved to satisfy personally his own inner being of love and justice! Then our balance would be more compatible with Scripture itself.

5. Christ the heavenly bridegroom: Bernard of Clairvaux

Christian mysticism

Christian mysticism came to full flower in Europe between the twelfth and the fourteenth centuries. It focused on Jesus Christ as the lover, indeed the bridegroom, of the Christian soul, and Bernard of Clairvaux (1090–1153) was the most popular exponent of it.

In spite of a natural shyness, and his constant ill-health due to his austere self-discipline, Bernard was a born leader, endowed with many and varied gifts. He preached and wrote with considerable eloquence, and was strongly committed to the reform of the monasteries. He was nevertheless drawn into ecclesiastical politics and exerted an enormous influence on successive popes, bishops and councils, and on the whole church. During the last two turbulent decades of his life he was widely regarded as 'the conscience of all Europe'.

At the same time, he was a diligent student of Scripture and an orthodox theologian. Indeed, his Christ-centred message was an essential aspect of his protest against an over-emphasis on the intellect and against the institutionalism and nominalism of the medieval church.

Bernard's best-known work is probably his *Sermons on the*

Canticle of Canticles. He was by no means the first scholar to develop an allegorical interpretation of the Song of Songs. Defending its inclusion in the Old Testament canon, the celebrated Jewish Rabbi Aqiba said: 'all the Scriptures are holy, but the Song of Songs is the Holy of Holies'.[20] There had also been Christian commentaries on the Song by early church fathers, one by Origen in the third century, and another by Gregory of Nyssa in the fourth. But Bernard's sermons were the most widely read and cherished.[21] He was known as 'the mellifluous doctor', and in Luther's opinion 'Bernard surpasses all the other doctors of the church'.[22]

During the last eighteen years of his life (1135–1153) Bernard preached eighty-six sermons on the Song of Songs, although even then he covered only the first two chapters of the book. In no sense was he writing a commentary, but rather a series of meditations for advanced believers who were 'ripe for the mystical nuptials of the Heavenly Bridegroom'.[23] His first eight sermons all had the same text, which is the second verse of the Song, namely: 'Let him kiss me with the kisses of his mouth.'

Needless to say, his treatment of it was a fanciful allegorization. For example, he elaborated three kisses (of the feet, the hand and the mouth), which symbolize three stages of the soul's progress towards perfection. To kiss Christ's feet is to prostrate ourselves before him in humble penitence, like Mary in the gospel story. This is the beginning of conversion. To kiss Christ's hand is to acknowledge that he is the giver of all good gifts, and that our relationship to him is based on his mercy, not on our merit. Few, however, reach the third kiss. This is 'the supreme kiss', when with fear and trembling we venture to raise ourselves 'to that divinely glorious mouth' and so enjoy the kiss of loving union with God, Father, Son and Holy Spirit.[24] Summed up in the declaration that 'my love is mine and I am his' (2:16), it expresses the ultimate union of the soul with God for which the mystic longs.

Many of us have probably been brought up to believe that Bernard's personal devotion to Christ was best expressed in his hymns. I am thinking specially of the following: 'Jesus, the very thought of thee / With sweetness fills the breast', and 'Jesus, the very thought is sweet / In that dear name all heart-joys meet', and

> Jesus, thou joy of loving hearts,
>> Thou fount of life, thou light of men,
> From the best bliss that earth imparts
>> We turn unfilled to thee again.

Although these hymns have been attributed for a long time to Bernard, hymnologists are now telling us that there is no evidence for this attribution. They are content to say simply that the hymns' Latin originals go back to the twelfth century. But at least an authority like Archbishop Trench could write that, if Bernard did not compose them, 'it is not easy to guess who could have written them', for 'they bear profoundly the stamp of his mind, being only inferior in beauty to his prose'.[25]

Before we leave Bernard of Clairvaux and his mystical attachment to Christ, we need to ask two questions.

First, what is the nature of Christian mysticism? Because the language of mysticism is used in Hinduism, Buddhism, Taoism, Neoplatonism, Judaism and Islam, as well as in Christianity, it is too readily assumed that to be a 'mystic' means the same thing in all religions. But this is not so. To be sure, everybody means by 'mysticism' some rather ill-defined experience like 'union with the ultimate'. But there is at least one fundamental difference between eastern mysticism and Christian mysticism. The objective of eastern mystics is to lose their individuality through absorption in the divine, like a drop of water becoming dissolved in the ocean. In Christian mysticism, however, the individual believer retains his or her identity. For God has created us with our own unique individuality, and has redeemed us so that we may become even more, not less, our true selves. Our destiny is not to lose ourselves, but by losing ourselves to find ourselves. To be 'in Christ' (a favourite expression of Paul's) is to be so intimately and organically united to him as to share his life. Jesus prayed that his followers might be 'one' just as he and the Father are one (John 17:21–23). But the three persons of the Trinity, although one, are yet eternally distinct.

The second question which needs to be asked is whether it is legitimate to use the Song of Songs as an allegory of the love between Christ and the Christian soul. In general, it is legitimate to use allegory to illustrate, but not to substantiate, a truth. That is, if a doctrine or duty is already established by the plain meaning of a biblical passage, then it is legitimate to use allegory to illustrate this truth. Thus Scripture teaches plainly and often that God and his people are committed to each other in a covenant of love. Therefore it is legitimate to use the Song of Songs, which expresses the love of bridegroom and bride for each other, in order to illustrate this truth.

In particular, the Song of Songs has been individualized too often and made to set forth the private and personal love which unites God and the individual. By contrast, the two prophets of divine love (Hosea and Jeremiah) paint a picture of God's love for his covenant people. For example, promises like 'I will betroth you to me for ever' are not spoken to individuals but to the unfaithful nation (Hos. 2:19). Similarly in the New Testament Paul writes that 'Christ loved the church and gave himself up for her' (Eph. 5:25). True, Paul could also write that 'the Son of God ... loved *me* and gave himself for *me*' (Gal. 2:20, my emphasis), but such flashes of individualism are rare, perhaps because of the risk of spiritual eroticism, a risk which – at least in language – the Christian mystics have not always managed to avoid.

6. Christ the ethical exemplar: Thomas à Kempis

An ascetic imitation of Christ

In Thomas à Kempis's book *The Imitation of Christ*, immensely popular and universally recommended, we see the late medieval church presenting Christ as the supreme model of Christian discipleship.

Thomas à Kempis was born in 1379 in Kempen (hence his name) in Germany. In 1400, aged twenty-one, he entered an Augustinian convent in the diocese of Cologne and was ordained in 1413. He remained in the same convent all his life, dying as its Superior in 1471, at the age of ninety-one.

He is said to have been shy and studious. He spent his time reading, writing, copying and praying.

In the Foreword to a new English translation of *The Imitation of Christ*, Dr L. M. J. Delaissé wrote that it 'has established itself in the course of the centuries, next to the Bible, as the most influential religious book of Christendom'.[26]

The book's appeal is probably due to its combination of asceticism and mysticism. Its first two books or sections are devoted to the development of an ascetic holiness. Recurrent themes relate to uprooting vices, resisting temptation, despising worldly vanities, having a humble opinion of oneself, not believing or thinking evil of others, bearing adversity and 'crosses', avoiding rash judgments, and preparing for the approach of death.

The third book, however, takes the form of a dialogue between 'the voice of Christ'; and 'the voice of the disciple', in which Thomas sometimes breaks out into passionate expressions of love for Christ. Here is an example from chapter 21:

> O thou most sweet spouse of my soul Jesus Christ, thou most pure Lover, Lord of all creation! Who wilt give me the wings of true liberty, that I may fly to a final rest in thee! O when will this spiritual grace be granted unto me, that in quietness of mind I may see how sweet thou art, O Lord my God? When shall I become one with thee? When, because of my ardent love will I no longer be conscious of self, but of thee alone …?[27]

Then a little later in the same chapter he bursts forth again:

> O Jesus, thou brightness of everlasting glory, thou comfort of the pilgrim soul … how long doth my Lord tarry ere he come? Let him come unto me, his poor servant, and make him joyful … Come, O come! for without thee there can be no blissful day or hour; for thou art my joy, and without thee my table is empty …[28]

> Let others seek what they please instead of thee; but as for me, nothing else doth nor shall delight me, but thou only, my God, my hope, my eternal salvation.[29]

Although Thomas's love for Jesus and longing for holiness are on the whole kept apart in his book, there are certainly some passages in which the two are integrated. For example, 'Blessed is he who understandeth what it is to love Jesus, and to despise himself for Jesus' sake. It behoveth the lover to forsake all things for the Belovèd ...'[30] Again, 'when Jesus is present, all is well, and nothing seems difficult; but when Jesus is absent, everything is arduous'.[31] And 'the noble love of Jesus inspireth us to do great things, and ever impelleth us to long for perfection'.[32]

So the goal and the motive are clear – to seek holiness out of love for Christ. It is summed up in one of Thomas's epigrams: 'he doeth much that loveth much'.[33] These emphases win our strong support, our profound admiration. Would that all of us who claim to follow Jesus Christ both hungered and thirsted after right-eousness, as Thomas did, and were on fire with devotion to Christ, as Thomas was!

It seems churlish and patronizing even tentatively to enter any caveat. Yet it is necessary at least to ask some questions. Was the church right in the late Middle Ages to present Jesus Christ as supremely an ethical exemplar, and the Christian life as an imitation of Christ? Certainly Jesus said 'follow me', and Paul wrote: 'Follow my example, as I follow the example of Christ' (1 Cor. 11:1). So what was missing in Thomas à Kempis's classic volume? I ask four further questions.

First, had Thomas grasped *the essence of the gospel invitation*, which is not to do good works in imitation of Christ, but first to put our trust in Christ crucified as our Saviour? He does not seem to have had any assurance of God's acceptance of him, for he lives in continuous fear of judgment, purgatory and hell. Moreover, his references to the love of Christ are almost entirely to his love for Christ rather than Christ's love for him. He never quotes the great affirmations that 'Christ's love compels us' (2 Cor. 5:14) and that nothing can separate us from the love of Christ (Rom. 8:35–39).

Secondly, had Thomas grasped *the way of holiness*, which is not by imitation of Christ but through union with Christ? It is not I living like Christ, so much as Christ living in me. As James Stalker put it, 'St Paul's whole teaching revolves between the two poles of righteousness through the death of Christ for us and holiness through the life of Christ in us.'[34]

Thirdly, had Thomas grasped *the context of Christian ethics*? His context, to quote Stalker again, was 'the little monotonous world of the cloister'.[35] But the New Testament context of the Christian life is the noisy, busy, challenging arena of the workplace and the marketplace. True, we are 'strangers and pilgrims' on earth (a phrase from 1 Peter 2:11, KJV, which Thomas quotes many times), but this does not necessitate withdrawal, as Thomas assumes. 'Desire the fellowship of God alone', he writes, 'and of his holy angels; and shun the acquaintance of men.'[36] Again, 'flee the press and tumult of the world as much as thou canst'.[37] He sees Christians as 'completely immersed' not in the world but 'in God'.[38] For in his view 'the greatest saints avoided the society of man, choosing rather to live unto God in solitude', and he added 'as did Jesus'.[39] But there is a serious disagreement or misunderstanding here. Jesus did indeed seek solitude for rest and prayer, as we saw when considering monasticism, but only in order to return fortified to the demands of his public ministry.

Fourthly, had Thomas grasped *the implications of imitation*? *The Imitation of Christ* is the appealing popular title given to his book, and probably accounts for much of its popularity. But when one begins to read, one is immediately disappointed by his failure to handle the theme as the New Testament does. Virtually the only following of Christ to which Thomas refers is the charge to take up our cross and endure suffering in imitation of Christ. Where, then, is any reference to imitating the humility of Christ in his incarnation and death (Phil. 2:5–8); to loving others as Christ loved us (Eph. 5:2) and forgiving others as God in Christ has forgiven us (Eph. 4:32); to purifying ourselves as he is pure (1 John. 3:3); to following in his steps in bearing unjust suffering without retaliation (1 Pet. 2:18–21); or to going out into the world in mission, just as he had been sent out by the Father (John. 17:18; 20:21)? These great New Testament themes, which elaborate what it means to imitate Christ, are absent from Thomas's book, to its considerable impoverishment.

One wishes that Thomas had kept more closely to the teaching of the New Testament and had held together Christ the Saviour and Christ the example (1 Pet. 2:21, 24), Christ for us and Christ in us, and the call to follow Christ both in withdrawal and in involvement.

7. Christ the gracious Saviour: Martin Luther

Justification by faith alone

It is hard for us to grasp in our day the heavy burden of sin and guilt under which medieval church people laboured. They were brought up to concentrate on the wrath of God, the awfulness of judgment and the pains of purgatory and hell. They lived in fear, striving to secure God's favour by good deeds of righteousness. For this was the teaching of the church.

The early Martin Luther was no exception. Born in 1483, his father was ambitious for him and sent him to both school and university. But all the time he was overwhelmed by a profound spiritual turmoil. Seeing a friend struck dead by lightning, he became gripped with the fear of death and of judgment. So he overed himself without reserve to the service of God and entered an Augustinian monastery, confident that here surely he would be able to save his soul. He prayed and fasted, and adopted other extreme austerities. 'I was a good monk', he wrote later. 'If ever a monk got to heaven by his monkery, it was I.'[40] But his ascetic regimen tended to increase rather than diminish his torment. He made his confession and did penance. He took the three vows of poverty, chastity and obedience. He plunged into his theological studies. He was ordained priest. He made a pilgrimage to Rome; and crawled on his knees up the twenty-eight steps of the *Scala Sancta*. But it was all to no avail. He became disillusioned with the church, convinced that it had lost the keys of the kingdom.

In 1512 Luther became Professor of Bible at the University of Wittenberg. At first his doubts and fears persisted. He determined to appease God, but could find no peace. 'When I looked for Christ', he once said, 'it seemed to me I saw the devil'.[41] This shocking statement reveals the false image of Jesus Christ that he was harbouring, owing to the intensity of his moral struggle. To him at that time Christ was angry not friendly, menacing not merciful, his judge not his saviour. Where might he find a gracious God? That was his anguished cry.

Now Luther turned to the Scriptures. In preparation for his

university lectures, he studied the Psalms in 1513–15, and the epistle to the Romans in 1515–16. He became disturbed by the prayer in Psalm 31:1, 'deliver me in your righteousness' and by the statement in Romans 1:17 that the righteousness of God is revealed in the gospel. If God's righteousness is his justice, he asked himself, how can it bring salvation or be part of the gospel? Luther wrestled with this question, because he still understood 'the righteousness of God' as expressed in *punishing* the unrighteous. *That* does not sound like good news!

> Night and day I pondered until … I grasped the truth that the righteousness of God is that righteousness whereby, through grace and sheer mercy, he *justifies* us by faith. Thereupon I felt myself to be reborn and to have gone through open doors into paradise. The whole of Scripture took on a new meaning, and whereas before 'the righteousness of God' had filled me with hate, now it became to me inexpressibly sweet in greater love. This passage of Paul became to me a gateway to heaven.[42]

Thus Luther's theology and experience came together. Through the clarified gospel of justification by grace alone in Christ alone through faith alone, Luther discovered that acceptance with God which he had been desperately seeking for years. He had not become an antinomian, as his critics sometimes suggest, declaring that good works do not matter, for he insisted that they are the fruit of faith. Nor was Luther an innovator; he had rather recovered the original apostolic gospel which the church had temporarily lost. He wrote in his commentary on the letter to the Galatians: 'This is the truth of the gospel. It is also the principal article of all Christian doctrine, wherein the knowledge of all godliness consisteth. Most necessary it is, therefore, that we should know this article well, teach it unto others, and beat it into their heads continually.'[43] It is this doctrine, he added, 'which maketh true Christians indeed',[44] for 'if the article of justification be once lost, then is all true Christian doctrine lost'.[45]

In every generation, therefore, the church needs to re-recover the doctrine of justification. Paul called it 'the gospel of God's grace' (Acts 20:24; cf. Gal. 1:6), and grace is the unmerited, unsolicited love of God. It was seen in its fullest splendour on the cross. It offers salvation to sinners as an absolutely free gift. It therefore leaves no room for human boasting. It gives glory to Jesus Christ alone – to Jesus Christ our gracious Saviour.

8. Christ the human teacher: Ernst Renan and Thomas Jefferson

Enlightenment scepticism

The so-called 'European Enlightenment' or 'Age of Reason', which flourished during the seventeenth and eighteenth centuries, constituted a frontal assault on the church's traditional beliefs. Its avowed intention was to declare the autonomy of the human mind, and so to replace revelation with reason, dogma with science, the supernatural with the natural, and a pessimistic view of the human condition with confidence in both the fundamental goodness of human nature and the consequent inevitability of social progress.

In this general attack on orthodox Christianity, the person of Jesus was not left unscathed. The Enlightenment presentation of him was of a merely human teacher. The most outspoken expression of this is to be found in the 'Lives of Christ' which were published from the end of the eighteenth to the end of the nineteenth centuries, some eighty of which Albert Schweitzer documented in his famous book, whose English title was *The Quest of the Historical Jesus*. The radical authors of these 'Lives', Schweitzer wrote, 'were eager to picture him as truly and purely human, to strip from him the robes of splendour with which he had been apparelled, and clothe him once more with the coarse garments in which he had walked in Galilee'.[46]

The most famous *Life of Jesus* was written by David Friedrich Strauss, and published in two volumes and 1,480 pages when he was only twenty-seven in 1835–36. Schweitzer devotes three chapters to him and declares that, although he was neither the greatest nor the deepest theologian, 'he was the most absolutely sincere'.[47] He found that, as a matter of integrity, he could not preach what he had previously believed. He goes through the gospels in great detail, incident by incident and parable by parable, applying his concept of 'myth' to them or pronouncing them to be purely legendary, although he did believe in Jesus' messianic self-consciousness. He became an instant celebrity at the centre of a theological storm, which ruined his career.

Better known to English readers is probably *La Vie de Jésus* by Ernst Renan (1863). As with Strauss, so with Renan, an outburst of dismay and anger greeted the publication of his *Life*. With Renan, however, criticism came from both sides. To the orthodox he was a heretic, but to liberals not liberal enough. Yet of his liberalism there is no doubt. Near the beginning of his book he wrote: 'That the Gospels are in part legendary is evident, since they are full of miracles and of the supernatural.'[48] Although Jesus believed he was the Messiah, he was no incarnation of God; the gospels are 'full of errors and misconceptions';[49] and instead of a real resurrection, 'the passion of one possessed [*d'une hallucinée*, referring to Mary Magdalene] gave to the world a resuscitated God'.[50]

But the reason why Renan's *Vie* has also attracted appreciative readers is the evident admiration and even devotion which its author had for Jesus. Renan writes of 'the sensitive and kindly heart of Jesus'[51] and of 'his gentle and penetrating genius'.[52] He writes even of Jesus' 'divinity'; but he does not mean it. After recounting his death Renan addresses Jesus personally. 'Rest now in thy glory, noble initiator. Thy work is completed; thy divinity is established.'[53] 'For thousands of years the world will extol thee ... Between thee and God men will no longer distinguish.'[54]

Yet we must not be deceived by this kind of rhetorical tribute. He says so himself. 'This sublime person ... we may call divine, not in the sense that Jesus has absorbed all the divine ... but in the sense that Jesus is the one who has caused his fellow-men to make the greatest step towards the divine.'[55]

But in the end he was only a man. 'Let us place, then, the person of Jesus at the highest summit of human greatness.'[56] For among the 'uniform mediocrity' of mankind, 'there are pillars that rise towards the sky'. 'Jesus is the highest of these pillars'.[57]

Here is Renan's conclusion:

Whatever unexpected phenomena may rise in future, Jesus will not be surpassed. His worship will constantly renew its youth, the tale of his life will cause ceaseless tears, his sufferings will soften the best hearts; and all the ages will proclaim that among the sons of men there is none born who is greater than Jesus.[58]

A particularly striking example of Enlightenment thinking was Thomas Jefferson, chief architect of the American Declaration of Independence (1776) and the third President of the United States (1801–1809). A man of genius, he was simultaneously inventor, architect, farmer, philosopher, statesman, diplomat and founder of the University of Virginia. At the same time he was a freethinker and a deist. Although he revered Jesus for his benevolence and ethical teaching, he rejected miracles as incompatible with nature and reason, and all mysteries like the Trinity. So he was determined to reconstruct a Christianity without dogma and a Jesus without miracles. He wrote:

When we shall have done away the incomprehensible jargon of the Trinitarian arithmetic, that three are one, and one is three ... when, in short, we shall have unlearned everything which has been taught since his [Jesus'] day, and got back to the pure and simple doctrines he inculcated, we shall then be truly and worthily his disciples.[59]

Consequently, using scissors and paste, Jefferson twice produced his own edition of the gospels, from which all miracles and mysteries had been eliminated. The first was the work of only two or three nights in the White House, and was entitled *The Philosophy of Jesus of Nazareth* (1804). It contained only his moral teaching, grouped in topics. The second so-called 'Jefferson Bible' appeared in 1820 and was called *The Life and Morals of Jesus of Nazareth*. It contained an outline of his life, ending abruptly with his burial: they 'rolled a great stone to the door of the sepulchre, and departed'. Those are the last words. There is no mention of the resurrection.

Jefferson claimed that his work was the product of common sense. As with the 'self-evident' truths of his Declaration of Independence, so in the teaching of Jesus he regarded it as a simple matter to abstract 'what is really his from the rubbish in which it is buried ... the diamond from the dunghill'.[60] But his mood was one of unwarranted self-confidence, and his criteria largely subjective. While Jefferson's two reconstructions have perished, the gospels themselves live on.

9. Christ the tragic victim: John Mackay

Good Friday without Easter

Jesus the ethical exemplar belonged to the Middle Ages, Jesus the gracious Saviour to the Reformation, and Jesus the human teacher to the eighteenth century Enlightenment. All three were European. It is time therefore to consider another ecclesiastical portrait of Jesus Christ, which began in Spain but then developed its own indigenous shape throughout Latin America.

In this examination I shall rely on a famous book published in 1932, entitled *The Other Spanish Christ*. Its author was a Scot, John A. Mackay, who, after studying in Spain and discovering the Iberian soul, spent twenty years as a Presbyterian missionary in Lima, Peru (where he was the first Protestant to hold the Chair of Philosophy in Peru's National University), in Montevideo, Uruguay and in Mexico City. Later, from 1936 to 1959, John Mackay became the distinguished President of Princeton Theological Seminary.

Mackay's classic book *The Other Spanish Christ: a study in the spiritual history of Spain and South America* retells the terrible story of the Spanish conquistadores, who vanquished and colonized the continent's native peoples by brute force at the beginning of the sixteenth century.

What was the picture of Jesus which Spanish catholicism introduced into Latin America? The Christ who came to Latin America, Mackay replies, was a figure of tragedy. 'Christ stands before us as the tragic victim.'[61] Spanish religious artists depicted Christ as 'bruised, livid, bloodless and blood-streaked', 'twisted Christs that struggle with death, and recumbent Christs that have succumbed to it ... They are the quintessence of unrelieved tragedy'.[62]

Of one particular picture Mackay writes: 'he is dead for ever. He has become the incarnation of death itself ... This Christ ... does not rise again'.[63] He then quotes the early twentieth-century existential philosopher, Miguel de Unamuno: 'this corpse Christ … lies horizontal and stretched out like a plain, without soul and without hope, with closed eyes facing heaven'.[64] Mackay comments: 'In Spanish religion Christ has been the centre of a cult of death,'[65] 'a Christ known in life as an infant and in death as a corpse, over whose helpless childhood and tragic fate the Virgin Mother presides'.[66]

Similarly, the creole Christ 'appears almost exclusively in two dramatic roles – the role of the infant in his mother's arms, and the role of a suffering and bleeding victim. It is the picture of a Christ who was born and died, but who never lived'[67] and (we might add) never lived again, that is, never rose.

It is surely very striking that about fifty years after John Mackay was in Peru, the late Henri Nouwen paid it a visit, and that both men – the Presbyterian missionary and the Roman Catholic priest – came to the same conclusion. Henri Nouwen wrote in his journal that in Lima's downtown churches 'the manifold representation of the suffering Christ became an overwhelming impression'.[68] 'But most haunting of all', Nouwen continued,

> was a huge altar surrounded by six niches in which Jesus was portrayed in different states of anguish: bound to a pillar, lying on the ground, sitting on a rock and so on, always naked and covered with blood … Nowhere did I see a sign of the resurrection, nowhere was I reminded of the truth that Christ overcame sin and death, and rose victorious from the grave. All was Good Friday. Easter was absent … The nearly exclusive emphasis on the tortured body of Christ strikes me as a perversion of the Good News into a morbid story that intimidates … people but does not liberate them.[69]

In drawing attention to this popular Latin American portrayal of the impotent Christ, I am not of course suggesting that this is the only picture known to Latin American Christians. For Mackay's book is deliberately entitled *The Other Spanish Christ*, in order to show that there is an alternative tradition, even if it has been almost lost. It is the tradition of the sixteenth-century Spanish mystics, whose precursor was the noble Raymond Lull.

Raymond Lull was born in Mallorca in 1236, and as a young man was a pleasure-seeking courtier and soldier. After his conversion, however, three life-goals formed in his mind: (1) to write a definitive book to prove that Christianity is true and Islam false, (2) to found colleges in which the missionary languages could be learned, and (3) to die as a martyr for Christ. He then made three missionary visits to North Africa, when he was fifty-six, seventy and eighty years old. On each occasion he had the courage to proclaim Christ publicly in Arabic in the city square. On the first two occasions he was arrested, imprisoned and banished. On his third visit an infuriated crowd dragged him to the seashore and stoned him to death.

Here is one of his most memorable statements: 'The image of the crucified Christ is found much rather in men who imitate him in their daily walk than in the crucifix made of wood ... He who loves not lives not. He who lives by the Life cannot die.'[70]

Then came the sixteenth-century Spanish mystics, of whom the most famous were San Juan de la Cruz and Santa Teresa de Avila. St John of the Cross is best known for his poems 'The Dark Night of the Soul' and 'A Spiritual Canticle of the Soul', while St Theresa is remembered for *The Way of Perfection* and *The Interior Castle*. Both were 'great solitary souls',[71] expressions of Iberian individualism. Both were passionately devoted to Christ, and St Theresa combined the Mary and the Martha. 'The Lord walks among the pots and pans', she was fond of saying to her nuns. She regularly wrote of Christ as 'His Divine Majesty'. Both John and Theresa in their different ways were also rebels against the establishment. Their tradition has been carried on into the twentieth century by Don Miguel de Unamuno, whom Mackay called a 'saintly Christian rebel',[72] and Ricardo Rojas, President of the University of Buenos Aires in the 1920s, author of the provocative book *El Cristo Invisibile* (1927), and radical critic of Latin American catholicism.

If John Mackay had been writing about Latin America in the second rather than the first half of the twentieth century, he would without doubt have included substantial sections on the rise of liberation theology and on the phenomenal growth both of the pentecostal churches and of the charismatic movement within the mainline churches. These developments are further aspects of *The*

Other Spanish Christ. We will consider pentecostalism now and liberation theology later.

Being now a worldwide phenomenon, pentecostalism must surely be attributed to the work of the Holy Spirit. At the same time, his activity is usually not direct but through current social circumstances. The best analysis is probably still Professor David Martin's book *Tongues of Fire : the explosion of protestantism in Latin America*. Against the background of rapid, threatening social change, pentecostalism offers shelter, or what has been called a 'haven for the masses', reproducing the closeness and protection of the *hacienda* (the Latin American ranch). Pentecostalism has four main characteristics: (1) *Latin authenticity*: it is indigenous (whereas the Roman Catholic priesthood is mainly foreign), enthusiastic and emotional; (2) *active participation*: it is lay and egalitarian, involving people who were previously voiceless, powerless and marginalized; (3) *material blessing*: it promises economic betterment, physical healing and freedom from anxiety; and (4) *a surrogate family*: pentecostalism 'creates a protective network and reproduces some of the solidarities and the structures of authority found on the *hacienda*'.[73]

To sum up, in the disorientation caused by the movement from *hacienda* to mega-city, and by modernization, pentecostalism offers 'a hope, a therapy, a community and a network'.[74] It provides an affirmation of personal worth and dignity, and so the discovery of a new identity.

We have seen, then, in the churches of Latin America, both that there are several different portraits of Christ and that they need each other. We must beware of imbalance. We have no liberty to proclaim the baby Jesus without the life to which his infancy led, nor his life and death without his glorious resurrection, nor the objective historical Jesus without personal devotion to him, nor the traditional, liturgical, respectable worship of him without any charismatic joy or spontaneity. Nor may we overlook the portrait of Jesus the liberator, with his clarion call to liberation, to which we now come.

10. Christ the social liberator: Gustavo Gutierrez

Good news for the poor

Jesus is presented to us in the New Testament as the world's supreme liberator. There can be no question about this, for he said so himself. 'If you hold to my teaching, you are really my disciples. Then you will know the truth, and the truth will set you free' (John 8:31f.). And Paul wrote to the Galatians: 'It is for freedom that Christ has set us free' (Gal. 5:1). So in every era of the church's history 'salvation' has been interpreted in terms of some kind of 'freedom'.

A quarter of a century ago, however, in the 1970s, the so-called 'liberation theology' was developed in Latin America. Its best-known exponents were Rubem Alves (*A Theology of Hope*, 1969), Gustavo Gutierrez (*A Theology of Liberation*, 1971) and Hugo Assmann (*Oppression-Liberation: a Challenge to Christians*, 1972). Orlando Costas distinguished between them by suggesting that 'if Alves is the prophet of the movement, and Assmann is the apologist, then Gutierrez is the systematic theologian'.[75]

The background to Gustavo Gutierrez' seminal book, which is sub-titled *History, politics and salvation*, is the social reality that Latin America is an oppressed continent. Although delivered at the beginning of the nineteenth century from the colonial rule of Spain and Portugal, the Latin American republics were still in political and economic bondage. Professor José Miguez Bonino, who delivered the first London Lectures in 1974 under the title *Christians and Marxists: the mutual challenge to revolution*, began his later book *Revolutionary Theology Comes of Age*[76] with a brief historical analysis. He pointed out that Christians entered Latin America in two distinct but equally oppressive stages, namely 'Spanish colonialism (Roman Catholicism) and North Atlantic neo-colonialism (Protestantism)'.[77] Not that the domination has been entirely from outside, however. Dom Helder Camara, formerly Roman Catholic Archbishop of Recife in North-East Brazil, kept protesting against 'internal colonialism', that is, continuing political and economic oppression by Latin America's own right-wing oligarchies and military governments.

There can be no doubt of the sincere compassion which Gutierrez and his fellow liberationists feel towards the oppressed. He calls the church to 'a more evangelical, more authentic, more concrete and more efficacious commitment to liberation'.[78] Several times he quotes with approval Marx's famous dictum that 'the philosophers have only *interpreted* the world ... the point however is to *change* it'.[79] Gutierrez sees the process of liberation and transformation as 'a quest to satisfy the most fundamental human aspirations – liberty, dignity and the possibility of personal fulfilment for all'.[80]

Defined thus, all Christians should surely be equally committed to liberation. Indeed, those of us who are Protestants may well feel ashamed that we were not in the vanguard of the liberation movement, and that we did not develop an evangelical liberation theology. For we believe that God made man male and female in his own image; that human beings, being God-like beings, have an intrinsic value, on account of which they must be served, not exploited; and that we should set ourselves in Christ's name against all dehumanizing tendencies, against anything and everything which impedes human freedom and fulfilment.

This raises an immediate question. The original liberation theology was addressed to socio-political and economic oppression. But since then other liberation theologies have arisen. There is Dalit theology, addressing the issue of caste among India's 'untouchables'; black theology in the United States and Africa, addressing the issue of race; feminist theology, addressing the issue of gender; and the theology of gay liberation, addressing the issue of sexual orientation.[81] Political correctness insists that they are all equally valid, and that no discrimination should be permitted in regard to caste, race, gender or sexual orientation.

The Christian perspective, however, is different. True, as Paul wrote, 'there is neither Jew nor Greek, slave nor free, male nor female, for you are all one in Christ Jesus' (Gal. 3:28). This text is a charter of Christian freedom, but it must be carefully and conscientiously interpreted. It affirms that, in our relationship to Christ by faith, ethnic, social and sexual distinctions are irrelevant. We are equal in value and dignity before him. These distinctions have not been abolished, however. Our ethnic origin is still an essential part of our identity. Also men are still men, and women

women, and have different sexual functions and roles.

So we need to redefine liberation. It is intended to secure our freedom from anything and everything *which inhibits human beings from being what God by creation and redemption intends them to be* – which will include marriage as the heterosexual, monogamous, loving and lifelong partnership which God instituted and Jesus Christ endorsed.

Another notable feature of liberation theology is its emphasis on *praxis* as 'a new way to do theology'.[82] The first step in 'doing theology', Gutierrez maintains, is not to open the Bible, but to make a serious commitment to the struggle for liberation. Thus the first text to be studied is not a biblical but a social text, namely the surrounding reality and our experience of it. Only then are we ready for the second step, namely biblical study. Theology is therefore defined as 'a critical reflection on Christian praxis in the light of the Word'.[83] And the essential context for taking both steps is 'base ecclesial communities', that is, grassroots groups of ordinary Christians.

Without doubt many have found this process both illuminating and challenging. Nevertheless, it may be questioned whether the two steps must invariably be taken in the same order, provided that the Word and the world engage creatively with one another. Indeed, it may be that by beginning with a serious study of social reality, the serious study of the biblical text has been neglected. Andrew Kirk complains of this: 'None of our authors has undertaken an exegetical study of the (popular) passages … Most of them make no attempt to verify exegetically the correctness of either their method or their use of the text.'[84]

This is particularly clear when one considers the liberationists' use of the exodus theme. They regard it as a paradigm for any and every rescue from oppression, with no adequate recognition that the exodus of Israel from Egyptian bondage was *sui generis*. Not only was it a mighty act of God (by his 'strong right arm'), but it took place in fulfilment of God's remembered covenant with Abraham, Isaac and Jacob (Exod. 2:24) and in preparation for its renewal at Mount Sinai (Exod. 19:4–6).

The same hermeneutical looseness is seen in relation to the vocabulary of salvation. Gutierrez does acknowledge the difference between salvation (from sin and death) and liberation (from poverty and oppression), but probably not clearly enough. One complaint about this has come from an unexpected source, namely Bishop K. H. Ting of Shanghai, for many years President of the China Christian Council. When introducing liberation theology to the students of Nanjing Seminary in 1985, he said: 'Liberation theology is such a good thing that it hurts us not to be able to endorse it in its entirety.' But 'the eternal theme of Christianity and its theology should not be political ... but should rather be reconciliation of humanity with God ... Reconciliation between God and humanity is the eternal theme of Christian theology'.[85]

Further clarification of this issue remains crucial. William H. Lazareth, who wrote the Introduction to Bonino's book *Revolutionary Theology Comes of Age*, found it necessary to ask these questions:

> The decisive issue for liberation theology is the relation of Christian freedom to political liberty. By what apostolic authority may we conflate liberation from sin, death and the demonic with liberation from injustice, oppression and poverty? In more personal terms, how do we relate the first-century activities of Jesus and Paul with the twentieth-century activities of Che Guevara and Camilo Torres? Are they similar, repetitious, distinguishable or unrelated?[86]

For myself I am glad that the Lausanne Covenant (1974) spoke forthrightly about this matter. Here is paragraph five entitled 'Christian Social Responsibility':

> We affirm that God is both the Creator and the Judge of all men. We therefore should share his concern for justice and reconciliation throughout human society and for the liberation of men from every kind of oppression. Because mankind is made in the image of God, every person, regardless of race, religion, colour, culture, class, sex or age, has an intrinsic dignity because of which he should be respected and served, not exploited. Here too we express penitence both for our neglect and for having sometimes regarded evangelism and social concern as mutually exclusive. Although reconciliation with man is not reconciliation with God, nor is social action evangelism, nor

is political liberation salvation, nevertheless we affirm that evangelism and socio-political involvement are both part of our Christian duty. For both are necessary expressions of our doctrines of God and man, our love for our neighbour and our obedience to Jesus Christ ...[87]

We must now return to Jesus the liberator, and to the conviction of idealistic young people that he is the champion of the poor and the oppressed. When Salvador Allende, the Marxist President of Chile, fell in 1973, a large mass for Marxist students was held in Quito, Ecuador. The preacher was Leonides Proaño, Bishop of Riobamba, who, although known as *obispo rojo* (the red bishop), was not in fact a Marxist, for he insisted that the motivation for his ministry was not Karl Marx but Jesus Christ, who identified with the poor. So at the mass for Allende he proclaimed the authentic and compassionate Jesus, Jesus the critic of the establishment, the radical Jesus of the gospels. During the question-time which followed, the students responded: 'If we had only known *this* Jesus, we would never have become Marxists.'

11. Christ the Jewish Messiah: N. T. Wright

Exile and exodus

One of the first heretical movements to arise in the early church was Docetism, the belief that the humanity, sufferings and death of Jesus were only apparent (from *dokein*, to seem) and not real. Based on the Greek view that matter was evil, docetists denied the genuine humanity of Jesus, and therefore both the incarnation and the atonement. The apostle John saw the seriousness of this teaching and confronted it in both his gospel and his letters. 'Many deceivers have gone out into the world', he wrote, 'who do not confess that Jesus Christ has come in the flesh; any such person is the deceiver and the antichrist!' (2 John 7, REB).

Some people in our day are guilty of the same heresy without realizing it. They know that nowadays it is more often the deity than the humanity of Jesus which is denied. So they give their time and energy to marshalling the evidence for his deity until in the process he is no longer an authentic human being.

Since Jesus was a human being, however, he was also a historical figure, who lived at a particular time in a particular place and within a particular culture. These particularities were all part of his historical reality. To deny them would be to reject some essential aspects of his identity.

In 1937 the Harvard scholar Henry J. Cadbury produced his book *The Peril of Modernizing Jesus*. He pointed out that the great Italian and Dutch masters 'plainly can make no claim to Palestinian verisimilitude'. They do not even try. Instead they modernize their figures. Thus, Adam is depicted in a luxuriantly Flemish Garden of Eden, Delilah cuts off Samson's hair with embossed silver shears, and Mary Magdalene wears a Flemish headdress, while all the time the background is either 'the Italian campagna or the polders of Holland'.[88] In contrast, writes Cadbury, the aim of his book was 'to minimize the modernness of Jesus', while at the same time recognizing his originality and not going to the opposite extreme, so that we 'over-archaize him'.[89] His third chapter is entitled 'The Jewishness of the gospels', in which he emphasizes the Jewishness of Jesus himself. For our tendency is to forget Jesus' first-century Palestinian context and to create a Jesus in our own likeness and to our own liking. We do to him what Pilate's soldiers did when they stripped him of his own clothes, put on him a scarlet military cloak, and mocked him. 'The soldiers put on Jesus their own kind of clothes.'[90] We tend to do the same thing in our day. We clothe him with 'our own thoughts'.[91]

It is in relation to the Jewishness of Jesus that I would like to refer to the work of a contemporary theologian, Dr Tom Wright.[92] He is a New Testament scholar of great ability, who has written both academic and popular books. He is also a doughty champion of Christian orthodoxy over against (for example) the radical reductionism of the 'Jesus Seminar'.

Dr Wright's main emphasis is that Jesus must be located within his context of first-century Palestinian Judaism; and his main hypothesis is that Israel's Babylonian captivity (beginning in 587 BC), although it ended *geographically* later in the sixth century, was continuing *theologically* in the first century AD. Israel was still under foreign domination. But now, at long last, the Messiah would rescue them in a new exodus, which would be the climax of history.

So Jesus, in proclaiming the arrival of the kingdom, was also announcing the end of the exile. His message was quite different from the popular options, however. These were (1) the Qumran option of separatism and quietism, (2) the King Herod option of political compromise, and (3) the Zealot option of violent revolution.

Instead of these, as Jesus walked from village to village, he summoned the people to repent (i.e. to reject the other options) and to accept his radical counter-agenda (i.e. the kingdom way of non-retaliation, mercy and love for the enemy). Thus Israel was being redefined and reconstituted, with the twelve apostles as its nucleus, and with Jesus as its centre.

Jesus' gift of forgiveness showed that the exile (the penalty of sin) was over. His healing miracles, ridding people of the disabilities (blindness, deafness, etc.) which would have excluded them from the Qumran community, showed that the kingdom community would be characterized by a basic inclusiveness. His welcoming of social outcasts and eating with them showed that the messianic banquet had begun. Further, his kingdom people must give up their preoccupation with their own identity and accept instead their vocation to be the light of the world. Through Jesus Israel would be renewed; through renewed Israel the world would be blessed.

Did Jesus then believe himself to be the Messiah? Yes, according to Dr Wright, who goes into great detail about the messianic implications of various texts. In particular he stresses two complementary symbolic actions, which Jesus performed deliberately, and 'which encapsulated his whole work and agenda'.[93]

First, Jesus cleansed the temple, indicating both that the present corrupt system was ripe for judgment and that he would replace it, so that in future God's personal presence would be found wherever he and his people were.

Secondly, the last supper was the new Passover meal, the kingdom-feast celebrating the end of the exile, the true exodus and the new covenant.

But the Messiah was also expected to fight the final battle against the enemy. This expectation Jesus also transformed. He would overthrow evil not by violence but by non-violence, by turning the other cheek. He saw the cross as the climax of his vocation to identify with Israel, to take upon himself the judgment that was threatening the nation, and to bear Israel's sufferings as her representative. He was vindicated as Messiah by the resurrection.

Did Jesus also believe that he was in some sense divine? To this question Dr Wright gives an ambivalent answer. At one point he writes bluntly 'I do not think Jesus "knew he was God".'[94] But this statement comes in the middle of a section about different kinds of 'knowledge'. He goes on to write that Jesus 'believed he had to do and be, for Israel and the world, that which according to Scripture only Yahweh himself could do and be'.[95] Thus, in the new exodus he was not merely the new Moses but the pillar of cloud and fire, leading the people to freedom; and now his last journey to Jerusalem, culminating in the triumphal entry, seems to have been a staged fulfilment of the expectation that one day after the exile Yahweh would return to Zion. In claiming to be the new temple, Jesus was implying that he was the *Shekinah*[96] in person, the presence of Yahweh among his people. Jesus also claimed a teaching authority superior even to Torah, making him 'not a new Moses but, in some sense or other, a new Yahweh'.[97] Or summing up, Dr Wright says: 'Jesus ... would embody in himself the returning and redeeming action of the covenant God.'[98] How could he advance these claims to divine authority and action, and not believe that he was God?

It is no doubt absurd to attempt to summarize in a paragraph or two the closely reasoned argument of several books. I am also conscious that I have not expressed sufficient appreciation of the comprehensiveness, freshness and reverence with which Dr Wright has developed his thesis. Yet not all scholars have felt able to accept his reconstruction. The debate will certainly continue. I have only a few questions to ask:

First, is it certain that the exile-exodus theme was central both to first-century Palestinian Judaism and to the understanding of Jesus?

Secondly, we are not told how Jesus came to learn who he was. Nor can we pry into his self-consciousness. But is it necessary, in the interest of maintaining his real humanness, to hold back from saying that he knew who he was? He certainly claimed divine authority to forgive, to teach and to judge.

Thirdly, fine things are said about the crucified Messiah as the representative of Israel, and about the cross as the truest window into the very heart of the loving God. Dr Wright also distinguishes clearly between 'historical' and 'theological' answers to the question why Jesus died. Nevertheless, I miss more than a passing glance at the crucial ransom-saying (Mark 10:45).

Fourthly, Tom Wright alludes many times to the climax and consummation of history. But he reverses the direction of Christ's 'coming' from 'a downward cloud-borne movement' to his exaltation from earth to heaven, involving his vindication.[99] Does this mean that the personal, visible and glorious parousia of Jesus Christ has been completely dissolved into apocalyptic imagery?

To conclude, I appreciate Dr Wright's determination to break down the barriers between the academy and the church, and his passionate commitment to mission. He writes of the opportunity for 'serious and joyful Christian mission to the post-postmodern world'.[100]

It is to the topic of mission that we turn next.

12. Christ the global Lord: Mission in the twentieth century

From Edinburgh 1910 to Lausanne 1974

It was the risen Jesus who made the great claim that all authority had been given to him in heaven and on earth (Matt. 28:18). In consequence, the church has always borne witness to his universal lordship. For God has super-exalted him, and given him the name above every other name (that is, the rank beyond every other rank), in order that every knee should bow to him and every tongue confess him 'Lord' (Phil. 2:9–11). This is the fundamental basis of the world-wide mission of the church, as has been well illustrated in the twentieth century.

In 1910 the World Missionary Conference was convened in Edinburgh, under the chairmanship of John R. Mott. It had been carefully prepared for over a period of eighteen months by eight international commissions, whose printed reports had been read in advance by the 1,200 or so delegates. John Mott himself claimed that in its plan, personnel, spirit and promise it was 'the most significant gathering ever held in the interest of the world's evangelization'.[101]

John Mott's book, *The Decisive Hour of Christian Missions*, exudes the euphoria that had been generated during the conference. In the light of spiritual awakenings in South East Asia, mass movements in India, the rapid progress of the gospel in Africa, the weakening hold of other religions and 'the rising spiritual tide in the non-Christian world',[102] Mott wrote of 'abundant ground for hopefulness and confidence'.[103] Indeed, 'the way is unmistakably being prepared for the acceptance of Christianity by large masses of the people in many lands'.[104] And using what we would regard as an unfortunate military metaphor, Mott continued: 'On the world-wide battlefield of Christianity ... victory is assured ... '[105]

The delegates left Edinburgh elated and inspired. They were under no illusions about the immensity of the task. They knew that there were still about 1,000 million non-Christians in the world, no more than one-fifth of whom had heard clearly about Christ. But they were determined. They agreed with John Mott that 'it is the church's duty to see that this long-standing reproach is completely removed'.[106] Also, 'it is high time that the church deliberately and resolutely attack some of the hitherto almost impregnable fortresses'.[107] They believed (somewhat naïvely) that under the influence of Christ other religions would gradually disappear, like the old gods of Greece and Rome.

Who could have guessed that within the next few years this missionary emphasis would have evaporated almost entirely? There were two main reasons. First came the horrors of the First World War in 1914. Not only were Christians divided by the conflict, but almost all international enterprises were put on hold. And when post-war reconstruction began, the world had changed and moved on.

Secondly, the spread of liberal theology between the wars called into question the content of the gospel and undermined people's confidence in it. This was very evident at the next two missionary conferences – at Jerusalem (1928) and Tambaram outside Madras (1938). Whereas at Edinburgh the mood had been confident, at

Jerusalem and Tambaram it was largely diffident and hesitant.

At Jerusalem (1928) a comparatively small group of about 200 gathered, although it was notable that about fifty of them belonged to what were now called the 'younger' churches. Their broad agenda therefore included relations between the older and the younger churches, in addition to such topics as race relations, urban and rural questions, religious education and the menace of secularism. Theologically, relativism reigned. Christianity could no longer be regarded as either unique or final. William Temple saved the conference from disaster by drafting the 'Message', which included the epigram about the gospel that 'either it is true for all, or it is not true at all'.

The World Missionary Conference at Tambaram (1938) brought about 500 delegates together, and the representatives of the younger churches were equal in numbers to, and on an equal footing with, those from the older churches. But the most noteworthy feature of Tambaram was the sharp encounter between William E. Hocking and Hendrik Kraemer. Hocking was Professor of Philosophy at Harvard. His book *Re-thinking Missions* had been published in 1932, so that conference participants had had time to peruse it. In it the old missionary certainties had gone. So had any exclusive claim for Christ. Seeking conversions was frowned upon, and should be replaced by seeking the best in all religions. The ultimate goal of mission was said to be the emergence of a world fellowship of faiths.

Hocking's sparring partner at Tambaram was Hendrik Kraemer, a Dutch Reformed layman and seasoned linguist-missionary in Indonesia. He had been invited to write a book for the conference. It was published in 1938 under the title *The Christian Message in a non-Christian World*. Influenced by Karl Barth (whose assault on liberalism in his commentary on Romans had appeared in 1919), he defended what he called 'biblical realism'. He maintained that there was a radical discontinuity between God's unique revelation in Jesus Christ and all human religion.

This debate continues today and has by no means been resolved. A year after Tambaram, the Second World War broke out, and again ecumenical relationships were largely suspended until it was over. Then in 1948 the first assembly of the World Council of Churches took place in Amsterdam, and in 1961, at its third assembly in New Delhi, the World Council of Churches and the International Missionary Council were amalgamated. Assurances were given that the merger would bring mission to the forefront of the World Council's agenda. But this has not happened. Instead, the World Council has continued to drift away from the biblical gospel.

Not that all conciliar leaders have followed. For example, Visser't Hooft, the first General Secretary of the World Council of Churches, wrote in his book *No Other Name*: 'It is high time that Christians should rediscover that the very heart of their faith is that Jesus Christ did not come to make a contribution to the religious storehouse of mankind, but that in him God reconciled the world to himself.'[108]

More striking still is this forthright statement by the late Bishop Lesslie Newbigin:

> The contemporary embarrassment about the missionary movement of the previous century is not, as we like to think, evidence that we have become more humble. It is, I fear, much more clearly evidence of a shift in belief. It is evidence that we are less ready to affirm the uniqueness, the centrality, the decisiveness of Jesus Christ as universal Lord and Saviour, the Way by following whom the world is to find its true goal, the Truth by which every other claim to truth is to be tested, the Life in whom alone life in its fulness is to be found.[109]

The fact is that during the last quarter of the twentieth century the missionary initiative passed from the World Council to the Lausanne movement, which was launched by Dr Billy Graham. The International Congress on World Evangelization was held in Lausanne, Switzerland, in 1974. Some 2,700 participants (50% from the developing world) came together from 150 nations, and after nine days of hectic activity endorsed the Lausanne Covenant which, according to a theologian from Asia, may prove to be 'the most significant ecumenical confession on evangelism that the church has ever produced'. It is all the more important because its background is that of 'pluralism' which insists on the equal legitimacy of every religion.

The Covenant consists of fifteen paragraphs, and I quote here from the third paragraph on 'The Uniqueness and Universality of Christ'. This is how the church proclaims 'Jesus Christ the global Lord':

> We affirm that there is only one Saviour and only one Gospel … We recognize that all men have some knowledge of God through his general revelation in nature. But we deny that this can save, for men suppress the truth by their unrighteousness. We also reject as derogatory to Christ and the Gospel every kind of syncretism and dialogue which implies that Christ speaks equally through all religions and ideologies. Jesus Christ, being himself the only God-man, who gave himself as the only ransom for sinners, is the only mediator between God and man. There is no other name by which we must be saved … Jesus Christ has been exalted above every other name; we long for the day when every knee shall bow to him and every tongue shall confess him Lord.[110]

Conclusion: Authenticity versus accommodation

We have made a rapid – and inevitably selective – survey of church history, considering a dozen of its influential movements and their leaders. Have you not been astonished by the church's extraordinary versatility, as it has painted and repainted the portrait of Jesus?

In doing so, the church's motives have been mixed. It is good to present Jesus in the best possible light, so as to commend him to the world. But it is not good, in order to do so, to eliminate from the portrait everything that might offend, including the offence of the cross. This is to pander to Christianity's 'cultured despisers', as Schleiermacher called them. There is always a price to pay for this kind of feeble-minded accommodation. Jesus is wrenched out of his original context. He becomes manipulated and domesticated, and what is then presented to the world is an anachronism, even a caricature.

How can we avoid making this mistake ourselves? How can we present Jesus Christ to the world in a way that is simultaneously authentic and relevant? A double discipline seems to be needed, negative and positive. The negative is to rid our minds of all preconceptions and prejudices, and resolutely to renounce any attempt to force Jesus into our pre-determined mould. In other words we must repent of Christian 'procrusteanism'. Procrustes, in Greek mythology, was a brutal robber who compelled his victims to fit the dimensions of his iron bed. If they were too short, he stretched them. If they were too long, he chopped off their feet. The Christian 'Procrustes' exhibits a similar inflexibility, forcing Jesus into his way of thinking and resorting to ruthless measures in order to secure his conformity. From Procrustes and all his disciples, good Lord deliver us!

The positive counterpart follows. We have to open our minds and hearts to whatever the biblical text gives us, and to listen to the witness of the whole New Testament to Christ, as we tried to in Part I. For the authentic Jesus is the original Jesus, the Jesus of the apostolic testimony in the New Testament. Much as we may admire the creative versatility of the church's many presentations of Jesus, we must keep returning to the New Testament pictures as the norm by which the church's portraits must be judged.

C. S. Lewis saw an analogy here with the appreciation of art. He wrote: 'We must look, and go on looking, till we have certainly seen exactly what is there. We sit down before the picture in order to have something done to us, not that we may do things with it. The first demand any work of any art makes upon us is surrender. Look. Listen. Receive. Get yourself out of the way.'[111]

This double discipline is never more necessary than in evangelism. For often it is not that people have rejected Christ, but that they have rejected a pseudo-Christ. Dr Peter Kuzmic, President of the Evangelical Theological Seminary in Osijek, Yugoslavia, has put it in this way:

We must *renew the credibility of the Christian mission*. Missions and evangelism are not primarily a question of methodology, money, management and numbers, but rather a question of authenticity, credibility and spiritual power ... In going out to evangelize in Yugoslavia, I frequently tell our seminary students that our main task may be simply to 'wash the face of Jesus', for it has been dirtied and distorted by both the compromises of institutional Christianity through the centuries and the antagonistic propaganda of atheistic communism in recent decades.[112]

So by close attention to the witness of the New Testament, and in the interest of authentic evangelism, hopefully our vision of Christ will continue to clarify. At all events, however blurred and distorted our image of him may still be now, we have been promised that when Christ appears in glory 'we shall see him as he is' (1 John 3:2), the authentic, the incomparable Christ.

PART III

THE INFLUENTIAL JESUS

(or how he has inspired people)

PART III: THE INFLUENTIAL JESUS
(or how he has inspired people)

Introduction: The story of Jesus

In Part II we considered the church's varied presentation of Christ down the centuries. In Part III we reverse the order and consider Christ's influence on the church, and indeed on the world. The question we are asking was well put by K. S. Latourette of Yale University towards the beginning of his massive, seven-volume work entitled *The History of the Expansion of Christianity*. It is this: 'Just what difference has it made to the world that Jesus lived?'[1]

The question is not as simple to answer as may appear at first sight. First, we have to distinguish between the influence of Christ on the world and the influence of civilization or culture, which is an amalgam of many (not only Christian) influences. Secondly, to quote Latourette again, 'we must also remark the close connection between the effect of Christianity upon its (social) environment and the effect of the environment upon Christianity'.[2] Thirdly, we must humbly acknowledge that Christianity (though not Christ personally) has had a *bad* as well as a *good* influence. I am thinking of some of the church's blindspots like the Crusades, the Inquisition, the failure to abolish slavery until 1,800 years after Christ, and the imperialism of some Christian missions during the past two centuries. Reflecting on such things as these, all we can do is bow our heads in shame.

Nevertheless, it is still possible to affirm – cautiously but confidently – that Jesus Christ has had an enormous influence for good, not only in art and architecture, music and painting, science, democracy and legal systems, but especially in moral standards and values such as the dignity of the human person.[3] Indeed, one would hardly be guilty of hyperbole if one were to claim: 'All the armies that ever marched, all the navies that ever sailed, all the parliaments that ever sat, and all the kings that ever reigned, put together, have not affected our life on earth as much as that one solitary life.'[4]

What fascinates me is that different Christians have been influenced by different aspects of Christ to undertake different tasks. Our focus in Part III is not now the story of the church (and its presentation of Christ) but the story of Jesus (and his challenge to the church). To be sure, the two stories overlap: for example, if Francis of Assisi influenced the way in which the church presented Christ (which he did), Christ also influenced the way in which Francis developed the Franciscan movement. Nevertheless the two influences are distinct. We will consider now the whole cycle of Jesus' career, from his first coming to the anticipation of his second, and see how each stage (whether episode or teaching in the gospels) has gripped somebody's imagination and inspired him or her to action.

1. The Bethlehem stable: Francis of Assisi

The nativity of the poor king

In 1926, the seven-hundredth anniversary of the death of St Francis, something like two million pilgrims visited Assisi, his birthplace in central Italy. At that time, Pope Pius XI officially confirmed the unofficial designation of Francis as 'Alter Christus', 'the second Christ', so closely was he deemed to resemble him.

What was it that inspired Francis to assume a life of absolute poverty and simplicity? It was partly Jesus' teaching, namely his call to self-denial and his mission charge to the Twelve. But in particular it was Jesus' example that Francis longed to imitate in strict and literal conformity. In particular, Francis saw in his birth in a stable the supreme expression of the Son of God's self-imposed poverty.

Three or four centuries seem to have elapsed after the birth of Christ before Christmas enjoyed a fixed position in the Western church calendar and Christians regularly celebrated it. This may have been due partly to a confusion. People spoke of Christ driving his chariot across the sky like the Sun God. In fact, because Christians worshipped on Sundays, and often turned East to do so, many pagans thought that Christians were sun-worshippers. Not till the fourth century did the Western church begin to celebrate December 25 (the birthday of the Sun God at the winter solstice, the shortest day of the year) as the nativity of Christ.

Francis found enormous inspiration from the circumstances surrounding the birth of Jesus. 'He spoke charming words concerning the nativity of the poor King and the little town of Bethlehem.'[5] He often called Jesus 'the Child of Bethlehem', and it was said of him: 'The Child Jesus had been forgotten in the hearts of many; but, by the working of his grace, he was brought to life again through his servant St Francis.'[2] So 'the birthday of the Child Jesus Francis observed with inexpressible eagerness over all other feasts, saying that it was the feast of feasts, on which God, having become a tiny infant, clung to human breasts'.[7]

Although the centrality of the cross is clear in the faith and life of Francis, he kept together in his heart and mind the incarnation and the crucifixion, Christ in the crib and Christ on the cross. For he saw them both as manifestations of divine humility and poverty, which he determined to imitate. He believed himself commissioned to proclaim the kingdom, serve the needy, forsake money and even do without spare clothing.

This does not mean that he rejected, or even undervalued, the material world or the good gifts of the good Creator. On the contrary, he is well-known for his celebration of God's creatures, hailing them as his 'brothers' or 'sisters', and finding joy in these relationships. His 'Canticle of the Sun' remains a beautiful expression of praise, not of course to nature but to the God of nature. He seems to have seen no dichotomy between an acknowledgment of the material world as God-given and a renunciation of material possessions.

Others, however, have felt an unresolved conflict here. G. K. Chesterton, for example, in his famous work on Francis,[8] entitles his first chapter 'The Problem of St Francis'. What was this problem? Chesterton, who is usually regarded as himself the master of paradox, found in Francis a mass of inconsistencies, and even contradictions. How can we reconcile Francis's joy in nature and his rigorous asceticism, he asked; his 'gaiety and austerity',[9] 'his glorifying gold and purple and perversely going in rags',[10] his 'hunger for a happy life' and 'thirst for a heroic death'?[11]

It is impossible to read the story of Francis without being profoundly moved, even if we cannot quite echo G. K. Chesterton's conclusion that Francis 'has lived and changed the world'.[12] Further, I venture to ask: Was not Francis's resolve to imitate Christ in all things too literal? Did he not fail to perceive the vivid, dramatic imagery which Jesus often employed? For example, in Luke 14:25–33 Jesus laid down three conditions without which a would-be follower, he said, 'cannot be my disciple'. First, he must 'hate' his father and mother, wife and children, brothers and sisters. Secondly, he must 'carry his cross' and follow Christ. Thirdly, he must 'give up everything he has'. Now we certainly have no freedom to water down this strong gospel medicine. Nevertheless, to 'carry the cross' is definitely not literal; Jesus did not require all his disciples to be crucified. Nor can the injunction to hate our close relatives be taken literally; the Jesus who told us to love even our enemies is not likely to tell us to hate our own family. So the third command (to renounce our property) is surely not to be taken literally either. This is not a cowardly evasion of the teaching of Jesus, but an honest desire to discover what he meant. The cost of discipleship involves putting Christ first in everything, before even our relatives, our ambitions and our possessions.

2. The carpenter's bench: George Lansbury

The dignity of manual labour

We know very little about Jesus' so-called 'hidden years' before his public ministry began. The only story that has survived from those days is Luke's account of how at the age of twelve he visited Jerusalem and got lost in the temple (Luke 2:41–51). The immediately preceding verse covers the twelve years between his birth and his Jerusalem visit, while the immediately following verse covers the eighteen years between the Jerusalem visit and his baptism. Both these verses (40 and 52) are therefore bridge verses; they tell us that he was growing in wisdom as well as in stature, and in favour with both God and man, and that the grace of God rested upon him. Presumably this is all we are meant to know, and all we need to know, about the first thirty years of Jesus' life on earth.

Throughout the four gospels the word 'carpenter' appears only twice. Matthew refers to 'the carpenter's son' (13:55), while Mark records the question asked by the villagers of Nazareth: 'isn't this the carpenter?' (6:3). We assume from this that Joseph had worked as a carpenter, that Jesus had been his apprentice, and that he took over from him, perhaps at Joseph's death.

The word *tektōn* could be used of any artisan or craftsman, but normally denoted a worker with wood, a carpenter, joiner or builder. As William Barclay put it, the *tektōn* could 'build you anything from a chicken-coop to a house'.[13] In other words, he was a handy man. At the same time Professor Martin Hengel emphasizes that 'Jesus himself did not come from the proletariat of day-labourers and landless tenants, but from the middle class of Galilee, the skilled workers.' He adds that *tektōn* meant 'mason, carpenter, cartwright and joiner all rolled into one'.[14] Justin Martyr, at about the middle of the second century, affirmed in his *Dialogue with Trypho a Jew* [15] that Jesus 'used to make ploughs and yokes'. In addition to farm implements, it seems probable that he will have learned to make and repair household furniture like tables, chairs, beds and cupboards.

It is important to remember that the Romans and the Greeks despised having to work with their hands. 'Among the Jews', however, wrote Alfred Edersheim, 'the contempt for manual labour, which was one of the painful characteristics of heathenism, did not exist. On the contrary, it was deemed a religious duty, frequently and most earnestly insisted upon, to learn some trade, provided it did not minister to luxury, nor tend to lead away from personal observance of the law.'[16] Thus the Talmud records the dictum of Rabbi Judah in the second century AD: 'He who does not teach his own son a trade, teaches him to be a thief.'[17] The Jews knew that work had been commanded by God as a consequence of the creation, not the fall.

The apostle referred a number of times in his letters to his own trade. In Acts 18:3 Luke calls him a *skēnopoios* which, since *skēnē* or *skēnos* is a tent, is usually translated 'tentmaker', although some commentators prefer 'leather worker' or 'saddler', since tents in the ancient world were normally made of leather. What is certain is that Paul worked with his hands and took pride in his labour.[18]

Having sketched this background, we are now ready to ask who has been inspired by the knowledge that Jesus had worked at a carpenter's bench?

We could begin our answer by referring to the Pre-Raphaelite

Brotherhood, those painters in the middle of the nineteenth century who set themselves to revive fidelity to nature in art. In 1850 one of their members, J. E. Millais, completed his painting 'Christ in the home of his parents' or 'The Carpenter's shop'. The child Jesus is at the centre of the picture. He has evidently injured himself with a nail; Joseph is leaning over to examine the wound; Mary is seeking to comfort Jesus with a kiss; and the youthful John the Baptist is carrying a bowl of water with which to bathe the injury. Jesus is leaning against the work bench, which seems to symbolize the altar of sacrifice, and penned sheep can be seen through the open door.[19]

Twenty-two years later Millais' friend Holman Hunt completed his picture 'The Shadow of Death'. We are once again in the carpenter's shop. But this time Jesus is an adult, stripped to the waist, and standing beside a wooden trestle. Pausing from his work, he stretches, raising his arms above his head and apparently appealing to heaven. As he does this, a dark shadow in the shape of a crucifix is cast on the wall behind him, where his tool rack looks like a horizontal bar and reminds us of the hammer and nails of crucifixion.[20]

Both pictures are deliberately symbolical. They speak powerfully of the cross, but say nothing about the dignity of manual labour. So in my searching I turned next to the Christian leaders of the early British labour movement. I began with James Keir Hardie (1856–1915), pioneer of the Scottish labour movement. He created a sensation when he entered the House of Commons in his workman's cloth cap and tweed suit. He was outspoken in his commitment to Christ, to whom he often referred as 'the Carpenter of Nazareth'. But the main inspiration for his work was not the example of Jesus Christ but his teaching, especially the Sermon on the Mount which he interpreted somewhat naïvely as a socialist manifesto.

Other and later labour leaders, however, drew encouragement from the fact that Jesus belonged to the working class. An anonymous trade unionist in 1921 wrote a short book entitled *Jesus the Carpenter and his Teaching*. 'At any rate', he wrote,

> the life of Jesus is the life of a working man. It may be said that it is far more and far greater! Be it so. Yet in the days of

his flesh he was a carpenter. We have not had many great poets, heroes, martyrs among us workers. But Jesus, the Carpenter of Nazareth, was of us. And therefore, in these days when so much is stirring in the minds of the workers, every one of us might well study the life and teaching of the Carpenter of Nazareth.[21]

Similarly, Ira Boseley, in his book called *Christ the Carpenter, his trade and his teaching*, which he dedicated to the Worshipful Company of Carpenters, says that he aimed to portray Jesus as 'the only perfect working man'.[22]

But the best example I have found of a leader who was inspired by Jesus the carpenter is George Lansbury, who dominated the British labour movement during much of the first half of the twentieth century.

George Lansbury was born in 1859 in rural Suffolk, but he never stayed in the country. He kept moving home, because his father worked on the railways, and he lived most of his life in the East End of London. Leaving school at the age of fourteen, he got a job as a coal heaver, unloading coal from barges and railways. Even at this tender age, he experienced the challenges of manual labour and the dehumanizing influences of poverty and hunger.

But George Lansbury's heart was in politics, and he spent more than half a century in local and national government. After a brief flirtation with the Liberal Party, and several abortive attempts to enter Parliament, he was eventually elected in 1910 as the Labour member for Bow and Bromley, but resigned his seat two years later. During the next decade, while he was without a seat in the House of Commons, he was nevertheless tirelessly active in the cause of the labour movement. He edited the *Daily Herald* and spoke at meetings all over the country.

In 1922 he returned to the House of Commons, but not until 1929 did he achieve cabinet rank as First Commissioner of Works, with special responsibility for the Royal Parks in London. He succeeded in making them available for the recreation of working-class people. In 1931 he became chairman of the parliamentary Labour Party and so leader of the opposition.

During all these years George Lansbury was immensely popular. His bulky physique, exuberant personality, ruddy complexion, side whiskers, booming voice, cockney accent, boyish smile and transparent sincerity endeared him to everybody. The distinguished historian A. J. P. Taylor described him in a footnote as 'the most loveable figure in modern politics'.[23] An even better measure of his widespread popularity is that he was well known to the children of London's East End, who would hail him when he visited their school with cries of 'Good old George'.[24]

Lansbury's motivation in his indefatigable political career was undoubtedly a combination of his socialism and his Christianity. Not that he saw a need to distinguish sharply between them. 'Socialism', he wrote, 'which means love, co-operation and brotherhood in every department of human affairs, is only the outward expression of a Christian faith.'[25] Again, 'Christianity and socialism dominated Lansbury's very being. In the former he found the principles and power of living. In the latter he found the system through which they could be expressed.'[26] He was passionate for a just society in which poverty, unemployment, hunger and homelessness have been abolished.

It seems to have been Fenwick Kitto, Rector of Whitechapel, who by his teaching and example led George Lansbury into a personal commitment to Christ. Kitto 'entered into our lives', he said. After being confirmed in the parish church, George became a Sunday-school teacher, and later preached in many churches.

Bob Holman has written: 'It is important to note that Lansbury's Christianity preceded his socialism, for the latter was to spring largely from his understanding of the former.'[27] In an East End Roman Catholic magazine an anonymous contributor wrote: 'We younger men will never be able to say what we owe to George Lansbury from the example he has set us all, of a consistent self-sacrificing life, of a constant and fearless witness to Jesus Christ.'[28]

George Lansbury admired the so-called 'working classes' for their courage, perseverance, mutual solidarity and sense of humour, and he steadfastly refused attempts to make him 'climb the social ladder'. He determined to retain his own East End culture. Bob Holman, his biographer, has written: 'Lansbury came home from, belonged to, and worked with and for the ordinary, working-class residents and, by his mode of life, he continued to be one of them.'[29]

Bob Holman traces this resolve back to Lansbury's theology: 'as a Christian, he was captivated by the Christ who applied the principle of love to himself to the extent that he came to earth as an ordinary carpenter, and submitted to a cruel death for the sake of others'.[30]

Theologically speaking, 'it would be difficult to exhaust the significance of the fact that God chose for his Son, when he dwelt among men, out of all the possible positions in which he might have placed him, the lot of a working man. It stamped men's common toils with everlasting honour'.[31]

Or to express the same truth in working-class language and syntax, J. Paterson Smyth wrote:

> I don't know right where his shed may have stood,
> But often as I've been a-planing my wood,
> I've took off my hat just when thinking of he,
> At the same work as me.[32]

3. The ministry of compassion: Father Damien and Wellesley Bailey

Touching untouchables

On a number of occasions in the gospels we read that Jesus was moved with compassion towards the leaderless crowds, the hungry, the bereaved, the blind, and especially the sick.[33] In fact it is quite clear that healing was an integral part of his public ministry. He went about 'teaching in their synagogues, preaching the good news of the kingdom and healing every disease and sickness' (Matt. 4:23; 9:35). That is to say, he not only announced the coming of the kingdom, but demonstrated its arrival by his works of compassion and power.

In consequence, Christians have been in the vanguard of those who have sought to develop a ministry of compassion to those who suffer sickness or pain. On entering the Mayo Clinic in Rochester, Minnesota, one is confronted by a stained-glass window, whose central panel bears the inscription 'To cure sometimes, to relieve often, to comfort always.'

This is not to deny that proto-hospitals were developed by Hindus and Buddhists before Christ, and by Jews as well. It is rather to claim that Jesus of Nazareth introduced into the world a new threefold motivation – his parable of the good Samaritan, his golden rule and his personal example, all of which demonstrated his respect for human persons made in the image of God.

Dr Frank Davey has written:

> Jesus reversed the social priorities of his day by demonstrating and teaching a special concern for the poor, the disabled, the outcast and the underprivileged. Such people had no claim to attention until Jesus became their champion … One cannot imagine Hippocrates showing much interest in a prostitute in trouble, a blind beggar, the slave of a soldier of the occupying power, a psychotic foreigner clearly with no money, an old woman with a chronic spinal condition. Jesus not only did so, he expected his followers to do the same.[34]

Jesus' respect for those the world despised was best exemplified in his encounter with a leprosy sufferer, close to the beginning of his public ministry:

> A man with leprosy came to him and begged him on his knees, 'If you are willing, you can make me clean.'
> Filled with compassion, Jesus reached out his hand and touched the man, 'I am willing,' he said. 'Be clean!' Immediately the leprosy left him and he was cured (Mark 1:40–42).

His compassion motivated him to touch an untouchable, and his action has been a continuing inspiration ever since. It was the famous Cappadocian church father, Basil of Caesarea, who seems to have founded in AD 369 the first large-scale Christian hospital. He erected a cluster of buildings, which, in addition to the hospital of 300 beds, 'included hospices for travellers, a hospice for the poor, a hospice for the aged, an isolation unit and a house for those suffering from leprosy, who were treated in isolation'.[35]

During the following centuries hospices for the care of leprosy victims spread throughout Europe. They were known as 'lazar (=

leper) houses' or *lazarettos*, the words being derived from Lazarus who came to be regarded as the patron saint of leprosy sufferers.

But perhaps nobody in the Middle Ages was so inspired by Jesus' example, and in turn became an inspiration to others, as St Francis of Assisi. The story may have become embellished over the years, but Francis confessed in his last testament that 'sweetness of soul' first came to him when he was confronted by a beggar with leprosy. At first, Francis spurred on his horse to get away from the beggar. Then suddenly he became overwhelmed with remorse that, 'having turned away from his brother's need, he was galloping away from God, who suffered in every man's suffering'. So he turned his horse around, dismounted, and kissed the leprous beggar's hand.[36] Francis's example was contagious. It is sometimes said that what people caught from him was not the disease but his care for the diseased. He went on to establish both a hospital for leprosy sufferers and a 'company of brothers' to look after them.

We jump now in our story to the middle of the nineteenth century and to two remarkable men who gave their lives to the care of leprosy sufferers. One was a Belgian Roman Catholic, Father Joseph Damien, born in 1840, who worked in Hawaii, and the other an Irish Protestant, Wellesley Bailey, who was born in 1846, worked in India, and became the founder of the Leprosy Mission.

In 1863 Father Damien sailed as a missionary to Hawaii and was horrified by the plight of the leprosy victims, who had been permanently banished to the island of Molokai. Here they eked out a miserable existence in disease, filth and poverty, without either family or church to sustain them. Father Damien volunteered to go and live among them. He buried their dead. He brought them hygiene. He built churches and chapels, cleaned their water supply, improved their homes and their hospital, constructed an orphanage, trained a choir, and served as their teacher, carpenter, mason, priest and friend. This selfless ministry continued for sixteen years, until one Sunday morning in 1885 during church worship the congregation was stunned when he began his sermon with the words 'We lepers ...', indicating that he had contracted the disease himself. He died on Molokai in 1889.[37]

Wellesley Bailey was born only six years later than Damien, but they worked at opposite ends of the world. It was while Wellesley Bailey was teaching at a mission school in North West India that he visited a small 'leper asylum' nearby and was appalled by what he saw. Later, he wrote,

> [The victims] were in all stages of the malady, very terrible to look upon, with a sad woebegone expression on their faces – a look of utter helplessness. I almost shuddered, yet I was at the time fascinated, and I felt, if ever there was a Christ-like work in this world, it was to go among these poor sufferers and bring to them the consolation of the gospel.[38]

Bailey was right. As he began to visit the asylum regularly, he saw the gospel completely changing the lives and outlook of the inmates. At the same time he set himself to improve their physical condition. So in 1872 he founded 'The Mission to Lepers in India', which later became 'The Mission to Lepers', and then, as it is today, 'The Leprosy Mission'.

What was his inspiration? He tells us:

> I desire now to give a little of my own experience amongst [the leprosy sufferers], and to lay before my readers a plan whereby all may help who are in sympathy with him who when on earth did not think the leper too loathsome to lay his hands upon, but who, 'moved with compassion', put forth his hand, and touched him, and saith unto him 'I will; be thou clean.'[39]

This fine Christian tradition of care for leprosy sufferers was carried on in the twentieth century by an illustrious succession of Christian leprologists like Stanley Browne (Nigeria and Zaire), Frank Davey (Nigeria and India) and Robert Cochrane, who, citing the example of Jesus, 'led a campaign against the prevailing social stigma'.[40] Next came Paul Brand, who discovered that the clawed hand, the loss of fingers and toes, and the unexplained sores and bruises in leprosy patients were caused not by some mysterious aspect of the disease itself, but by their loss of sensation, their inability to feel pain.[41]

In our day, Aids is sometimes described as 'the modern-day leprosy', carrying a similar stigma and outlawed by a similar taboo. But Jesus set the compassionate example 'by reaching out and *touching* – an act of unimaginable courage in those days'.[42]

4. The Sermon on the Mount: Leo Tolstoy, Mahatma Gandhi and Martin Luther King, Jr

The challenge of non-resistance

Everybody who knows anything about Christianity is to some degree familiar with Jesus' Sermon on the Mount, which was probably an extended period of instruction. Most people also know that it contains the prohibition 'Do not resist an evil person' and the command 'Love your enemies' (Matt. 5:39, 44). Not only so, but Jesus practised what he preached. As the apostle Peter wrote: 'When they hurled their insults at him, he did not retaliate; when he suffered, he made no threats' (1 Pet. 2:23). Instead, he prayed that God would forgive those who were crucifying him (Luke 23:34).

Generations of people, both Christian and non-Christian, have been challenged and inspired by Jesus' combination of sermon and example, word and deed – by his endurance and self-control, his love for his enemies and his total freedom from the spirit of revenge. The radical reformers of the sixteenth century (various Anabaptist groups) and the peace churches today (e.g. the Mennonites, Quakers and United Brethren) are committed to total pacifism, and derive their mandate and their motivation from Jesus' Sermon on the Mount, as exemplified in his behaviour.

My concern in this chapter is to consider three individual leaders of the late nineteenth or early twentieth centuries, who all confessed the inspiration they had received from Jesus' sermon and suffering, namely the Russian novelist, Leo Tolstoy (1828–1910), the Indian social reformer, Mahatma Gandhi (1869–1948), and the American civil-rights campaigner, Martin Luther King, Jr (1929–1968).

Tolstoy was born into an aristocratic home, spent a dissolute youth, and then turned to serious writing. His best-known novels remain *War and Peace* and *Anna Karenina*, but for our purposes we need to consider his short work *What I Believe*. In it Tolstoy describes how in a time of personal crisis he read and re-read the Sermon on the Mount, and suddenly understood (he claimed) what the whole church for 1,800 years had misunderstood.

This was that Jesus meant what he said when he called his followers to non-resistance.[43] It is impossible to believe in Christ, he continued, and at the same time 'to work for the establishment of property, law courts, government and military forces ...',[44] because police, courts and army all use violence to resist evil and are therefore incompatible with the law of love. If only Christ's commands were obeyed literally, 'all men will be brothers, and everyone will be at peace with others'.[45] Then in the last chapter, defending himself against naïvety, he betrays his ingenuous view of human beings as being all basically good, rational and amiable.

Mahatma Gandhi, or 'Gandhiji' as Indians respectfully refer to him, is of course the father of modern India. Having studied law in London and practised it in South Africa, where he was insulted on account of his colour, he returned to India in 1914 and led the Civil Disobedience Campaign. He longed for an India freed from colonialism, casteism and materialism.

Already as a child Gandhi had learned about *ahimsa*, 'refraining from harming others'. But then as a young man in London he read the Hindu classic, *The Baghavad Gita*, and the Sermon on the Mount. 'It is that Sermon which has endeared Jesus to me', he said, and it is known that he constantly reflected on it, especially through the eyes of Tolstoy. For in South Africa he read Tolstoy's *The Kingdom of God is within you*, was profoundly affected by it, and determined when he returned to India to put his ideals into action. He described his policy as *satyagraha*, best translated 'truth-force', the attempt to win opponents by the power of truth and 'by the example of suffering willingly endured'. 'The state represents violence in a concentrated and organized form', he said. So in the perfect state which he envisaged, the police would still exist, but seldom use force; punishment would end; prisons would be turned into schools; and litigation be replaced by arbitration.[46] In all this Gandhi found inspiration in Jesus. 'Though I cannot claim to be a Christian in the sectarian sense', he said, 'the example of Jesus' sufferings is a factor in the composition of my undying faith in non-violence which rules all my actions ...'[47]

It is impossible not to admire Gandhi's humility and sincerity. Nevertheless, his policy must surely be judged unrealistic. He said he would resist the anticipated Japanese invaders by a 'peace brigade'; he urged the Jews to offer a non-violent resistance to Hitler; and he appealed to the British to cease hostilities. But, as Jacques Ellul commented, Gandhi had not considered the context. 'Put Gandhi into the Russia of 1925 or the Germany of 1933. The solution would be simple: after a few days he would be arrested, and nothing more would be heard of him.'[48]

Our main disagreement with Tolstoy and Gandhi, however, must not be that their position is unrealistic, but that it is unbiblical. We cannot interpret Jesus' command not to resist evil as an absolute prohibition of the use of force (including the police), unless we are prepared to say that the Bible contradicts itself and the apostles misunderstood Jesus. For the New Testament teaches (e.g. in Rom. 13) that the state has divine authority to punish the wrongdoer, that is, to 'resist one who is evil', forcing him to pay the penalty of his evil. This truth may not be twisted, however, to justify the institutionalized violence of an oppressive regime. It justifies only the 'minimum necessary force' to arrest wrongdoers and bring them to justice.

It is clear, then, that the state's duty is quite different from the individual's. In Romans 12:17 the individual is told 'Do not repay anyone evil for evil' (surely an echo of 'do not resist one who is evil'), and never to avenge himself, but leave it to the wrath of God; for it is written, '"It is mine to avenge, I will repay", says the Lord.' In other words, punishment is God's prerogative, and he exercises it through the law courts, as Paul goes on to write in Romans 13:4, namely that he (a duly authorized representative of the state) 'is God's servant, an agent of wrath to bring punishment on the wrongdoer'. This is not incompatible with the teaching and conduct of Jesus. He emphatically did not retaliate, but instead 'he entrusted himself [and his cause] to him who judges justly' (1 Pet. 2:23). To sum up this antithesis, Jesus was not prohibiting the administration of justice, but rather forbidding us to take the law into our own hands, and bidding us instead to love our enemies and be altogether free of malice and revenge. As has often been said, the way of the devil is to return evil for good; the way of the world is to return evil for evil and good for good; the way of Christ is to overcome evil with good (Rom. 12:21).

One person who understood this distinction was Martin Luther King, Jr. He had learned as much from Gandhi as Gandhi had from Tolstoy, although I think he understood Jesus' teaching better than either. Founder of the Southern Christian Leadership Conference, he was committed to non-violence and led the famous march to Washington in 1963, which was followed in 1964 and 1965 by the Civil Rights Acts. So on the one hand, he frequently acknowledged his debt to the Sermon on the Mount. On the other, he knew the necessity of legislation, indeed of enforceable laws, if ever racial discrimination were to be banned.

One of King's most eloquent sermons, entitled 'Loving your enemies', was composed in a Georgia jail. He described how 'hate multiplies hate ... in a descending spiral of destruction' and is 'just as injurious to the person who hates' as to his victim. Love, however, 'is the only force capable of transforming an enemy into a friend'. He went on to apply his theme to the racial crisis in the US. For over three centuries African-Americans had suffered oppression, frustration and discrimination. But King and his friends were determined to 'meet hate with love'. Then they would win both freedom and their oppressors, 'and our victory will be a double victory'.[49]

5. The love for children: Thomas Barnardo

'An ever-open door'

A love for children and a concern for their welfare are such essential elements of Christian culture that we tend to take them for granted. But they have not always been assumed. Child sacrifice, for example, was practised in various pagan religions, and its practice by the Ammonites to pacify their god Milcom or Molek was regarded by the Old Testament prophets with outrage and horror.

There seems in the ancient world to have been no law against, and no ethical disapproval of, either abortion or infanticide. Parents had full rights to pronounce life or death on their children.[50] For instance, among the first-century BC Oxyrhynchus papyri a letter was found from a man called Hilarian to his expectant wife Alis: 'If it is male, let it live; if it is female, expose it.'[51]

It is true that the Hippocratic Oath, which doctors took, included the undertaking 'I will not give a pessary to a woman to cause abortion.' Much of the oath may not have been written by Hippocrates (460–377 BC), 'the father of medicine', but by his disciples. Nevertheless, as W. H. S. Jones has written: 'It is indeed hard to believe that the nucleus, at least, of the Oath does not go back to the "great" Hippocrates himself.'[52] Yet this part of the oath was regularly breached, since in the permissive society of Greece and Rome the destruction or exposure of unwanted children became normative practice. On the other hand, Christians opposed it on theological and moral grounds. For example, Tertullian in his *Apology* accuses the Romans of infanticide, and then continues:

> In our case, murder being once for all forbidden, we may not destroy even the fetus in the womb while as yet the human being derives blood from other parts of the body for its sustenance. To hinder a birth is merely a speedier man-killing; nor does it matter whether you take away a life that is born, or destroy one that is coming to the birth. That is a man (*sc.* a human being) which is going to be one; you have the fruit already in its seed.[53]

After Constantine's conversion in AD 312, abortion became a crime, and orphanages for unwanted children were established in Rome, Athens and elsewhere. And this recognition of the sanctity and dignity of children the world owes largely to Jesus Christ. The Synoptic gospels describe two separate occasions on which he welcomed children and commanded childlikeness. The first was when little children ('babies' according to Luke 18:15) were being brought to him that he should place his hands on them and bless them. But when the disciples rebuked those who brought them, Jesus was indignant and said:

'Let the little children come to me and do not hinder them,

for the kingdom of God belongs to such as these. I tell you the truth, anyone who will not receive the kingdom of God like a little child will never enter it.' And he took the children in his arms, put his hands on them and blessed them (Mark 10:13ff.; cf. Matt. 19:13ff.; Luke 18:15ff.).

The second occasion was prompted by a discussion on who would be the greatest in the kingdom of God. This time Jesus took the initiative to call a little child and to have him stand among them. He then insisted that unless adults convert and become like little children they will never enter the kingdom. So it is those who humble themselves like a child who are the greatest in the kingdom (Matt. 18:1ff.; Mark. 9:35ff.; Luke 9:46ff.).

Among all those who have been inspired by Jesus' respect for children, one of the most striking is Dr Thomas Barnardo (1845–1905). Converted to Christ at the age of seventeen, he entered the London Hospital as a medical student four years later, intending to go to China as a medical missionary. But within a few months events occurred which changed the direction of his life. He discovered the pitiable existence in the East End of London of destitute children, and in 1870 at the age of twenty-five he opened his first home for them in Stepney. He decided to remain in London and to give his life to the rescue of that 'most helpless and needy of all God's creatures – the destitute child'.[54] In forty years he raised £3.25 million, established a network of homes for the reception, care and training of homeless, needy and afflicted children,[55] and rescued 60,000 boys and girls from destitution. Today we might call him the patron saint of street kids.

Thomas Barnardo's dedicated ministry to children had a dramatic beginning. Among the street boys he knew was John Somers, known as 'Carrots' because of his flaming red hair, aged eleven. He often slept out somewhere between Covent Garden and Billingsgate. On one of his midnight forays, Barnardo chose five homeless boys to be accommodated in his home. 'Carrots' pleaded to be included, but there was no room. So Barnardo promised him the next vacancy.

A few mornings later, as a porter was moving a large sugar

hogshead lying with its open end to the wall, he disturbed a sleeping boy, by whose side lay another also apparently sleeping. One of the two, as slippery as an eel, made his escape, but when the porter touched the other, there was no response or movement ... the boy was dead. It was 'Carrots'. The verdict at the Coroner's inquest was 'Death from exhaustion, the result of frequent exposure and want of food.'

This tragedy burned itself into Barnardo's sensitive soul ... Gradually a resolution shaped itself in his heart. 'Never again!' he said, 'Never again!' ... He fixed a prominent sign-board outside the Stepney home which read in three-foot letters 'NO DESTITUTE CHILD EVER REFUSED ADMISSION.'[56]

To this he later added the words 'AN EVER-OPEN DOOR' – where shelter, food, clothing and medical attention, if necessary, could be provided at once at any hour of the day or night.[57]

Later still Dr Barnardo was able to claim: 'We receive children whom no other charitable institution will touch ... children in the last stage of lingering disease; children who are lame, halt and blind; children who, as a result of a long course of neglect and suffering, can be admitted only to die. The one condition of eligibility is destitution ...'[58]

But what motivated this extraordinarily comprehensive charter? Barnardo's widow surely uncovered his secret incentive. In *The Memoirs of the Late Dr Barnardo* she wrote:

Everywhere Barnardo sought out the children ... For he loved them ... He loved them all ... In the unselfish ardour of youth he loved the worst best, with that passion which takes delight in unselfish service ... Amongst a people professing to follow One who said 'Suffer little children to come unto me ...', the children starved in the gutters, and there were few to care.[59]

Just after Barnardo's death, a memorial poem appeared in *Punch*, written by its editor, Sir Owen Seaman. It has eight verses. Here are its first two:

'Suffer the children unto me to come,
  The little children', said the voice of Christ,
And for his law whose lips today are dumb
  The Master's voice sufficed.

'Suffer the little children –' : so he spake
  And in his steps that true disciple trod,
Lifting the helpless ones, for love's pure sake,
  Up to the arms of God.[60]

6. The washing of feet:
Samuel Logan Brengle

A necessary lesson in humility

The washing of feet, whether by oneself or by somebody else, was practised throughout much of the ancient world. Most of it in the Bible was the provision of water to guests, so that they might wash their own feet;[61] to wash somebody else's feet was regarded as a signal act of condescension and humility, in fact the work of a slave.[62]

Jesus' act of washing the feet of his apostles, during his last evening with them, was rich in symbolism and significance. Indeed, Jesus himself indicated that there was mystery here, more than met the eye, when he said: 'You do not realise now what I am doing, but later you will understand' (John 13:7).

First, it was *a drama*, setting forth that the hour had arrived, and that he had come from God and was returning to God (vv. 1–3). So he 'got up from the meal' (v. 4a), as he had risen from his throne. He 'took off his outer clothing' (v. 4b), as he had laid aside his glory. He 'wrapped a towel around his waist' (v. 4c), as he had taken the nature of a servant. He 'poured water into a basin and began to wash his disciples' feet' (v. 5), as he had humbled himself and became obedient to death – even death on a cross. Then, 'when he had finished washing their feet, he put on his clothes and returned to his place' (v. 12), as he was about to return to the Father. It sounds like a deliberate dramatization of the five or more stages of his career which Paul delineated in the Christian hymn he quoted in Philippians 2.

Secondly, it was *a sign*. He claimed to be their 'Lord' and

'Teacher' (vv. 13–14). But instead of assuming the authoritarian manner of most masters, he humbled himself to serve them. Their master became their slave. What more evidence do we need to demonstrate his deity?

Thirdly, it was *a parable* of the universal need to be made clean from sin. Indeed, Jesus said to Peter: 'Unless I wash you, you have no share with me' (that is, 'in my kingdom', v. 8, NRSV). The implication of Peter's protest was to declare the cross unnecessary.

Fourthly, it was *an example*. Jesus said so: 'I have set you an example that you should do as I have done for you' (v. 15). That is, if we transpose Jesus' teaching into our own culture, there is no work too servile or menial for love to undertake.

The church, however, has tended to interpret Jesus' teaching too literally. The so-called *pedilavium*, or liturgical feet-washing, was observed for many years, especially in association with baptism, in the churches of both the East and the West. Canon 3 of the Seventeenth Synod of Toledo (AD 694) censured its non-observance and made it obligatory on Maundy Thursday (the day before Good Friday) 'throughout the churches of Spain and Gaul'. And still today Mennonites teach that feet-washing is a necessary ordinance in addition to baptism and the Lord's Supper. Seventh Day Adventists observe it quarterly as 'the ordinance of humility', and so do some Baptist groups.[63]

In particular, an occasional, ceremonial performance by leaders of church and state is supposed to be a symbol of their humility. Thus in 1530 Cardinal Wolsey (not exactly a paragon of lowliness) 'washed, wiped and kissed the feet of fifty-nine poor men at Peterborough'.[64] Still today, on Maundy Thursday in the Church of the Holy Sepulchre in Jerusalem, the Patriarch of the Greek Orthodox Church washes the right foot of twelve senior clergy representing the apostles, while in Rome the Pope does likewise, a custom restored by John XXIII after the lapse of about ninety years.

One of the most interesting examples of the literal interpretation of Christ's command is found among English kings and queens, beginning with King John in 1213. In addition to washing feet, he gave thirteen pence to thirteen men, which came to be known as the Royal Maundy money. The distribution of the Royal Maundy continues in our day. The recipients are elderly people who have given a lifetime of voluntary service and are in financial need. Their number is the same as the years of the Queen's age. Green, white and red purses are distributed, containing specially minted silver coins, in lieu of food and clothing. Although there is no feet-washing, the officials still wear white linen towels as aprons, and all the principal participants (including the Sovereign) still carry nosegays of fragrant herbs and flowers – as they did in days of plague, in order to ward off risk of infection.[65]

But all this is very literal. I think Calvin was right in saying 'Christ does not enjoin an annual ceremony here, but tells us to be ready, all through our life, to wash the feet of our brethren.' And not to wash them literally, but to live a life of love, and of humble and sacrificial service.[66]

A striking example of this is Samuel Logan Brengle, who became the first American-born Commissioner of the Salvation Army. He was a young Methodist minister when he first met William Booth, although he had a secret ambition to become successful and famous, a bishop perhaps. In 1887 he crossed the Atlantic to join the Army. But at first Booth was suspicious of him: 'Brengle', he said to him, 'you belong to the "dangerous classes"' (by which he meant the clergy). 'You've been your own boss so long that I don't think you'll want to submit to Salvation Army discipline.'

In spite of these misgivings, however, it was agreed to give Brengle a trial. In order to instil in him some necessary humility, he was sent to Leamington to train as a cadet, and his first assigned duty was to blacken the boots of his fellow-cadets. He found himself in a dark, little, underground cellar 'with eighteen pairs of muddy shoes, a can of blacking, and a sharp temptation'. Brengle was dismayed, even rebellious. 'Have I followed my own fancy 3,000 miles', he asked himself, 'in order to black boots?' Then,

in imagination he saw a picture: Jesus was the central figure, and he was washing the disciples' feet! His Lord, who had come from ... the glories of heaven and the adoration of its hosts – bending over the feet of uncouth, unlearned fishermen, washing them, humbling himself, taking the form of a servant! Brengle's heart was brought low. 'Dear Lord', he whispered, 'thou did'st wash their feet; I will black their boots.' And with an enthusiasm heretofore unknown to the boot-blacking profession, he tackled his job, a song on his lips, and peace in his heart.[67]

Brengle never forgot this humbling of his pride. 'He lived ... a Christ-like life', wrote his biographer, 'and Christ-likeness ... was the essence of the holiness experience he taught ... His name is a household word among Salvationists ... He occupies a high place among the movement's saints, and is still spoken of in Army circles with something approaching awe.'[68] And all because of a vision of Jesus washing feet!

To bring the record up to date, Chuck Colson, sentenced to imprisonment for his share in Watergate, was later transferred to the federal prison camp at Maxwell Air Base, where he was assigned to work in the laundry. 'It was ferociously hot in the summer', he wrote, and his job involved 'endless sorting of sweat-soaked underwear and brown work uniforms'. 'My assignment to the laundry was also, I'm convinced, another step in my ego-busting process. There was a certain lesson in humility in washing the clothes of other people, not too far removed from washing their feet.'[69]

7. The cross:
Toyohiko Kagawa

The revelation of the love of God

The cross of Christ has been an inspiration to millions. In fact, of all his works and words, nothing has been more stimulating than the cross. All Christians should be able to say with Paul that 'Christ's love compels us' (2 Cor. 5:14), 'leaves us no choice' (NEB), or even 'tightens its grip on us', so that we determine to live no longer for ourselves but for him who died for us.

As my example of how the cross motivates people, I have chosen an Asian Christian leader, namely Toyohiko Kagawa (1880–1960). He was born in Kobe, Japan. His father was an aristocrat, a wealthy businessman, a cabinet minister, and an advisor to the Emperor, while his biological mother was a *geisha*, a Japanese dancing girl. Both his parents died when he was only four years old, and he was then sent to live on the family farm with his stepmother. Here he was physically abused, unwanted and unloved, and he bore the scars of loneliness for the rest of his life.

While he was at school in Tokushima, he was introduced to some American Presbyterian missionaries, especially Dr Harry Myers who became his mentor. Immensely impressed by the teaching and example of Jesus, Kagawa learned the Sermon on the Mount by heart and began to pray daily: 'O God, make me like Christ.' Then at the age of fifteen he was baptized. This was too much for his relatives, however. His uncle disowned and disinherited him.

On Christmas day 1909, aged twenty-one, he moved out of Kobe Theological Seminary, wheeling all his possessions in a handcart, in order to live among the poor in the terrible Shinkawa slum. His windowless shack measured only six feet by six, yet he shared it with anybody who needed care and shelter, sometimes several at a time. He lived on two bowls of rice gruel a day and wore the same ragged suit for several years. It is not surprising that he was often ill. He was also misunderstood, maligned and attacked. But he never retaliated and never gave in. One of his biographers, William Axling, wrote of him at that time as follows:

> He visited the sick; he comforted the sorrowing; he fed the hungry; he lodged the homeless; he became an elder brother to the prostitutes, visiting them when they were ill and providing them with medicines. Parents turned to him for advice. Young people brought him their tangled life-problems. Criminals made him their father-confessor ... The children swarmed around him.[70]

These experiences, together with his continuing studies at seminary, convinced him of the need to go beyond philanthropy to social action. So when the dockers of Kobe went on strike, they turned to him for leadership, and he organized them into Japan's first labour union. He also took up the cause of the tenant farmers and helped to organize the first nation-wide peasant farmers' co-operative. As a result of his solidarity with the workers, Kagawa was dubbed an agitator, the police black-listed him, detectives shadowed him, and in due course he was arrested, dragged to the police station, and consigned to prison for thirteen days. Yet, stung by his writings, the government declared its intention to abolish the slums in Japan's six largest cities.

After the terrible earthquake, which destroyed Yokohama and two-thirds of Tokyo, and killed about 100,000 people, Kagawa was active in reconstruction. But he never lost his evangelistic zeal. In 1928 he had a vision of one million Japanese people turning to Christ, and 'the central theme of his preaching was the cross of Christ as the revelation of the love of God'.[71]

Before the Second World War he was arrested three times for subversive peace propaganda. But after the war (which for him meant four years of acute anguish) the Prime Minister appealed to him in these terms: 'Only Jesus Christ was able to love his enemies … Help me to put the love of Jesus Christ into the hearts of our people.'[72] And the Emperor gave him a half-hour private audience in which to explain to him the meaning of the cross.

Kagawa's books were immensely popular, and when a new one was published, long queues would form outside the bookshops. All his works alluded in some way to the cross.

First, although his beliefs about atonement and redemption were not clearly formulated, yet Kagawa affirmed strongly that Christ 'offered himself for the sins of others.'[73] 'Only a sinner weeping over his sins can comprehend the marvel of this love.'[74] 'To me, born a child of sin, this redemptive love fills and thrills every fibre of my being. It stirs within me a poignant sense of gratitude.'[75]

Secondly, 'the cross is the crystallization of love'.[76] That is, it exhibits both God's love for us and the measure of love we should show to others. 'As in a single word, Christ's love-movement is summed up in the cross. The cross is the whole of Christ, the whole of love.'[77]

Thirdly, Kagawa saw in the cross something altogether unparalleled. 'The fact', he wrote, 'unique in the whole world, of Christ's sacrificing himself and shedding the blood of redemption for the sins of the race, is the very revelation of love itself.'[78] Finally, here is perhaps his most eloquent personal statement:

I am grateful for Shinto, for Buddhism, and for Confucianism. I owe much to these faiths. The fact that I was born with a spirit of reverence, that I have an insatiable craving for values which transcend this earthly life, and that I strive to walk the way of the golden mean, I owe entirely to the influence of those ethnic faiths. Yet these three faiths utterly failed to minister to my heart's deepest need. I was a pilgrim journeying upon a long, long road that had no turning. I was weary. I was footsore. I wandered through a dark and dismal world where tragedies were thick. Tears were my meat day and night ... Buddhism teaches great compassion ... But since the beginning of time, who has declared, 'this is my blood of the covenant which is poured out for many unto remission of sins?' [79]

With that unanswered question we leave Kagawa. His creed was that 'the cross is the centre of Christianity',[80] and his favourite hymn was 'Jesus keep me near the cross'.

8. The resurrection: Joni Eareckson Tada

'I'll be on my feet dancing'

On 30 July 1967 an athletic girl of seventeen called Joni Eareckson had a diving accident in Chesapeake Bay. It left her a total quadriplegic, paralysed from the neck down.

At first in hospital she fought bravely against her condition, determined that she would walk again. But gradually she came to the realization that her injury was permanent, and that she was never going to regain the use of her hands or feet. She tells her story in her first book with great honesty.[81] She felt overwhelmed with the whole spectrum of human emotions – bitterness, frustration, resentment, anger and even suicidal depression. She also experienced what she called 'rebellious temper tantrums against God'.

Through a period of rehabilitation and therapy, however, and through the strong support of her parents, sisters, boyfriend and other friends, she gradually climbed out of her deep black hole. She began to trust God and face the future with realism. She learned to paint with her mouth. She became a popular public speaker and writer. And she developed JAF Ministries ('Joni and Friends') for the support of people with disabilities.

At the heart of her transformation was her rediscovery of the Bible. She relearned its great doctrines. She was helped by the vision of Jesus on the cross, 'immobilized, helpless, paralysed', as she was. But what helped her most was the resurrection. 'I have hope for the future now', she wrote. 'The Bible speaks of our bodies being "glorified" in heaven ... I now know the meaning of being "glorified". It's the time, after my death here, when I'll be on my feet dancing.'[82]

It is essential to note that what sustains Joni is the Christian expectation of a *bodily* resurrection. It would have been no great comfort to be assured of a mere survival of death. And to believe in a resuscitation, a restoration to this life, would have meant the horror of a further imprisonment in her wheelchair. 'I can scarcely believe it', she wrote,

I with shrivelled, bent fingers, atrophied muscles, gnarled knees, and no feeling from the shoulders down, will one day have a new body, light, bright, and clothed in righteousness – powerful and dazzling. Can you imagine the hope this gives someone spinal cord-injured like me? Or someone who is cerebral palsied, brain-injured, or who has multiple sclerosis? Imagine the hope this gives someone who is manic depressive. No other religion, no other philosophy promises new bodies, hearts and minds. Only in the Gospel of Christ do hurting people find such incredible hope.[83]

Whether knowingly or not, Joni was echoing some fine words of Archbishop William Temple:

It may be safely said that one ground for the hope of Christianity, that it may make good its claim to be the true faith, lies in the fact that it is the most avowedly materialist of all the great religions. It affords an expectation that it may be able to control the material, precisely because it does not ignore it or deny it, but roundly asserts alike the reality of matter and its subordination. Its most own central saying is: 'The Word was made flesh', where the last term was, no doubt, chosen because of its specially materialistic associations. By the very nature of its central doctrine

Christianity is committed to a belief in the ultimate significance of the historical process, and in the reality of matter and its place in the divine scheme.[84]

Temple was alluding to the three great material truths, namely creation, incarnation and resurrection.

Whenever Christians recite the Apostles' or the Nicene Creed, we declare our belief in two resurrections – the resurrection of Jesus Christ (which is past) and the resurrection of our body (which is still future). And these are related to one another, for Jesus 'will transform our lowly bodies so that they will be like his glorious body' (Phil. 3:21). Again, 'just as we have borne the likeness of the earthly man [Adam], so shall we bear the likeness of the man from heaven [Christ]' (1 Cor. 15:49). Between our present and future bodies, however, there will be both continuity and discontinuity, as is the case of Jesus. His resurrection body was recognizably the same, yet it also had amazing new powers. This paradox of sameness and difference was well illustrated by Paul's botanical metaphor. The seed determines the identity of the flower – thistle seeds produce thistles, not figs, Jesus said (Matt. 7:16), but the flower far surpasses its seed in beauty. Similarly our present body is weak and perishable, whereas our resurrection body will be strong and imperishable (1 Cor. 15:35–44). To sum up, the Christian hope is not the immortality of the soul, but the resurrection and transformation of the body.

It is the physical nature of the resurrection which has inspired Joni Eareckson. She is excited, she writes, 'over how like the Rock of Gibraltar heaven is'. 'We shall touch and taste, rule and reign, move and run, laugh and never have reason to cry.'[85]

Joni describes a Christian convention at which the speaker, at the close of his message, asked his audience to kneel for prayer. She watched as they did so. But of course she couldn't do it herself. So she couldn't stop the tears. It was particularly hard for her because, brought up in a Reformed Episcopal Church, she had been accustomed to kneeling for prayer. Then she remembered the resurrection:

Sitting there, I was reminded that in heaven I will be free to jump up, dance, kick and do aerobics. And although I'm sure

Jesus will be delighted to watch me rise on tiptoe, there's something I plan to do that may please him more. If possible, somewhere, sometime before the party gets going, sometime before the guests are called to the banquet table at the Wedding Feast of the Lamb, the first thing I plan to do on resurrected legs is to drop on grateful, glorified knees. I will quietly kneel at the feet of Jesus.[86]

Joni writes repeatedly in her books, 'I can't wait.'

9. The exaltation: Henry Martyn

Zeal for the honour of Christ's name

In some New Testament passages the resurrection and exaltation of Jesus appear to be telescoped into a single event. Yet his resurrection and ascension were separated from one another by forty days, and in addition they carry a different significance. The resurrection celebrates his conquest of death and the ascension his exaltation to the supreme position of honour and authority at the right hand of the Father. A good example of the telescoping is Paul's statement that, because Christ humbled himself to the depths on the cross, therefore he has been exalted to the heights, and given the name above every name (that is, the dignity beyond every dignity), in order that every knee should bow to him and every tongue confess him Lord (Phil. 2:9–11).

Here lies the supreme missionary motivation. It is neither obedience to the great commission, nor compassion for the lost, nor excitement over the gospel, but zeal (even 'jealousy') for the honour of Christ's name. Thus Paul writes of his vocation to preach to the Gentiles 'for his name's sake' (Rom. 1:5), and John describes some early missionaries as having gone out 'for the sake of the Name' (3 John 7). He does not even identify the name, but we recognize it. It is the name above every name. No incentive is stronger than the longing that Christ should be given the honour that is due to his name.

I know no more striking example of this zeal than Henry Martyn. He was a Cornishman, born in Truro in 1781. At the tender age of fourteen he went up to St John's College, Cambridge. He had many interests. He loved walking and horse-riding in the countryside, and had artistic gifts in music, painting and poetry. Then through the sudden death of his father and the witness of his younger sister Sally, he sought and found mercy in Christ.

His studies concluded with his being nominated 'Senior Wrangler', which is the most highly placed student in mathematics, and in 1802 he became a Fellow of his college. The following year he was ordained as Charles Simeon's curate at Holy Trinity Church, Cambridge. He stayed for only two years, however, because some time previously he had announced his intention to go overseas as a missionary.

So in July 1805, aged twenty-four, he set sail for Calcutta, India, turning his back both on a brilliant academic career and (at least, he thought, for the time being) on Lydia Grenfell, the woman he loved. 'My heart was sometimes ready to break with agony', he wrote, 'at being torn from its dearest idol'.[87] For some eight years Henry and Lydia continued to correspond, but she declined his proposal, and they never married.[88]

Henry Martyn proved to be an exceedingly gifted linguist. He mastered Urdu (closely related to Hindi), Persian and Arabic, the three principal languages of the Moslem world, and his Urdu New Testament has remained the basis of all subsequent translations. Then he sailed for Shiraz, Iran, where, despite the intense heat, he completed his Persian New Testament within a year. He was helped by an Islamic scholar named Mirza Sayyid Ali, who one day told him about a recent victory over the Russians in which Crown Prince Abbas Mirza, son of the Shah, with his troops had killed so many Russian Christians that 'Christ from the fourth heaven took hold of Mahomet's skirt to entreat him to desist'.[89]

Imagine the scene. Christ is kneeling before Mohammed. How did Henry Martyn react? 'I was cut to the soul at this blasphemy', he said. Mirza Sayyid Ali was surprised and asked what was so offensive to him. He replied: 'I could not endure existence if Jesus was not glorified; it would be hell to me if he were to be always thus dishonoured.' His scholar-friend was astonished and again asked why. 'If anyone pluck out your eyes', Henry Martyn replied, 'there is no saying why you feel pain; it is feeling. It is because I am one with Christ that I am thus dreadfully wounded.'[90] One of his biographers accuses Henry Martyn of a 'high degree of touchiness'.[91] But no, it was his zeal for the honour of the exalted Christ.

On 21 October 1811 Henry Martyn wrote his last letter to Lydia, telling her that he was thinking of her incessantly. Four months later his Persian New Testament was finished. He prepared two ornate copies for presentation to the Shah and the Crown Prince, but they never reached them. Henry Martyn left Shiraz on horseback, and two months later arrived in Tabriz. He was already in a state of high fever from TB, but he set out again, expecting to reach Constantinople, some 1,400 miles away, within another two months. Then in early October he made his last diary entries, being in considerable pain. He managed to ride on for ten more days, but died on October 16, 1812 in Tokat, Armenia, only thirty-one years old.

What motivated Henry Martyn to visit both India and Persia as a missionary, to risk injury at the hand of fanatical Moslems, to learn three languages, to persevere in his translation work, in spite of constant ill-health, and to put his vocation before his love for Lydia? It was his determination that the exalted Christ be given his due honour. Henry Martyn 'belongs to that band of missionary saints', wrote one of his biographers, 'devoured by a consuming zeal, which gave them no rest, but drove them ever onwards to greater endeavours for the furtherance of the kingdom of God'.[92] His favourite hymn, another biographer tells us, was Isaac Watts' paraphrase of Psalm 72:

> Jesus shall reign, where'er the sun
> Does his successive journeys run;
> His kingdom stretch from shore to shore,
> Till moons shall wax and wane no more.[93]

10. The gift of the Spirit: Roland Allen

The Holy Spirit is a missionary Spirit

'Being therefore exalted at the right hand of God, and having received from the Father the promise of the Holy Spirit, he has poured out this which you see and hear' (Acts 2:33, RSV).

So said Peter in the climax of his sermon on the day of Pentecost. The final act in the saving career of Jesus, following his resurrection and exaltation, was his gift of the Spirit to his waiting and expectant church.

Of all the Holy Spirit's many ministries, the New Testament emphasis (though often overlooked) is on mission. Pentecost was essentially a missionary event. Indeed, the gap between the first and second comings of Christ, between the ascension (when he disappeared) and the parousia (when he will reappear) is, in God's purpose, to be filled with the worldwide mission of the church. As the late Bishop Lesslie Newbigin put it, 'the church is the pilgrim people of God. It is on the move – hastening to the ends of the earth to beseech all men to be reconciled to God, and hastening to the end of time to meet its Lord who will gather all into one'.[94] Indeed, the two ends will be reached simultaneously for, as Jesus said, 'this gospel of the kingdom will be preached in the whole world as a testimony to all nations, and then the end will come' (Matt. 24:14).

One person who was greatly inspired by this link between Christ's gift of the Spirit and the church's mission was Roland Allen. Born in 1868 in Bristol, England, he felt called from childhood to be a missionary. 'From my earliest years', he wrote, 'I was as firmly convinced of my vocation as I was of my existence.'[95] He was ordained in 1892, and three years later sailed for Northern China. Although he served there for only eight years (he was invalided home in 1903), he developed some radical convictions about the indigenous nature of the church, and spent the next forty years writing about them. He also visited East Africa, India and Canada, and settled for a while in Kenya.

His first, best known and most influential book was *Missionary Methods: St Paul's or Ours?*[96] He began with these provocative words:

> In little more than ten years St Paul established the church in four provinces of the Empire – Galatia, Macedonia, Achaia and Asia. Before AD 47 there were no churches in these provinces; in AD 57 St Paul could speak as if his work there was done, and could plan extensive tours into the far West

without anxiety lest the churches which he had founded might perish in his absence for want of his guidance and support.[97]

For 'nothing can alter or disguise the fact that St Paul did leave behind him at his first visit complete churches'.[98] Indeed, 'the first and most striking difference between his action and ours is that he founded "churches" whilst we found "missions".'[99]

By contrast, as Roland Allen surveyed what was then known as 'the mission field', he saw 'three very disquieting symptoms'. First, everywhere Christianity was still an exotic, a foreign plant. Secondly, everywhere Christian missions were dependent on foreign finance and leadership. Thirdly, everywhere he saw the same foreign forms of Christian life, bearing 'a most astonishing resemblance one to another', with no cultural originality. Thus Christian missions were 'exotic, dependent, uniform' – the very opposite of indigenous.[100] Instead, 'we desire to see Christianity established in foreign climes putting on a foreign [i.e. indigenous] dress and developing new forms of glory and of beauty'.[101]

Paul's missionary method was to plant a church and then retire, in order to give place to Christ. But was he not risking disaster? If all missionaries were to withdraw, would they not expose the church to false teaching and moral failure? Roland Allen saw these questions as a crisis of faith. Could God not be trusted to look after his own church? The only precautions Paul took were that he left behind him, when he withdrew, the Old Testament Scriptures, a local pastorate and his own apostolic teaching.[102] But above all, Allen wrote, Paul 'believed in the Holy Ghost ... as a Person indwelling his converts. He believed therefore in his converts. He could trust them. He did not trust them because he believed in their natural virtue or intellectual sufficiency. But he believed in the Holy Ghost in them'.[103] He was confident that the Spirit would stablish, strengthen and settle them.

Roland Allen's principles are still being debated, for there are significant differences between Paul's situation and ours, which perhaps Allen did not sufficiently allow for. Moreover, as Alexander McLeish wrote in his *Memoirs*, Roland Allen was 'always a rebel in spirit'.[104]

Nevertheless, in his emphasis on the indispensable role of the

Holy Spirit in mission he cannot be faulted. 'His main concern and interest was in no usual sense in the place of the Holy Spirit.'[105] It dominated his thinking. To him the Acts was a missionary book and the Spirit was a missionary Spirit.[106] His vision for an indigenous church was of a church relying on Christ's gift of the Holy Spirit.

11. The second coming:
Anthony Ashley Cooper (Lord Shaftesbury)
A programme for social reform

The 1662 Prayer Book gave directions how to find the date of Easter Day for 500 years up to the year AD 2199. And according to an Act of Parliament in 1732 the American Episcopal Prayer Book enabled its readers to calculate the church calendar as far ahead as AD 8500. These Anglican churches do not exactly encourage their members to live in lively expectation of the Lord's return! A notable exception, however, was Anthony Ashley Cooper, who on his father's death became the seventh Earl of Shaftesbury.

Born in 1801, he had an unhappy childhood, neglected and abused by his parents. His only solace was their housekeeper, Anna Maria Milles, who told him Bible stories, taught him to pray, and seems to have led him to personal faith in the Lord Jesus Christ.

At the age of sixteen, while at Harrow School, he saw a group of drunken men drop a poor man's coffin in the street, cursing and laughing as they did so. He was sickened and disturbed by this incident, later calling it 'the origin of my public career', for then and there he resolved to dedicate his life to the cause of the poor and the weak.[107]

He entered Parliament in 1826, aged only twenty-five, and soon began his programme of humanitarian reform, seeking to remedy some of the worst consequences of the Industrial Revolution. His unremitting labour continued for nearly sixty years, and the legislation for which he was largely responsible represents an astonishing achievement.

In 1842 The Coal Mines Act prohibited underground work in mines and collieries by women and girls, and reduced the hours worked by boys. In 1845 The Lunacy Act secured the humane treatment of the insane, and appointed fifteen 'Commissioners in Lunacy', of which he was one for forty years. In 1847, 1850 and 1859 he piloted The Ten Hours Factory Acts through Parliament, which regulated working hours for women and children. He was the acknowledged leader of all this factory reform. In 1851 The Common Lodging House Act sought to end the insanitary and overcrowded conditions of these lodging houses, laid down acceptable standards and permitted local authorities to inspect and supervise them. Even this list is far from complete. Ashley Cooper also founded the Ragged School Union and busied himself on behalf of boy chimney-sweeps, flower girls, orphans, prostitutes, prisoners, handicapped people and crippled children. Although his parliamentary bills were several times defeated, he refused to give up. 'I must persevere' his journal records.

What motivated him? To begin with, he believed and loved the gospel. 'I am essentially, and from deep-rooted conviction,' he wrote in his diary, ' ... an Evangelical of the Evangelicals'.[108] This means that in particular he emphasized 'the divinity of Christ, his atoning sacrifice and his coming kingdom'.[109] And his good works of love and justice were the natural outflow of his faith.

During the 1830s, however, he became firmly and vitally convinced of the second coming of Christ. 'It entered into all his thoughts and feelings', wrote Edwin Hodder; 'it stimulated him in the midst of all his labours; it gave tone and colour to all his hopes for the future'.[110] For 'there is no real remedy, he often said, for all this mass of misery, but in the return of our Lord Jesus Christ. Why do we not plead for it every time we hear the clock strike?'[111]

'I cannot tell you', Ashley Cooper once said to Edwin Hodder, his authorized biographer, 'how it was that this subject first took hold upon me; it has been, as far as I can remember, a subject to which I have always held tenaciously. Belief in it has been a moving principle in my life; for I see everything going on in the world subordinate to this one great event.'[112]

It is not surprising, therefore, that Ashley Cooper's favourite text was the second from last verse in the Bible: '"Yes, I am coming soon." Amen. Come, Lord Jesus' (Rev. 22:20). His life-long diary, to which he committed his private thoughts, is sprinkled all through with this ejaculation. It was a motto he had inscribed in

Greek on the flaps of the envelopes he used every day.[113] A few years before he died, he left instructions that this text (Rev. 22:20) should be one of three engraved on his tombstone. And on his deathbed he kept muttering 'Come, Lord Jesus'.

Anthony Ashley Cooper, seventh Earl of Shaftesbury, died in 1885. So richly had he deserved the epithet 'the poor man's earl' that tens of thousands of people, from all walks of life, lined the route taken by the cortège carrying his body from his home in Grosvenor Square to Westminster Abbey. There was a great outpouring of public grief, love and respect. Representatives of the homes, asylums, schools and societies that he had founded carried banners, on which were emblazoned sentences from Matthew 25: 'I was an hungered and ye gave me meat', 'I was thirsty, and ye gave me drink', 'I was a stranger and ye took me in', 'naked and ye clothed me', 'I was sick, and ye visited me', 'I was in prison, and ye came to me' (vv. 35–36, AV). Even the pouring rain could not dampen their spirits.

'My Lords,' exclaimed the Duke of Argyll, in a political speech delivered soon afterwards, 'the social reforms of the past century have not been due to a political party: they have been due to the influence, the character and the perseverance of one man: I refer, of course, to Lord Shaftesbury.' *The Times* also acknowledged him as a man who 'changed the whole social condition of England'.[114]

And why? What had been his incentive? He tells us. Towards the end of his life he said: 'I do not think that in the last forty years I have lived one conscious hour that was not influenced by the thought of our Lord's return.'[115]

12. The last judgment:
William Wilberforce

The abolition of slavery and the slave-trade

My last example of someone who was profoundly influenced by Jesus Christ is William Wilberforce. He constantly remembered this fact, that one day he would have to stand before the judgment seat of Christ.

Wilberforce once summed up his life ambitions in these terms: 'God Almighty has set before me two great objects, the suppression of the slave trade and the reformation of manners.'[116]

I propose to consider his two goals in the reverse order. Wilberforce's influence on English moral values and standards can be attributed mainly to his famous book with its cumbersome title: *A Practical View of the Prevailing Religious System of Professed Christians, in the higher and middle classes in this country, contrasted with real Christianity*. Published in 1797, reprinted five times the same year, translated into five European languages, and popularly known as *Real Christianity*, it made a sensational impact.

Most of its chapter headings begin with the words 'Inadequate Conceptions of ...', since his purpose, from his extensive knowledge of the Bible, was both to expose the inadequacies of 'nominal' or 'professed' Christianity and to clarify the essentials of 'real', 'true', 'vital' or 'practical' Christianity. The chief difference between them, he insisted, 'consists in the differing place given to the Gospel'.[117] Its foundational doctrines are 'the corruption of human nature, the atonement of the Saviour, and the sanctifying influence of the Holy Spirit'.[118] From these truths, believed and experienced, flows a radically new life, inspired by gratitude to God, characterized by love, holiness and humility, and permeating every part of us, both private and public.

Wilberforce was painfully aware, as he wrote, that religion and morals were in serious decline in contemporary England. 'The Bible lies on a shelf unopened',[119] he complained. Above all, 'the fatal habit of considering Christian morals as distinct from Christian doctrines has imperceptibly gained strength ... Even in the majority of sermons today one can scarcely find a trace of biblical doctrine.'[120]

In particular, Wilberforce became incensed with Britain's involvement in the slave-trade. Its horrors have been described thus:

> the sudden night raid on some peaceful native village (sc. in West Africa), the dragging of men and women and children in chains to the coast, the long slow voyage across the Atlantic, the filth and stench of the poisonous hold, where the slaves were packed in layers, and then the work on the sugar plantations beneath the overseer's whip.[121]

Wilberforce entered Parliament as the member for Yorkshire at the age of twenty-one in 1780, and seven years later put down a motion about the slave-trade. He was not a very prepossessing figure. Small of stature, he had poor eyesight and an upturned nose. When Boswell heard him speak, he pronounced him 'a perfect shrimp', but later conceded that 'presently the shrimp swelled into a whale'.[122] He also encountered the determined opposition of vested interests. But in spite of all the problems, he persevered. In 1789 he addressed the House of Commons about the slave-trade in these terms: 'So enormous, so dreadful, so irremediable did its wickedness appear, that my own mind was completely made up for Abolition ... Let the consequences be what they would, I from this time determined that I would never rest until I had effected its Abolition.'[123]

So Abolition Bills (relating to the trade) and Foreign Slave Bills (prohibiting the involvement of British ships) were debated in the Commons in 1789, 1791, 1792, 1794, 1796, 1798 and 1799. Yet they all failed, until the Abolition of the Slave-Trade Bill finally passed in 1807. Then, following the Napoleonic Wars, Wilberforce directed his energies to the abolition of slavery itself. But in 1825 ill health compelled him to resign from the House, and Thomas Fowell Buxton took over the campaign's leadership. In 1833 the Abolition of Slavery Bill was passed by an overwhelming majority in both Houses of Parliament. Three days later Wilberforce died. He was buried in Westminster Abbey, in recognition of his forty-five years' persevering struggle on behalf of the African slaves.

Not that Wilberforce battled alone. He was certainly the campaign's acknowledged leader, but he could not have won it without a groundswell of support from the country, and especially from his close friends in south London, whom the wit Sydney Smith, one of the founders of *The Edinburgh Review*, nicknamed 'The Clapham Sect', although in Parliament they were dubbed 'The Saints'.

The Clapham Sect's agenda was enormous. Indeed, 'the most striking feature of evangelical charity in the Victorian era', wrote Dr Kathleen Heasman, 'is its vast dimensions'.[124] So what motivated them? Here is the answer given by R. C. K. Ensor, the radical journalist and historian: 'No-one will ever understand

Victorian England who does not appreciate that among highly civilized ... countries it was one of the most religious that the world has known.' Ensor was referring to evangelical religion, whose second essential in his opinion was

> its certainty about the existence of an after-life of rewards and punishments. If one asks how nineteenth-century English merchants earned the reputation of being the most honest in the world ... the answer is: because hell and heaven seemed as certain to them as tomorrow's sunrise, and the Last Judgment as real as the week's balance-sheet.[125]

John Venn, Rector of Clapham (1792–1813), laid much stress in his sermons on our moral accountability to God. It was this, wrote Michael Hennell,

> which gave the Clapham Sect that entire integrity which acted as salt and leaven in the House of Commons; it was this sense of accountableness to God that enabled the Anti-Slave Trade team to persevere with their campaigns during a major European war and in the face of twenty-five years of defeat, disappointment and disillusionment.[126]

Michael Hennell also tells us that the young prime minister William Pitt once asked Henry Thornton (the banker member of the Clapham Sect) why he had voted against him on one occasion. Thornton replied: 'I voted today so that if my Master had come again at that moment I might have been able to give an account of my stewardship.'[127]

Wilberforce could have said the same thing. His strong sense of duty to his neighbour arose from his sense of accountability to Christ, his Saviour, Lord and Judge.

Conclusion: The radical nature of Christ's influence

That Jesus exercised a powerful influence on the development of the human story is widely recognized by historians. Here is

Kenneth Scott Latourette's summary at the end of his seventh volume:

> In this world of men, with its aspirations and its struggles ... there appeared one, born of woman ... To most of ... his contemporaries he seemed a failure ... Yet no life ever lived on this planet has been so influential in the affairs of men. From it has grown the most nearly universal fellowship, the Christian church, that man has known ...
>
> From that brief life and its apparent frustration has flowed a more powerful force for the triumphal waging of man's long battle than any other ever known by the human race. Through it millions have had their inner conflicts resolved in progressive victory over their baser impulses. By it millions have been sustained in the greatest tragedies of life and have come through radiant. Through it hundreds of millions have been lifted from illiteracy and ignorance, and have been placed upon the road of growing intellectual freedom, and of control over their physical environment. It has done more to allay the physical ills of disease and famine than any other impulse known to man. It has emancipated millions from chattel slavery and millions of others from thraldom to vice. It has protected tens of millions from exploitation by their fellows. It has been the most fruitful source of movements to lessen the horrors of war, and to put the relations of men and nations on the basis of justice and peace.[128]

This is not to claim that all these developments can be attributed exclusively to the influence of Jesus Christ, for many other people have left a wholesome mark on society. Nor is it to pretend that the Christian record has been spotless, for it has been grievously blemished by blind spots and blunders, of which we are ashamed. Nevertheless, in every place and every generation, wherever the name and story of Jesus have been known, the radical nature of his influence can be traced.

Behind the whole massive scientific enterprise there lies a belief in the rationality and uniformity of the created order stamped upon it by its Creator.

Behind the democratic process there lies the paradox of our

humanness which Jesus taught – our dignity by creation, demanding that we be governed only by consent, and our depravity by disobedience, demanding that political power be dispersed.

Behind the drive for universal education lies Jesus' respect for children, requiring the development of their God-given potential.

Behind the quest for justice and human rights, for improved conditions in factory, mine and prison, and for people's health of body, mind, soul and community there lies the value of every human person for whom Jesus both lived and died.

Behind the current concern for the natural environment there lies the call to be responsible stewards of it, which Jesus inherited from the early chapters of Genesis, even if his followers have been slow to discern their duty.

Behind the search for harmonious race relationships there lies the conviction of the fundamental equality of all human beings, made in the image of God, irrespective of colour, culture or creed, which Jesus taught in his parable of the good Samaritan.

Behind human families as the foundation of human society there lies God's institution of heterosexual monogamy which Jesus endorsed, together with the health-giving sexual restraint which it presupposes.

All these foundational social principles were taught and/or confirmed, directly or indirectly, by the words and deeds, the attitudes and example of Jesus Christ.

But, as Thomas Carlyle wrote in his famous book *On Heroes and Hero-worship* (1841), movements do not just arise; they presuppose innovative personalities. That is why I have chosen to tell the stories of a dozen such leaders, whose imagination has been fired, compassion aroused and action inspired by Jesus – by the Bethlehem stable or the carpenter's shop, by his ministry of compassion or his Sermon on the Mount, by his love for children or his washing of feet, by his cross, resurrection, exaltation or gift of the Spirit, by his second coming or his final judgment.

One more question must detain us. It is prompted by the long story of the church, and is asked by Bishop Stephen Neill: 'What kind of a stone could it be that, once thrown into the pool of human existence, could set in motion ripples that would go on spreading until the utmost rim of the world had been reached?'[129]

My answer is: 'Only the incomparable Christ.' And if we are prepared to take the risk of familiarizing ourselves with his story, and exposing ourselves to his personality, example and teaching, we shall not remain unscathed. Rather we too shall feel the power of his influence and say with Paul that the love of Christ tightens its grip upon us, until we are left with no alternative but to live – and die – for him (2 Cor. 5:14).

PART IV

THE ETERNAL JESUS

(or how he challenges us today)

PART IV: THE ETERNAL JESUS
(or how he challenges us today)

Introduction: 'The Revelation of Jesus Christ'

In Parts II and III we took a look at church history, and considered both how the church has presented Christ and how Christ has inspired the church. We now return to the New Testament, in particular to the book of Revelation, which I deliberately omitted from my original survey.

It may seem strange that, after the three broad surveys of Parts I to III, I should now narrow down my focus to just one New Testament document, and devote the whole of Part IV to the book of Revelation. Why?

The first reason is that the book of Revelation, being an apocalypse, in fact *the* Christian apocalypse, belongs to a particular literary *genre*, and on that account requires special treatment.

Secondly, it contains within itself a gallery of pictures of Jesus Christ. In every other New Testment book it has seemed possible to isolate its distinctive emphasis. Each gospel and each epistle has its particular theme. But this is not so with the book of Revelation, which contains a variety of portraits of Christ. It presents him as the first and the last, the lamb and the lion, the thief in the night, the King of kings, the divine judge and the heavenly bridegroom. These and other metaphors come tumbling out of John's fertile mind. We must do justice to this portrait gallery.

Thirdly, the book of Revelation is the climax of the New Testament. Irrespective of the dates when the New Testament documents were composed, the church has been wise to order the canon in such a way that it begins with the story of Jesus (the four gospels) and the story of the early church (the Acts); it continues with twenty-two letters of apostolic instruction about the Christian faith, life and hope; and it concludes with the book of Revelation, which brings eternity near.

For these reasons the book of Revelation deserves special, individual attention.

Readers' reactions to the book of Revelation are remarkably varied.

Some Christians are obsessed with it. They suppose that, together with the apocalyptic chapters of the book of Daniel in the Old Testament, it contains a secret history of the world, especially of contemporary events and people, and that they have the key to decipher it. So they predict, often with great self-confidence, the developing world-scene and treat us to lurid descriptions of the final Battle of Armageddon.

For example, Edward Irving, who helped to found the Catholic Apostolic Church in 1832, wrote a learned commentary on the Hebrew text of Daniel, in which he found references to Napoleon Bonaparte, to Louis XVI as the 'raiser of taxes', and to Britain as God's 'faithful witness'. He also predicted that by 1867 the millennium would have dawned.

Then in our generation, in his immensely popular book *The Late Great Planet Earth* (1970), Hal Lindsey made the mistake of identifying the ten horns of the beast in Daniel and Revelation as the ten member-states of the European Union. When he wrote, there were six. But in 1981, with the addition of Greece, they became ten. Now, however, they number fifteen! Hal Lindsey was naturally discomfited when this happened. His explanation, given in a one-sentence parenthesis, was that '*more* than ten nations could at one point be admitted' but that 'in the final stages it will number ten'.[1] Hal Lindsey was also proved mistaken in predicting that the year 1980 could well be the climax of history.[2]

Such self-styled prophets have so often been proved wrong in their predictions that one would expect their successors to develop a greater measure of humility.

Other Christians, far from becoming obsessed with Revelation, go to the opposite extreme of neglect. They know that the book contains much bizarre imagery. As we read it, we encounter a lamb, a lion and a huge red dragon, together with two fearsome monsters, one emerging out of the sea and the other appearing from inland. The seals of a scroll are broken, trumpets are blown, bowls are poured out, and there are frequent earthquakes, hail storms, flashes of lightning and peals of thunder. Readers are understandably mystified and even intimidated by these unfamiliar phenomena. So they fight shy of the book or, if they begin, they quickly give up in despair, and the book becomes the Cinderella of the New Testament.

A third and positive reaction is exemplified by Professor Richard Bauckham, who is a scholarly specialist in the book of Revelation. He begins his studies entitled *The Climax of Prophecy* with these words: 'The Apocalypse of John is a work of immense learning, astonishingly meticulous literary artistry, remarkable creative imagination, radical political critique, and profound theology.'[3] This expert evaluation should encourage us to persevere. So should the special blessing which is promised in the third verse both to the lector who reads the book in the public assembly and to those who hear the reading and take to heart what they hear (1:3; cf. 22:18f.).

Four principles of interpretation

Consider now these four principles of interpretation.

First, *the Revelation is full of symbolism*. Indeed, many people ask impatiently why John resorted to so much strange symbolism, because it makes his book hard to understand. There are probably two explanations. To begin with, John is handling transcendent truths which could not be expressed in straightforward prose. Secondly, it would be not only impossible but imprudent of him to do so. John is writing about the refusal of Christians to worship the Emperor and about the overthrow of the Empire, which would have been regarded by the authorities as seditious. Further, the symbols in the Revelation are to be understood, not visualized. If we were to attempt to visualize them, the result would often be grotesque. For example, God's redeemed people are said to be wearing robes which have been 'made ... white in the blood of the Lamb' (7:14). Now I confess that I have never tried to launder dirty linen in lamb's blood, but the concept is rather revolting, and the consequence would not be to make it white. The interpretation is beautiful, however, namely that the only righteousness which qualifies us to stand in God's presence is due to the atoning death of Jesus Christ, in whom we have put our trust.

Secondly, *the Revelation addresses the past, the present and the future*. Indeed these are the three classical theories of inter-pretation. The 'praeterist' view regards almost all the book as alluding to the past, in fact to the events of the early centuries AD, especially the overthrow of the Roman Empire. Then the 'historicist' view reads the book as telling the story of the church stage by stage during the whole period between the first and second comings of Christ, including our own generation. But this presupposes a Western horizon, and there is much disagreement about the details. The third or 'futurist' view expects most of the book to be fulfilled immediately before the parousia. But in this case it has been irrelevant for the last 1,900 years or more. It is surely unnecessary to be forced to choose between these three, for God's Word is intended to speak to the church in every age. It seems better, therefore, to adopt a 'parallelist' view, which sees every section of the book as recapitulating the whole 'inter-adventual' period between the two comings of Christ, each concluding with a scene of judgment and salvation. John sees the visions consecutively, but the realities they symbolize do not happen consecutively.

Thirdly, *the Revelation celebrates the victory of God*. It depicts conflict between God and Satan, the lamb and the dragon, the church and the world, the holy city Jerusalem and the great city Babylon, the bride and the harlot, those marked on their foreheads with the name of Christ (7:2ff.; 14:1; 22:4), and those marked with the name of the beast (13:17; 14:9, 11; 16:2; 19:20). Revelation depicts more than conflict; it celebrates conquest. The book's perspective is that already Christ 'has conquered' (5:5; cf. 12:9–10), and that his people are meant to share in his victory. 'To him who overcomes, I will give the right to sit with me on my throne, just as I overcame and sat down with my Father on his throne' (3:21). Thus, as Professor Swete wrote at the beginning of the twentieth century, 'the whole book is a *Sursum corda*', a summons to Christian believers to 'lift up their hearts', and to see their tribulations in relation to a victorious, reigning and returning Christ.[4]

Fourthly, *the Revelation focuses on Jesus Christ*. The first three words of the book's Greek text are *apokalupsis Iesou Christou*, that is, an apocalypse or revelation of Jesus Christ. True, many commentators think that this is a subjective genitive, so that it is Jesus Christ who reveals the contents of the book. But it seems to me much more likely that the genitive is objective, so that the book is above all else an unveiling of the greatness and glory of Jesus Christ. For this is what a beleaguered and persecuted church needs more than anything else, not a series of prophecies about the past or the future, nor even a coded panorama of church history, but a disclosure of the incomparable Christ, once crucified, now resurrected and reigning, and one day returning in power and great glory.

We need now to consider the context of the book. John has been banished to the island of Patmos in the Aegean Sea, on account of his faithful preaching of the Word of God and his testimony to Jesus (1:2, 9). He describes himself as the 'companion' of his Asian readers, since he shares with them 'the suffering and kingdom and patient endurance' which are theirs 'in Jesus' (1:9). And now he is instructed to share with them everything he has seen (1:10), in particular his vision of Christ. What has he to say?

Every commentator supplies his own structural analysis of the book of Revelation, so that the many different proposals form what Professor G. K. Beale has called 'a maze of interpretative confusion'.[5] My plan is not to increase the confusion with yet one more analysis, but rather to concentrate on the ten most striking Christological visions in the book. Each contributes something fresh to its composite 'revelation of Jesus Christ' in the fullness of his person and work.

1. Christ claiming to be the First and the Last, and the Living One (Rev. 1)

A vision of the resurrected and eternal Christ

First, then, in chapter 1 (vv. 17–18) we see *Christ claiming to be the First and the Last, and the Living One*. Indeed, before we read these words, already the earlier verses have given us a rich Christology. Even in the opening salutation (vv. 4–5a), which in most letters is merely a conventional formula, John manages to include a greeting from the Trinity. He wishes his readers grace and peace 'from him who is, and who was, and who is to come' (the Eternal Father); and 'from the seven spirits before his throne' (presumably the one Holy Spirit, as in verse 10, but said to be seven to indicate his ministry in and through the seven churches); and 'from Jesus Christ', who is then given an exalted threefold designation 'the faithful witness, the firstborn from the dead, and the ruler of the kings of the earth' (vv. 4 and 5), the latter being particularly audacious, since it is exactly what the Roman Emperor claimed to be.

After this greeting comes a personal doxology to Christ (vv. 5b–6), celebrating what he has done for us, namely that he loves us, that he has set us free from our sins by his sacrificial death, and that he has made us 'a kingdom and priests' to serve his God and Father (vv. 5, 6). Then this doxology is immediately followed by an acclamation (v. 7), declaring that Christ is coming back. His coming will be a historical event which somehow will be simultaneously glorious (the clouds symbolizing the glory of God's presence), visible (our eyes will see him) and universal (for 'every eye will see him', of both the penitent and the impenitent).

And the introduction ends with a divine statement in which God repeats that he is the One 'who is, and who was, and who is to come' (v. 8), and adds that he is both 'the Alpha and the Omega', and 'the Almighty'.

What is remarkable about these opening eight verses (the greeting, the doxology, the acclamation and the statement) is that in them John, unselfconsciously and unsystematically, alludes to every event in the saving career of Jesus, and so to the essence of the apostolic gospel. He refers to the Lord's earthly ministry ('the faithful witness'), his sacrificial death ('he has freed us from our sins by his blood'), his decisive resurrection ('the firstborn from the dead'), his supreme exaltation ('the ruler of the kings of the earth'), his saving achievement (he 'has made us to be a kingdom and priests') and his visible return ('he is coming with the clouds'). And all this in the epistolary introduction before the serious business of the letter has even begun!

In verses 9–11 John sets the scene for his first and defining vision of the glorified Christ. It was a Sunday. He was in exile on the island of Patmos. And he was 'in the Spirit', as the revealing and inspiring Spirit took hold of him. Then, before he saw the vision he heard a voice. Loud and peremptory, like the blast of a trumpet, and evidently the voice of Christ himself, it commanded John to write down on a scroll what he was about to see, and to send it to the seven churches of the Roman province of Asia, beginning with Ephesus, the capital and the nearest to Patmos, and continuing north and then south-east on the circular road which linked them all together.

Turning round to see whose voice it was, John's attention was first caught by seven golden lampstands. They were only the framework, however. Much more important was the person standing among them, in their midst. He is called 'someone like a son of man', that is, resembling a human figure, an expression borrowed from the book of Daniel whose chapters 7 and 10 supply much of the following description.

John was struck by the figure's clothing. He was dressed in a long robe that reached down to his feet and was secured by a golden sash round his chest. It seems to have been the garment of a king, a priest or a judge.

Next, John described various parts of his body. Both his head and his hair were as white as wool or snow, which was Daniel's description of 'the Ancient of Days', that is, of God himself (Dan. 7:9). Now transferred to Christ, it shows that the human figure was also a divine figure. His eyes blazed like fire, piercing hearts; his feet were strong and stable as brass, and his voice was as loud as the breakers crashing on the cliffs of Patmos.

In his right hand the son of man was holding seven stars, to be identified later; out of his mouth there jutted a sharp, double-edged sword, symbolizing his powerful word; and his face shone like the sun in all its brilliance – the face from which on the day of judgment the impenitent will cry out to be hidden (6:16).

It is not surprising that, in reaction to such a glorious vision, like Ezekiel (1:28) and Daniel (8:17; 10:9) before him, John should fall prostrate at his feet as if he were dead. Though not surprising, it is nevertheless anomalous, for he lay dead at the feet of the Living One!

But the same Christ who inspired awe brought comfort. He placed his right hand on John and said to him 'Do not be afraid.' Yet how could he not be afraid? It was not only the vision that caused him fear, but the whole situation in which he found himself. He was in exile. What did the future hold for him and for the Christian communities in Asia for which he was responsible? Emperor Domitian was demanding to be addressed as *Dominus et Deus Noster* ('our lord and god'), which loyal Christians who had confessed Jesus as Lord could never do. Already a man called Antipas in Pergamum had paid for his faithful witness with his blood (2:13). Who would be next in the annals of Christian martyrdom?

That these things were in John's mind is evident from the fact that, in his coming letter to Smyrna, Christ will announce himself in the very words of this vision, as 'the First and the Last, who died and came to life again' (2:8). He will go on to warn Smyrna of affliction, slander, suffering (adding again 'Do not be afraid', v. 10), prison and persecution, and will urge all church members 'Be faithful, even to the point of death, and I will give you the crown of life' (2:10).

To such a church, enduring persecution and facing the possibility of martyrdom, Christ's message is more than the command 'Do not be afraid' (1:17 and 2:10). It is also the basis of Christian fearlessness, which is twofold. First, Christ shares the eternity of God. For the title he claims 'I am the First and the Last' (1:17) is virtually identical with God's claim 'I am the Alpha and the Omega' (1:8). Secondly, he calls himself 'the Living One', not in the sense that he survived death, or that he was resuscitated and brought back to this life, only to die again, but that his dead body was resurrected and simultaneously transformed. Consequently he is now 'alive for ever and ever', victorious over death, never to die again. Further, because of his resurrection victory he 'holds the keys of death and hades',[6] that is to say, he has authority over them.

So because Christ is both the Eternal One and the Resurrected One, death has lost its terrors and we have every reason to rejoice, and not be afraid.

In the last two verses of chapter 1 John is instructed to write down his vision, which will include both 'what is now' and 'what will take place later'. He is also informed that the seven stars in Christ's right hand are 'the angels of the seven churches', symbolic probably of the local church leaders (or perhaps of their heavenly counterparts), and that the seven lampstands are the churches themselves, shining like lamps in a dark world (Matt. 5:14).

So the first 'revelation of Jesus Christ' is of the risen and eternal Christ. His resurrection is foundational. He is presented throughout, in spite of the onslaughts of the devil, as victorious, having won a decisive victory over evil by his death and resurrection.

2. Christ supervising his churches on earth
(Rev. 2 – 3)

Seven marks of an ideal church

The scene changes. Our vision is now focused not so much on the glorious human-divine figure of Christ, as on the churches among which, we are told, he walks (2:1), and to which he instructs John to write.

It is immediately noteworthy that all seven letters to the seven churches have an identical outline.

First comes *an announcement* of both the recipient and the author of the letter. The recipient is the 'angel' of each church. The author is of course Christ, but he describes himself differently in each letter, taking up one or two appropriate phrases from the opening vision. For example, he writes to Smyrna (2:8): 'These are the words of him who is the First and the Last, who died and came to life again ...'

Secondly comes *an assertion*, which begins in each case with the two words *I know*. Christ knows his churches intimately, for he is the one 'whose eyes are like blazing fire' (2:18), 'who searches hearts and minds' (2:23), and 'who walks among the seven golden lampstands' (2:1). As he patrols and supervises his churches, he knows everything about them, different in each case. 'I know your deeds', he says, five times, but then he makes such assertions as these: 'I know your hard work and perseverance'; 'I know your affliction and your poverty'; 'I know where you live'; 'I know your love, faith and service'; 'I know your reputation'; 'I know your opportunities'; 'I know your lukewarm complacency.'

Thirdly, Christ sends each church *a message* adapted to their situation, for each is either praiseworthy or blameworthy, and receives either commendation or criticism accordingly. Most receive a call to repent, and with it a warning and an exhortation.

The fourth part of each letter is *an appeal*, and in this case it is the same: 'he who has an ear, let him hear what the Spirit says to the churches'. It is an exceedingly significant sentence. First, although each letter was penned by John, yet through it the Spirit was speaking. Secondly, although John's letters may have been written months previously, yet through them the Spirit was still speaking (present tense). Thirdly, although each letter is addressed to a particular church, the Spirit was speaking to 'the churches' (plural).

Finally, each letter concludes with *a promise* to Christian overcomers. Generally speaking, it is a promise of eternal life, but this gift is described differently in phrases borrowed from the climax of Revelation 21 and 22.

Since seven was the perfect or complete number (at least in the circles of the author and his readers), it seems legitimate to regard the seven individual churches of the province of Asia as together representing the universal church. And since one particular feature is emphasized in each church, we may perhaps regard these seven features as the marks of an ideal church.

Love. This is the first mark of an ideal church. The church in Ephesus had much to commend it. Christ knew its hard work and perseverance, its intolerant attitude to evil, and its theological discernment. A few years later, at the beginning of the second century, Bishop Ignatius of Antioch, on his way to Rome to be executed as a Christian, wrote to the Ephesians in very laudatory terms: 'You all live according to truth, and no heresy has a home among you; indeed you do not so much as listen to anyone if they speak of anything except concerning Jesus Christ and his truth.'[7]

Yet Jesus had something against the Ephesian church: 'You have forsaken your first love' (2:4). All the Ephesians' virtues did not compensate for this lack. It was no doubt at the time of their conversion that their love for him had been ardent and fresh, but now the fires had died down. One remembers Yahweh's complaint to Jeremiah about Jerusalem: 'I remember the devotion of your youth, how as a bride you loved me ...' (Jer. 2:2). As with Jerusalem so with Ephesus, the heavenly bridegroom sought to woo his bride back to the first ecstasy of her love. 'Remember the height from which you have fallen! Repent and do the things you did at first' (2:5). Without love, everything is nothing.

Suffering. If the first mark of a living church is love, the second is suffering. A willingness to suffer for Christ proves the genuineness of our love for him.

Christ knew the afflictions, the poverty and the slander which the church in Smyrna was having to endure. Perhaps these sufferings were associated with the local emperor cult, for Smyrna boasted of her temple in honour of the Emperor Tiberius. From time to time citizens were required to sprinkle incense on the fire burning before the Emperor's bust and to confess that Caesar was lord. But how could Christians deny the lordship of Jesus Christ? In AD 156, the venerable Polycarp was Bishop of Smyrna. He faced this same dilemma. In the crowded amphitheatre the proconsul urged him to swear by the genius of Caesar and revile Christ, but Polycarp refused, saying 'For eighty-six years I have served him, and he has done me no wrong; how then can I blaspheme my king who saved me?' He was burned at the stake rather than deny Christ.[8]

More than half a century before this, Christ had already warned the Smyrnaean church that severer trials were coming, including prison and perhaps death. 'Be faithful, even to the point of death', Jesus said to them, 'and I will give you the crown of life' (2:10).

Truth. The church in Pergamum was dedicated to truth. So Jesus introduces himself as the one who has a sharp two-edged sword issuing from his mouth, symbolizing his word. He describes the Pergamum church as living 'where Satan has his throne', for Pergamum was a centre of pagan worship. But 'we must conclude', wrote Colin Hemer, 'that the expression "throne of Satan" refers primarily to the emperor cult as enforced from Pergamum at a time of critical confrontation for the church'.[9] Yet, in spite of opposition, and even the martyrdom of Antipas, the church had remained true to Christ's name and had not renounced its faith in him, even though some church members had succumbed to false teaching which condoned idolatry.

Holiness. Jesus writes next to the church in Thyatira and emphasizes that holiness is another mark of a living church. He begins in terms of warmest commendation, for he knows their love and faith, service and perseverance. These are four fine virtues and include the triad of faith, hope and love.

But unfortunately this was not the complete picture. For, alongside the church's sterling Christian qualities, it was guilty of moral compromise. The church tolerated an evil self-styled prophetess, symbolically named Jezebel after Ahab's wicked wife, who was leading Christ's servants astray into sexual immorality as well as idolatry. Christ had given her time to repent, but she had been unwilling, so that judgment would come upon her.

The holiness of self-control and Christ-likeness is another essential characteristic of a living church. Tolerance is not a virtue if it is evil that is being tolerated. God still says to his people: 'Be holy, because I am holy.'

Sincerity. Christ's letter to Sardis is the only one which contains no commendation of any kind. Instead he complains: 'you have a reputation of being alive, but you are dead.' This church does not seem to have tolerated error or evil, or to be deficient in love or faith or holiness. It showed every sign of life and vigour. Yet its reputation was false.

Scripture has much to say about the difference between reputation and reality, between what human beings see and what God sees. 'The LORD does not look at the things man looks at. Man looks at the outward appearance, but the LORD looks at the heart' (1 Sam. 16:7). To be obsessed with appearance and reputation leads naturally to hypocrisy (which Jesus hated) and tells us that sincerity characterizes a true and living church.

Mission. In writing to Philadelphia, Jesus describes himself as holding the key of David with which he was able to open closed doors and close open ones. In consequence he was able to say to the church in Philadelphia: 'See, I have placed before you an open door that no-one can shut' (3:8). The most likely meaning is that this is the door of opportunity, as when Paul wrote that in Ephesus 'a great door for effective work has opened to me' (1 Cor. 16:9). This means that mission is another mark of a true church. To quote G. K. Beale, all the letters to the churches 'deal generally with the issue of witnessing for Christ in the midst of a pagan culture'.[10]

Perhaps it is emphasized in the letter to Philadelphia because of its strategic location. Philadelphia was situated in a broad and fertile valley which commanded the trade routes in all directions. Sir William Ramsay wrote that the intention of the city's founder had been to make it a centre for the spread of Greek language and civilization. 'It was a missionary city from the beginning.'[11] So it may be that Christ was intending that what Philadelphia had been for Greek culture, it was now to be for the spread of the gospel. The door was wide open. Even though the church was comparatively weak, it must go boldly through the open door with the good news.

Wholeheartedness. There can be no doubt about Christ's message to the church in Laodicea: he wants his church to be characterized by wholeheartedness. He is very outspoken. He prefers his disciples to be either hot in their devotion to him or icy cold in their hostility rather than tepid in their indifference. He finds tepidity nauseating.

Directly opposite Laodicea, across the River Lycus, stood Hierapolis, whose hot springs sent lukewarm waters over the cliffs of Laodicea, leaving limestone deposits which can still be seen today. So the adjective 'Laodicean' has entered our vocabulary to denote people who are lukewarm in religion, politics or anything else. Laodicea seems to represent a church that is outwardly respectable but inwardly superficial, one of the purely nominal churches with which we are familiar.

When the metaphor changes to naked, blind beggars, one begins to wonder whether the Laodicean church members were genuine Christians at all. Then it changes again to that of an empty house. Christ stands on the threshold, knocks, speaks and waits. If we open the door, he enters, not only to eat with us, but to take possession. This is the essence of the wholeheartedness to which Christ calls us.

Thus the risen Lord reveals himself as the chief pastor of his flock. Patrolling, inspecting and supervising his churches, he has an intimate knowledge of them, and is able to pinpoint the seven marks that he would like every church to display: love for him and the willingness to suffer for him, truth of doctrine and holiness of life, and commitment to mission, together with both sincerity and wholeheartedness in everything.

We have also watched the church hard-pressed by sin, error and lethargy within, and by tribulation and persecution without, especially by the temptation to forsake Christ for Caesar and by the real risks of martyrdom.

So with Revelation 4 we turn abruptly from the church on earth to the church in heaven, from Christ among the flickering lampstands to Christ in the very centre of the unchangeable throne of God. It is the same Christ, but from an entirely different perspective.

3. Christ sharing God's throne in heaven (Rev. 4 – 5)

The throne, the scroll and the Lamb

'After this I looked, and there before me was a door standing open in heaven. And the voice I had first heard speaking to me like a trumpet said, "Come up here, and I will show you what must take place after this"' (4:1). It was the open door of revelation, and as John looked through the door what he saw developed in three stages: first, *a throne*, from which God rules over the universe; secondly, *a scroll*, the book of history, closed, sealed, and held in God's right hand; and finally, *a lamb*, as slain, who alone is worthy to open the scroll, to interpret and control history.

John's vision of a throne (4:1–11)

It is immensely significant that, when John peeped through the open door, the very first thing he saw was a throne, symbol of the sovereignty, majesty and kingly rule of God. His vision has a strong Old Testament background in Ezekiel 1 and Daniel 7.[12] The throne is mentioned seventeen times in Revelation 4 and 5.

The churches of Asia were small and struggling; the might of Rome seemed invincible. What could a few defenceless Christians do if an imperial edict were to banish them from the face of the earth? Already the powers of darkness seemed to be closing in upon them. Yet they need have no fear, for at the centre of the universe stands a throne. From it the wheeling planets receive their orders. To it gigantic galaxies give their allegiance. In it the tiniest living organism finds its life.

Everything John saw in his vision was related to the throne. He uses seven prepositions to indicate the centrality of the throne of God.

On the throne somebody was sitting (v. 3). The occupant of the throne is not described, because God is indescribable. All John saw was brilliant colours like flashing jewels, 'jasper and carnelian', meaning perhaps diamonds and rubies.

Encircling the throne there was an emerald rainbow (v. 3), symbolizing God's covenant mercy and reminding us that God's exalted throne is at the same time a throne of grace (cf. Gen. 9:8–17).

Surrounding the throne were twenty-four other thrones (v. 4), on which were seated twenty-four elders, presumably representing the twelve tribal heads of Old Testament Israel and the twelve apostles of Jesus Christ. Their white clothing and golden crowns indicated their righteousness and their authority.

From the throne issued flashes of lightning, rumblings and peals of thunder (v. 5a), reminiscent of the revelation of God on Mount Sinai, tokens of the presence and power of the Holy One.

Before the throne seven lamps were blazing (v. 5b), which are the seven spirits of God, namely the Holy Spirit in all his many ministries, not least in relation to the seven churches. For church and Spirit go together.

In front of the throne there stretched an infinite expanse like a sea of glass (v. 6a), speaking to us of God's transcendence and unapproachability.

In the centre, around the throne, as a kind of inner circle, were four living creatures (v. 6b). They were 'covered with eyes in front and behind' (expressing their ceaseless vigilance), and resembling a lion, an ox, a man and an eagle, representing 'whatever is noblest, strongest, wisest and swiftest in animate nature'.[13] Day and night all nature never stops singing the praise of the Lord God Almighty, and as they do so, the twenty-four elders join in. Thus nature and church, the old creation and the new, unite in proclaiming God as worthy of worship because by his will all things were created and continue to have their being.

We pause and reflect whether this is our vision of ultimate reality. Our vision of the future tends to be too negative. We seize on the assurances of the book of Revelation that one day there will be no more hunger or thirst, no more pain or tears, no more sin, death or curse, for all these things will have passed away.

It would be better and more biblical, however, to focus not so much on these absences, as on the cause of their absence, namely the central dominating presence of God's throne. For when God takes his power and reigns without rival, and the kingdom will have come in its fullness, then everything incompatible with his reign will be destroyed and God will be 'everything to everyone' (1 Cor. 15:28, RSV). Meanwhile, we are called to anticipate on earth the God-centred life of heaven, to live our lives now in conscious relationship to the throne, so that every thought, word and deed comes under God's rule.

John's vision of a scroll (5:1–6)

Looking now more closely at the throne and its occupant, John notices in his right hand a scroll. It has writing on both sides and is sealed with seven seals. John does not tell us what it is, but from what follows when the seals are broken, it is the book of history, the sealed record of the unknown future, 'what must take place after this' (4:1).[14]

In John's vision (5:2) a mighty angel appears and asks in a loud voice exactly what all of us would like to ask, namely: 'Who is worthy to break the seals and open the scroll?', that is, to disclose the future, let alone control it? For the future is in the hand of God. Who else is worthy to know it? There was no answer to the angel's challenging question. So John says (v. 4) 'I wept and wept.' He was overcome with emotion, with deep disappointment that nobody was fit to open the scroll or even look inside it.

Let's try to imagine the situation. The Christian church was a tiny community in the midst of the mighty Roman Empire. Not only were Christians an insignificant minority, but they were a persecuted minority as well. Everybody seemed to be against them. Christians could cling to the throne; but what secrets would the scroll contain? Did their sufferings have any meaning? Did God have a plan? Did history have a plot? Who could give them a clue to the mystery of history?

Then (v. 5) one of the elders came forward and spoke up. He told John not to weep, and added 'See, the Lion of the tribe of Judah, the Root of David' (that is, the Messiah), 'has triumphed. He is able to open the scroll and its seven seals', and so to reveal the contents and the meaning of history.

It was a dramatic moment. John looked to see this triumphant lion, and to his astonishment he saw instead a Lamb, looking as if it had been slaughtered, and yet standing in the very centre of the throne, sharing it with God (see 3:21). In this central position he was surrounded by both the four living creatures (nature) and the elders (the church). He is also described as having seven horns and seven eyes, which are identified as 'the seven Spirits of God sent out into all the earth' (v. 6).

Thus our attention is redirected from the throne to the scroll, and now from the scroll to the Lamb.

John's vision of the Lamb (5:7–14)

The Lamb now took action. He came to the throne-occupant and took the scroll from his right hand. This was the signal for the four living creatures and the twenty-four elders to fall prostrate before the Lamb and sing a new song, declaring his worthiness to take the scroll and open its seals not now because of the creation, but because of the redemption:

> 'because you were slain,
>> and with your blood you purchased men for God
>> from every tribe and language and people and nation.
> You have made them to be a kingdom and
>> priests to serve our God,
> and they will reign on the earth' (5:9–10).

Next, millions of angels joined in, proclaiming the worthiness of the Lamb, because he had been slain, to receive seven blessings, since all power and wisdom must be ascribed to him.

And finally (v. 13) John heard every creature throughout the whole universe ascribing praise and honour 'to him who sits on the throne and to the Lamb'. The four living creatures endorsed it with their amen, and the twenty-four elders fell down and worshipped.

It is a most magnificent vision of the whole creation on their faces before God and his Christ, and truly amazing that the Lamb is bracketed with the occupant of the throne as sharing it with him and receiving equal praise.

However, the drama also provokes questions. Why is Jesus Christ the only person who is worthy to open and explain the scroll? What is it about the Lamb of God which uniquely qualifies him to interpret it? Clearly it is because he was slain, and because of what he achieved by his death. But what is it about the cross that makes it the key to history?

First, the cross illumines history because it speaks of *victory*. The reason why the Lamb was able to open the scroll is because he has triumphed (5:5). The same verb has been used at the conclusion of each of the seven letters to the churches. A promise is given to him who overcomes. For example, 'To him who overcomes, I will give the right to sit with me on my throne, just as I overcame and sat down with my Father on his throne' (3:21). Thus the cross is represented in the New Testament as victory not defeat, as triumph not tragedy. For, as Paul wrote, on the cross Christ dethroned and disarmed the principalities and powers of evil, triumphing over them in the cross (Col. 2:15). True, they are still alive and active, for they have not yet conceded defeat. Nevertheless, they have been conquered and are under Christ's feet (e.g. Eph. 1:22). This is the great truth of *Christus Victor*, which the church has sometimes forgotten. The first reason why the Lamb alone can interpret history with all its evil is that he triumphed over evil at the cross.[15]

Secondly, the cross illumines history because it speaks of *redemption*. The repeated use of the title 'the Lamb' will immediately have reminded Jewish readers of the Passover. For just as the Passover lamb was sacrificed, its blood sprinkled and the people spared, so Christ our Passover has been sacrificed for us, so that we might be redeemed and might celebrate the festival of redemption. Thus history has a twofold plot-line. There is world history (the rise and fall of empires) and there is salvation history (the story of the redeemed people of God). Moreover, we dare to say that the former is explicable only in the light of the latter; that what God is doing against the backdrop of world history is to call out from every nation a people for himself; and that only the cross makes this possible.

Thirdly, the cross illumines history because it speaks of *suffering*. For the sufferings of the Christ, although unique in their redemptive significance, were nevertheless the prototype of the sufferings of the people of God. Because he suffered, his people are called to suffer. Because he went to the cross, he calls us to take up our cross and follow him. So John moves on from the Lamb slain (in ch. 5) to the souls of the martyrs, slain because of their faithful testimony (in ch. 6). Thus those who are called to suffer for Christ, whose sufferings are so hard to understand and to bear, learn to see them in the light of the sufferings of Christ.

Fourthly, the cross illumines history because it speaks of *weakness*, and specifically of power through weakness. This paradox is seen in its most dramatic form in Christ and the cross, and in John's vision in Revelation 4 and 5. For at the centre of God's throne (symbol of power) stands a slain Lamb (symbol of weakness). In other words, power through weakness, dramatized in God on the cross and the Lamb on the throne, lies at the heart of ultimate reality, even of the mystery of almighty God himself.

4. Christ controlling the course of history (Rev. 6 – 7)

The seven seals and the two communities

Having celebrated the Lamb's unique right to open the scroll, and having seen him take it from the throne-occupant (5:7), John now watches as the Lamb breaks the seven seals one by one. After each of the first four is broken, one of the living creatures shouts in a voice like thunder 'Come!' and behold a horse and its rider appears. These are the famous 'four horsemen of the Apocalypse', well known to Christian artists.

The first horse was white; and its rider held a bow, was given a crown, and 'rode out as a conqueror bent on conquest'. Because he belongs to the series of apocalyptic horsemen, many commentators conclude that he too symbolizes disaster, in his case military conquest. But throughout Revelation white stands for righteousness; crowns and conquest belong to Christ; and in 19:11–15 the rider on a white horse is named 'Faithful and True', 'the Word of God' and even 'King of kings and Lord of lords'. So we are assured that, before the other horsemen spread the horrors of war, famine and death, Christ rides first at the head of the cavalcade, resolved to win the nations by the gospel. And he succeeds! For in the next chapter we see a countless multitude standing before God's throne, drawn from all the nations, the fruit of his international mission.

The second horse is fiery red, symbolizing bloodshed, whether through war, civil strife or persecution (see Matt. 10:34). The third horse is black, symbolizing famine conditions, as rocketing inflation makes staple foodstuffs too expensive to buy, and luxury goods available only to the wealthy. The fourth horse is pale green (like a corpse), symbolizing death and hades, that is, both the event and its domain. They were given authority over a quarter of the population to kill by sword, famine, plague and wild animals.

Instead of the appearance of another horse, the breaking of the fifth seal revealed the souls of Christian martyrs 'under the altar' (the place of sacrifice), who were appealing for justice. As George Eldon Ladd has commented, 'it is the blood of the martyrs crying for vindication, not the martyrs themselves crying for personal vengeance'.[16] In response they were told to wait a little longer until the tally of the martyrs was complete.

After the breaking of the sixth seal, there was a great earthquake, followed by the most appalling cosmic convulsions. The sun turned black and the moon red; the stars fell and the sky disintegrated; and all mountains and islands were dislodged. These are not to be interpreted as literal events, however, but as social and political upheavals described in familiar apocalyptic imagery. They will lead up to the day of judgment, when human beings along the whole social spectrum from kings to slaves will run for cover, hoping to escape. They will scream to the mountains to fall on them and hide them from the face of God and the wrath of the Lamb (cf. Is. 2:19).

This opening drama of the first six seals gives us a general overview of history between the first and second comings of Christ. It will be a time of violent disturbance and suffering, but the eye of faith looks beyond these things to Christ who is both the crowned and conquering rider on the white horse and the Lamb who breaks the seals, controlling the course of history.

We now have to wait until 8:1 for the seventh seal to be broken. Instead, John treats us to an interlude which stresses the security of the people of God. Revelation 7 describes two human communities. The first (vv. 1–8) numbers 144,000 and is drawn from the twelve tribes of Israel; the second (vv. 9–17) is a huge unnumbered multitude drawn from all nations, languages and tribes. At first sight they seem to be two distinct groups (numbered and unnumbered, Israel and the Gentiles), and several ingenious attempts have been made to distinguish between them. But on closer inspection it becomes clear that both are pictures of the same redeemed community of God, although viewed from different perspectives. In the first the people are assembled like soldiers in battle array – the church militant on earth; in the second they are assembled before God, their conflicts past – the church triumphant in heaven.

Take the first community. They are called 'the servants of our God' (v. 3), and are sealed or stamped on the forehead to indicate that they belong to him. The number 144,000 is an obvious symbol for the complete church (12 x 12 x 1,000); they are later identified (14:3) as those 'who had been redeemed from the earth'. And the only reason why they are represented as the twelve tribes of Israel is that throughout the New Testament the church is seen as 'the Israel of God', 'the true circumcision', and 'a chosen people, … a holy nation, a people belonging to God' (Gal. 6:16; Phil. 3:3; 1 Pet. 2:9), in whom God's covenant promises are being fulfilled.

What then are we told about the second crowd? It is 'a great multitude that no-one could count, from every nation, tribe, people and language' (v. 9). In it God's promise to Abraham is fulfilled, to give him a posterity as numerous as the sand and the stars, and through it to bless all the families of the earth (Gen. 12:1ff.).

Next, the unnumbered crowd are standing before the throne of God and of the Lamb, enjoying the blessings of their kingly rule. They are wearing white robes of righteousness and waving palm branches of victory. They are also singing loud songs of worship, ascribing their salvation to God and the Lamb. The angels, elders and living creatures also join in, falling on their faces and worshipping God. For the life of heaven is a continuous joyful celebration, and earthly choirs and orchestras are rehearsing for the eschatological concert.

How then can we make sure that we belong to this redeemed, international throng? One of the elders expressed this very anxiety by asking a question: 'These in white robes – who are they, and where did they come from?' (7:13). He then proceeded to answer his own question. On the one hand, 'they have washed their robes and made them white in the blood of the Lamb'. We cannot possibly stand before God's dazzling throne in the soiled and tattered rags of our own morality, but only if we have sought cleansing from the Lamb who died for us. On the other hand, they 'have come out of the great tribulation'. Since all the redeemed are being described, this cannot refer to the specific period between the appearance of Antichrist and the parousia of Christ. It must be a description of the whole Christian life, which the New Testament repeatedly designates a time of tribulation (*thlipsis*. See e.g. John 16:33; Acts 14:22; Rev. 1:9). Therefore, 'they are before the throne of God' (7:15). For only those who suffer with Christ will be glorified with him (cf. Rom. 8:17).

The chapter ends with glorious assurances (vv. 15–17) that God will shelter his people; that they will never again suffer from hunger, thirst or scorching heat; that – in the boldest reversal of roles – the Lamb will be their shepherd; and that God will wipe away all their tears.

5. Christ calling the world to repentance (Rev. 8 – 11)

The seven trumpets, the little scroll and the two witnesses

It is generally agreed that chapters 8 to 11 of Revelation are difficult to interpret. They begin with the breaking of the seventh seal, which was followed by 'silence in heaven for about half an hour'. There was neither vision nor voice, perhaps to indicate that the seventh section of the scroll had no content of its own but consisted rather of the seven trumpets that came next.

John also tells us, in his introduction to these chapters (vv. 3–5), that an angel's incense and the prayers of God's people were ascending to the throne of God. He implies that the divine reply of thunder and lightning, symbols of his judgment, was in direct response to the church's prayers (cf. 6:9–17).

Now seven angels were given seven trumpets. It is important to remember, as the drama develops, that the breaking of the seven seals and the blowing of the seven trumpets are not consecutive, but symbolize the same period, stretching between the two comings of Christ, although from different perspectives.

What, then, is the distinctive perspective of the trumpets? What is its vision of Christ?

I suggest that we should see the word *warning* flashing in red lights all over these chapters, for their overriding purpose is to jolt the unbelieving world out of its complacency and self-centredness, to summon it to repentance and to warn the impenitent of the righteous judgment of God. This is the dominant message of these chapters: a call to repentance and a warning of judgment.

Some may respond that this is not the immediately obvious meaning of these chapters. So how can I justify it? Consider these six arguments:

First, although the trumpet was used in the Old Testament for several purposes, for example to assemble the people in an emergency and to 'summon people's attention to God's communication',[17] one of its main functions was in warning. Thus Ezekiel wrote that if a watchman 'sees the sword coming against the land and blows the trumpet to warn the people', then the people will be held responsible for their reaction (Ezek. 33:1–6. Cf. Joel 2:1).

Secondly, John deliberately draws an analogy between the judgments he describes and the plagues of Egypt. He alludes, for example, to water becoming blood, a heavy hailstorm, a swarm of locusts, and thick darkness.[18] And the purpose of those plagues in Egypt was to bring Pharaoh and his court to repentance.

Thirdly, the first five of the seven trumpets herald calamities on earth, sea, fresh waters, sky and human beings, in each of which one third suffers. This deliberate limitation sends a warning signal to the other two-thirds. The judgments were partial, not final.

Fourthly, people's negative response to the trumpets shows that repentance had been hoped for: 'The rest of mankind that were not killed by these plagues still did not repent of the work of their hands' (that is, idolatry); 'Nor did they repent of their murders …' and other sins (9:20–21). In spite of continuous divine warnings, they remained defiantly impenitent.

Fifthly, the natural disasters symbolized by the trumpets were God's indirect warnings; they were accompanied by the direct warnings of his Word. The little scroll represented the proclamation of the gospel, and God's two witnesses represented the missionary church. As they preached, they were 'clothed in sackcloth' (11:3), dramatizing the repentance they sought (Luke 10:13).

Sixthly, even if the ministry of the two witnesses was not effective, it was hoped that their persecution and martyrdom might succeed in arousing the world's repentance.

These six arguments constitute a strong case. We can then

understand the seals, the trumpets and the bowls as relating to the same period between Christ's comings, but from a different point of view. The seven seals describe what Christ *allows* in his world (since things happen only when he breaks the seals). The seven bowls (still to come) describe how Christ *judges* his world. But the seven trumpets (which come between the seals and the bowls) describe how Christ *warns* the world and summons them to repentance.

Consider then the meaning of the trumpets.

The calamities which are now listed (damage to earth, sea, fresh water and the solar system) are not to be regarded as particular, let alone recognizable, events. The huge blazing mountain of the second trumpet, for example, is not a reference to the eruption of Mount Vesuvius in AD 79, although this eruption may have supplied some of the imagery. Instead they are natural disasters, which may occur to anybody at any time in any place. If they are meant to be taken literally, then they contribute to the hazards of life on earth. And they are warnings in the sense that the collapse of the tower of Siloam was, which Jesus interpreted as a call to repentance (Luke 13:4). But they are much more likely to be figurative and to allude to such happenings as environmental disaster (the green things of the first trumpet), economic chaos (the destroyed ships of the second), human tragedy (the bitterness of the third) and barbarian behaviour (the darkness of the fourth).

But the future will be even worse. John sees an eagle flying in mid-air and calling loudly to all the inhabitants of the earth. 'Woe! Woe! Woe!' it cries, in order to indicate that the fifth, sixth and seventh trumpets will bring even more intense suffering and will therefore be renamed the first, second and third woes.

If the first four trumpets describe damage to nature, the fifth (9:1–11) and sixth (9:12–21) describe damage to human beings. John sees a swarm of locusts (at least that is what he calls them) which came out of the smoke that billowed from the opened abyss and darkened sun and sky. The one thing locusts are known for (consuming all vegetation) these creatures are expressly forbidden to do. Instead, they attack the unbelieving world (which had not received God's seal) and inflict on them a sting as painful as a scorpion's. But they have no authority to kill, and though their human victims will long to die, they will not be able to kill themselves.

John's description of them is extremely vivid. He tells us what they looked like in his vision, or what they reminded him of. Eight times he repeats the word 'like'. In general they were like war horses, and their head-dress like a golden crown. Their faces were like human faces, their hair like a woman's, and their teeth like lions'. Then, reverting to their warlike nature, their armour was like an iron breastplate, and their whirring wings like the thunder of horses and chariots charging into battle. Their king is called 'Destroyer', since they are bent on destruction. But what impressed John most was their power to inflict severe pain. Three times in chapter 9 he tells us that they sting like a scorpion (vv. 3, 5, 10), and three times he refers to their ability to torture, cause agony (v. 5) or torment (v. 10), causing pain so acute that they long to die (v. 6).

These venomous creatures are of course not literal. Nor does John give us any hint that they are demonic hordes. Is it possible then, remembering Jesus' teaching that all kinds of evil lie buried in the human heart (Mark 7:21–23), that this is what John is graphically illustrating? Professor Thomas Torrance identifies the star with the key as the Word of God. For nothing 'opens the bottomless pit of human nature' like the gospel.[19] The gospel reveals to us and others the deep depravity of our fallen nature. Often it is hidden, but at times it breaks the surface, to our acute embarrassment. It convicts us painfully of sin, for there is no pain more painful than that of a tormented conscience. It leads some to repentance and faith, but others to harden their hearts and so perish.

John is aware that the sixth trumpet (9:12–21) would bring even more acute suffering than any of the five previous ones. So he emphasizes that permission for it had come direct from God in answer to his people's prayers (v. 13; cf. 8:3–5), and that it would sound only at the exact moment that had been decreed by God (v. 15). These permissions were necessary because of the escalation of suffering; the sixth trumpet will bring a license actually to kill one third of the human race (vv. 15, 18). Further, whereas after the fifth trumpet the agents of divine judgment were locusts, now they are horsemen. The cavalry numbered 200 million and were assembled symbolically at the River Euphrates, from which Israel's Assyrian and Babylonian enemies had come, and where Rome felt threatened by the Parthian hordes. The mounted troops John saw were formidable indeed – their breastplates were red, blue and yellow, their horses' heads were like lions' heads, and out of their mouths came the three plagues of fire, smoke and sulphur. But their power to inflict injury and death was in their snake-like tails as well.

Once again this is not a description of literal events, but nor is it to be explained away as meaningless. The sixth trumpet seems to symbolize violent death, whether by war or terrorism or persecution, and has a special relevance to us who have lived through much of the twentieth century, perhaps the most violent of all centuries. One would also have hoped that the horrors of war would bring unbelievers to repentance. But John records in his vision that those who survived death did not repent either of their idolatry (the worst breach of the first table of the law) or of their other sins (mostly those in breach of the second table). See Revelation 9:20–21.

The little scroll and the two witnesses

As between the sixth and seventh seals, so between the sixth and seventh trumpets, there is an interlude. It features a little scroll (10:1–11) and two witnesses (11:1–13). The little scroll is brought down from heaven by a 'mighty' angel (who seems to be none other than Jesus Christ himself), and John is commissioned to preach it. The two witnesses, on the other hand, seem to represent the missionary church. These two gospel ministries need to be understood in relation to the warning trumpets. Now that the world has largely rejected the negative message of warning, much as Pharaoh had hardened his heart and refused to repent, the positive proclamation of the gospel is all the more essential. For Christ is still calling the world to himself; his patience is not exhausted; and the end has not yet arrived.

As John describes his vision of 'another mighty angel coming down from heaven', it is evident that he is no mere angel. True, he is throughout called an 'angel', but why should he not be 'the angel of the Lord', who appeared in those Old Testament theophanies which seem to have been pre-incarnate appearances of the Son of God?

At all events, John seems to have deliberately assembled a

number of divine features in his description. The 'angel' was robed
in a cloud (symbol of the presence of God), and had a rainbow over
his head (symbol of the covenant mercy of God). His face shone
like the sun, and his legs were like fiery pillars, as in John's original
vision of Christ in chapter 1. He was holding a little scroll which
lay open in his hand, perhaps (some commentators think) the very
same scroll that he had taken from the Father's hand in chapter 4.
It was closed then; it is open now. Having planted one foot on the
sea and the other on the land, this colossus stood astride the whole
planet, with all things under his feet. He then roared like a lion,
reminding us that the sovereign Lord has spoken (Amos 3:8) and
that he is himself the Lion of the tribe of Judah (Rev. 5:5). And
when seven thunders spoke, only he understood them, though he
was forbidden to divulge their meaning. The evidence seems
overwhelming that this is Jesus Christ.

At this point the 'angel' swore by the eternal Creator that there
would be 'no more delay', for when the seventh trumpet is blown
'the mystery of God' (his revealed salvation and judgment) will be
accomplished.

What then about the little scroll? A voice told John to take it
(which he did) and eat it, digesting its contents (which he also did).
Its taste in his mouth was sweet as honey, but it turned his stomach
sour. Jeremiah and Ezekiel before him had both had a similar
experience (Jer. 15:16; Ezek. 3:1ff.). Thus John was recommis-
sioned to take the gospel to all nations (Mark 13:10), but was at
the same time warned that the sweetness of the message of
salvation would be followed by the bitterness of judgment for those
who rejected God's word.

Before the second half of the interlude takes place (involving the
'two witnesses'), John is told to measure the sanctuary of God, the
altar and the worshippers. With Ezekiel 40 – 48 in our minds (the
rebuilding of the temple), we may say that 'measuring' like 'sealing'
symbolizes the protection of God's true people. The outer court
(perhaps the nominal church), however, is not to receive the same
security, because it has been handed over to the unbelieving
nations, who will trample the holy city (that is, persecute the
church) for forty-two months, which is the same as three and a half
years, the traditional apocalyptic period of tribulation (cf. Dan.
9:27; 12:7).

Suddenly, in 11:3, Christ's 'two witnesses' are introduced with neither warning nor explanation, and their dramatic biography is told. It seems clear that they represent the witnessing and suffering church. They are given power to prophesy (that is, to preach the gospel) for 1,260 days, which is the same church-age period as the forty-two months or the three and a half years. In other words, the witness, the persecution and the divine protection of the church will last for the same period of time (11:2–3; 12:5–6, 14).

But why is the witnessing church symbolized by 'two witnesses'? It seems to be due to several factors. First, there was the Old Testament requirement of a minimum of two witnesses to validate testimony in a law court (e.g. Deut. 19:15; John 8:17). Secondly, Jesus had sent out the seventy two by two. Thirdly, the witnesses are identified with the two olive trees and two lampstands of Zechariah 4:1–6. These were two Israelite leaders, namely the priest Joshua and the governor Zerubbabel. Fourthly, they are further identified (vv. 5–6) with Moses (turning water into blood, Exod. 7:20) and Elijah (stopping the rain, 1 Kings 17:1), representing the law and the prophets.

Throughout this period of their prophetic ministry the two witnesses will be persecuted and protected simultaneously. But when their testimony is finished, an unidentified 'beast that comes up from the Abyss' (v. 7), perhaps Antichrist, will attack, overpower and kill them. Their bodies will be left lying in the street of the city which is given four symbolic names: Babylon ('the great city'), Sodom (symbol of immorality), Egypt (symbol of oppression) and Jerusalem ('where also their Lord was crucified'). For a short time representatives of all unbelieving peoples will refuse them burial (the acme of disrespect), gloat over them and celebrate their murder, that is, rejoice that their witness has been silenced. And the reason for their glee? It is that the church's faithful witness has caused them great torment of mind and conscience (v. 10).

After a short period, however, the martyred and silenced church will be resurrected by God (its testimony revived), causing terror in the watching world, and finally will be exalted to heaven, to the consternation of its enemies. This will be accompanied by a severe earthquake, causing devastating damage and huge casualties, and spread terror among the survivors. They will give glory to God, some by conversion, others by submission on the day of judgment.

The title I have given these four chapters (8–11) is 'Christ calling the world to repentance'. Under this rubric the trumpets are his warning judgments, while the scroll and the two witnesses are the church's faithful preaching of the gospel. Both caused 'torment' in unbelievers (9:5, 10; 11:10), but these divine warnings did not lead them to repentance (9:20f.). So now it is too late. The seventh trumpet (or third woe) is about to sound, and with it the end will have come.

After the sounding of the seventh trumpet, John records a threefold sequel, the most significant feature of which is the sequence of time references, which are all in the aorist or perfect tense, indicating what has now taken place irrevocably: 'the kingdom of the world *has become* the kingdom of our Lord ...' (v. 15); '... you *have taken* your great power and *have begun* to reign' (v. 17); 'your wrath *has come*. The time *has come* for judging ...' (v. 18); 'Then God's temple *was opened* ...' (v. 19). All these statements indicate the finality of what has happened, either concluding the past or inaugurating the future.

First, loud voices in heaven proclaimed the kingdom. Of course the kingdom of God came with Jesus, but now the rule over the world has passed into the hands of our Lord and of his Christ, of whom together it is then said in the singular, 'he will reign for ever and ever' (v. 15).

Secondly, the twenty-four elders representing the completed church prostrated themselves before the eternal and almighty God, worshipping him that he has taken his power and begun to reign and that the time has come to judge the dead, to reward the people of God both small and great, and to destroy the destroyers of the earth.

Thirdly, John saw God's sanctuary open (declaring free access into his presence), and in it the ark of his covenant (speaking of his mercy). At the same time (symbolizing his final judgment), there came thunder and lightning, an earthquake and a great hailstorm.

Thus John has again brought us full circle from the beginning to the conclusion of the gospel era, and with 12:1 the whole cycle will begin again.

6. Christ overcoming the devil and his allies (Rev. 12 – 13)

The woman, the dragon, the male child and the two beasts

Each time that John recapitulates his story, as it stretches from Christ's first coming to his second, there is persecution, conflict, victory and celebration. This is very clear in chapters 12 – 14.

Consider the *dramatis personae* in the opening vision of chapter 12. There are three chief actors: a pregnant woman entering labour, the male child she bears and an enormous red dragon with seven crowned heads and ten horns symbolizing his powerful empire.

There is no doubt of the identity of the dragon, since John refers to him in verse 9 as 'that ancient serpent called the devil and Satan'. Nor is there any question about the male child the woman bears, for his destiny is to 'rule all the nations with an iron sceptre'. He is the Messiah, the King of kings (v. 5; cf. Ps. 2:9). But who is the mother who gives birth to her son? A popular Roman Catholic interpretation is that she is the Virgin Mary. But Mary was not persecuted as this woman is. She appears, in fact, to be not an individual at all but a corporate figure representing the church of both Old and New Testaments in continuity. The strongest hint occurs in verse 1 where she is clothed with the sun, with the moon under her feet and a crown of twelve stars on her head. This reminds us of Joseph's dream in which sun, moon and stars (representing his father, mother and brothers) bowed down before him (Gen. 37:9).

In other words, this glorious lady, who gave birth to the Messiah, is a symbol of the people of Israel, from whose twelve patriarchs the human ancestry of the Christ is traced (Rom. 9:5). The twelve stars in her crown seem to indicate this.

Three visions (12:1–17)

Having identified the three main actors, we are ready to look at the three visions of Revelation 12, which all tell the same story of the defeat of the devil, the victory of Christ and the protection of the church.

First comes the vision of *the woman, the child and the dragon* (vv. 1–6). As the woman went into labour, the dragon stood over her, determined (we think of King Herod's malice) to devour her child the very moment he was born. But when she was delivered, her son was snatched up to God and his throne. And then the woman fled to the desert to a place prepared for her by God, where she will be taken care of for 1,260 days (which is forty-two months or three and a half years), the whole period of the church's ministry and persecution (cf. 11:2–3). Thus the first vision (of the woman, the child and the dragon) is a marvellous condensation of the gospel story from the Messiah's birth in fulfilment of the Old Testament to his resurrection and ascension, and on to the time of the persecution and protection of the church. It is also an expression of the age-long 'enmity' between the serpent and the woman (Gen. 3:15).

Secondly, there is the vision of *two armies locked in battle* (vv. 7–12). This second vision does not depict events subsequent to those of the first, but is superimposed on it as its heavenly counterpart. Michael, a leading archangel first mentioned in Daniel, together with his army of good angels, engages the dragon and his demonic forces in war. But (v. 8) the dragon and his forces were not strong enough. They were soundly defeated and lost their place in heaven. So the great dragon (who leads the whole world astray) was hurled down to earth. That is, his power to deceive was broken, as is evidenced by the mission of the church and the millions who have been converted to Christ. We also know from the rest of the New Testament that it was at the cross that Christ decisively vanquished the devil, and by the resurrection that his victory was vindicated.

Indeed, Christ's great conquest is now celebrated in song (vv. 10–12). For what have now 'come', and so become available to us, are 'salvation' (for which Christ died), 'power' (the gospel being God's power for salvation), 'the kingdom of our God' (which broke into history through Christ) and 'the authority of his Christ' (who said that universal authority now belonged to him). These blessings are now ours because Satan the accuser has been overthrown. For Satan is both the deceiver of the nations, who leads the world astray (v. 9), and the accuser of the church (v. 10), who slanders God's people day and night. But now that Christ has died for our sins, there is no condemnation for those who are in him (Rom. 8:1, 33). Meanwhile there is both joy in heaven and woe to the earth because the devil has come down, filled with fury.

Thirdly, there is the vision of *the dragon's continuing hostility to the woman* (vv. 13–17). Hurled down to earth, the devil relentlessly pursued the woman who had given birth to the Messiah. We note, therefore, that the woman who gave birth to the child symbolized the Old Testament people of God, whereas the woman who was pursued by the devil symbolized the New Testament people of God. There is an essential continuity between them. She fled into the desert (enjoying a new exodus), where she was cared for by God. So the devil became enraged and went off to make war against the rest of her offspring, that is, the church of later generations, whose members obey God's commandments and faithfully bear witness to Jesus. Obedience and testimony are two essential marks of the messianic community.

The dominant theme of this chapter has been the decisive overthrow of the devil. He was foiled in his resolve to devour the Christ-child, who instead was snatched up to God. He was foiled in his engagement in spiritual warfare, and instead was hurled down to the earth. He was foiled in his attempts to destroy the woman, who instead was rescued by God. Although Christ's victory was achieved once for all on the cross, God's people have been given a way to enter into it themselves. 'They overcame him', John wrote (v. 11), 'by the blood of the Lamb, and by the word of their testimony', and by their readiness for martyrdom, for they did not shrink even from death.

The beast out of the sea

The three visions of Revelation 12 have left the dragon standing by himself on the seashore (13:1). But he did not remain alone for long. Three allies joined him and are introduced to us one by one. They are called 'the beast out of the sea', 'the beast out of the earth' and 'Babylon', a gaudy prostitute. They seem to masquerade as a diabolical parody of the Trinity. They all also represent the city and empire of Rome, although from three different perspectives.

First, the beast out of the sea represents Rome as *a persecuting power* (13:1–10). Secondly, the beast out of the earth represents

Rome as *an idolatrous system* (13:11–18), with special reference to the cult of Caesar. This beast is also later called 'the false prophet' (16:13; 19:20; 20:10). Thirdly, Babylon the harlot represents Rome as *a corrupting influence* (14:8). These are a portrayal, writes Richard Bauckham, of 'the oppressive power of Rome, the imperial cult and the corrupt civilization of Rome'.[20]

The Jews were always afraid of the sea. It seemed to them a continuation of the primeval chaos, and even a symbol of hostility to God. The raging of the nations was like the raging of the sea (Is. 17:12). So a monster emerging out of the sea would be a particular horror. This one had twelve crowned horns, symbolizing extraordinary imperial power, and seven heads, standing perhaps for the seven hills on which Rome was built (17:9). He also had fierce features resembling a leopard, a bear and a lion. Whereas in Daniel 7:3ff. these represented three successive world powers, here in Revelation they are combined into one, to indicate the beast's extreme ferocity. But specially important was the fact that the dragon delegated to the beast 'his power, his throne and great authority' (v. 2).

A strange detail is that one of the beast's seven heads had a fatal wound, which nevertheless had been healed. The best explanation is probably that it represented Nero, who committed suicide in AD 68, but was believed – according to legend – to have survived or come alive again, which he certainly did figuratively when his successor Domitian resumed his policies. Moreover these events were a parody of the death, resurrection and parousia of Christ.

The rest of the passage about the beast out of the sea concentrates on his use and abuse of power. Men worshipped the dragon because he had given his authority to the beast. But they also worshipped the beast. For forty-two months (throughout the church age) the beast exercised his blasphemous and slanderous ministry. He was also given power to persecute the church. In fact, all the earth's inhabitants, if their names had not been registered in the book of life which belongs to the Lamb slain before the creation of the world, will worship the beast. This scenario is a challenge to God's people to endure, to be faithful and to refuse to compromise.

The beast out of the earth

The beast who emerged out of the earth looked very different from the first beast. Instead of having ten crowned horns and seven heads (an impressive show of power), he was modest enough to have only one head, and his two horns were lamb-like, masquerading as a counterpart to Christ the Lamb. At the same time, his voice was as loud and menacing as a dragon's, or perhaps as *the* dragon's, whose representative he was.

More important than his appearance was his ministry. He had no independent role. Instead, having received his authorization from the first beast, the second beast's ministry related wholly to the first beast, to whom he seems to have been entirely subservient. The second beast (1) made the earth's inhabitants worship the first beast; (2) performed magic on behalf of the first beast, deceiving the inhabitants of the earth (cf. Matt. 24:24); (3) ordered the people to set up an image or statue in honour of the first beast; (4) was given power to make the first beast's image live and speak, and to cause those who refused to worship the image to be killed; and (5) forced everybody, small and great, to receive the mark of the first beast, so that nobody could buy or sell without it.

As for the name of the beast, or the number of his name, this certainly 'calls for wisdom' and has in fact generated much ingenuity! If the beast symbolizes a literal, historical figure, there is something approaching a consensus among scholars about his identity, namely that he represents Nero, since the Hebrew letters for 'Nero Caesar', when converted into numbers, total 666. But numbers in Revelation are almost always symbolical. It has been pointed out, therefore, that, since seven is the perfect number, six falls short of it and represents imperfection. More-over, as G. K. Beale has written, 'the triple repetition of sixes connotes the intensification of incompleteness and failure …' Or, more simply, 666 'indicates the completeness of sinful incom-pleteness'.[21]

If this is the identity of the first beast, however, who is the second, who serves the first with sickly obsequiousness? The best guess is that he is provincial Asia's high priest, who was responsible for the imperial cult and presided over its ceremonial. Thus the dragon gave his authority to the first beast (13:4), the first gave his to the second (13:12), and the second required everybody to worship the first.

Certainly the imperial cult, together with official pressure to conform to it, lies behind many passages in the book of Revelation. Although verses 14 and 15 must include all idolatry or worship of God-substitutes, their most direct allusion is to the imperial cult, with its mention of setting up an image in honour of the beast and of the death penalty for those who refused to worship it.

It was about the year 29 BC that the Emperor Augustus (who reigned until AD 14) permitted the establishment of the cult in Asia Minor by the building of a temple in his honour in Pergamum. By the end of his reign the cult was flourishing in thirty-four cities, and Tiberius, his successor, continued the tradition.[22] But it was the Emperor Domitian (AD 81–96) who took the cult to extremes. He had a huge statue created in his honour in Ephesus. 'He even insisted upon being regarded as a god, and took vast pride in being called "master" and "god".'[23] 'With no less arrogance', he dictated a circular letter which began '"Our Master and our God bids ..." and so the custom arose of henceforth addressing him in no other way even in writing and in conversation ...' [24]

The main celebrations of the cult took place on New Year's Day, which was the Emperor's birthday, and in connection with a personal visit by him. On such occasions there was pressure on everybody to participate. Pliny the Younger, about AD 112, in one of his letters to the Emperor Trajan, explained how he discharged Christians who 'did reverence, with incense and wine, to your image which I had ordered to be brought forward, and especially because they cursed Christ ...'[25] Other Christians, however, who refused to conform, paid the price of their courage, like Antipas in Pergamum (2:13) and Bishop Polycarp in Smyrna, who have been mentioned already.

Babylon the harlot

If the dragon's first two allies were the beasts from the sea and from the earth, the third was Babylon, 'the great city', portrayed as a lewd prostitute. She is only just mentioned here (14:8), where her fall is anticipated on account of 'the maddening wine of her adulteries'. She is much more fully described in chapters 17 and 18. The dragon's three allies, then, when John was writing, were Rome the persecutor (the first beast), Rome the idolater (the second beast or false prophet) and Rome the seductress (Babylon the harlot).

Thus 'our struggle is not against flesh and blood, but against the rulers, against the authorities, against the powers of this dark world and against the spiritual forces of evil in the heavenly realms' (Eph. 6:12). And the Revelation allows us to peep behind the scenes and see the subtle strategy of Satan. We can see him in the early chapters of the Acts wielding the same three weapons. First, he tried to crush the church by force. Secondly, he tried to corrupt the church by the hypocrisy of Ananias and Sapphira. Thirdly, he tried to mislead the church by false teaching, distracting the apostles from their ministry of the Word and so exposing the church to heresy. All over the world today the same threefold assault on the church is mounted by the devil – physical (persecution), moral (compromise) and intellectual (false teaching).

7. Christ standing on Mt Zion with his redeemed people (Rev. 14:1 – 15:4)

The radical alternative: salvation and judgment

The Lamb and the 144,000 (14:1–13)

John now gives us another of his welcome interludes. It would be hard to conceive a sharper contrast than the one he depicts between chapter 13 and chapter 14. It is an immense relief to turn from the dragon and his first beast, whose habitat is the unruly sea, to the Lamb who stands on firm and holy ground; from persecution and the threat of martyrdom to security in Mount Zion; from the incompleteness of 666 to the completeness of 144,000; and from those who have received the mark of the beast on their forehead (13:16) to those who have the name of the Lamb and of his Father written on their forehead.

John now hears some marvellous music, which he likens to a waterfall, a clap of thunder and an orchestra of harpists. In addition to the orchestra there was a choir, who sang a new song before the heavenly audience. No-one knew the words of the song except the

144,000, but presumably it celebrated the victory of the Lamb.

As for the 144,000, John gives them a fivefold description: (1) they 'had been redeemed from the earth' by the blood of the Lamb (5:9); (2) they are pure and undefiled, meaning not that celibacy is morally superior to marriage, but that they had been faithful to Christ as his virgin bride; (3) they 'follow the Lamb wherever he goes', even to suffering and death (Mark 8:34); (4) they were 'purchased from among men and offered as firstfruits to God and the Lamb'. So they were only the beginnings; the full harvest would follow (vv. 14–16); and (5) they were people of integrity, uncontaminated by any falsehood or hypocrisy.

Thus assured of the security of God's redeemed people, we are ready to hear the messages brought by three angels one after the other. Basic to their ministry is the conviction that 'the hour of his [sc. God's] judgment has come' (v. 7), that is, the time for separating or sifting (the fundamental meaning of *keisis*) the true from the false.

The first angel proclaimed the gospel, which John describes as both 'eternal' in its validity and universal in its scope ('every nation, tribe, language and people'). His proclamation included a summons to his hearers to respond, to fear and glorify God, and to worship the Creator.

The second angel made an advance announcement of the fall of Babylon, expressing the certainty of this future event by means of a so-called 'prophetic past tense'. Babylon deserved this fate because it had intoxicated and seduced the nations.

The third angel issued a loud warning to anyone who worships the beast and its image (instead of the Creator), and who receives its mark. He will drink the wine of God's wrath. He will be tormented in the presence of the Lamb and the angels. The smoke of their torment rises for ever and ever. There is no rest for them day or night. I do not myself think that the anxious question whether the nature of hell is an eternal conscious torment or an ultimate eternal annihilation can be settled by a simple appeal to these sentences. For one thing, we need to keep reminding ourselves that the content of Revelation is symbolic vision not literal reality. Further, the essence of hell is separation from God, whereas these sentences speak of torment 'in the presence of the ... Lamb'. What is clear is that hell is an eternal destruction, whatever the precise nature of this destruction may be, and that there will be no respite from it.

These warnings about the fate of the impenitent, John adds, constitute a call 'for patient endurance on the part of the saints who obey God's commandments and remain faithful to Jesus' (v. 12). They are assured of final vindication. If they 'die in the Lord', whether in martyrdom or by natural causes, they are truly 'blessed' (v. 13). For they will rest from their labour (in contrast to the wicked for whom there will be 'no rest'). Moreover, their deeds will follow them and give evidence of their loyalty.

The harvest and the vintage (14:14–20)

Jesus himself used the harvest metaphor to illustrate spiritual truths. Evangelism is reaping a harvest (Matt. 9:37; John 4:35–38.). The work of the Messiah would be to gather his wheat into the barn and to burn up the chaff (Matt. 3:12). And judgment on the last day will involve separating the weeds from the wheat (Matt. 13:37–39).

The paragraph which is now before us divides the final judgment into two parts. Two figures appear, each with a sharp sickle (vv. 14, 17), and each receives a loud command to take his sickle and reap (vv. 15, 18). The second is explicitly a vintage, and concludes with the grapes being thrown into 'the great winepress of God's wrath' (v. 19). We can only assume, therefore, that the former is a grain harvest and represents the in-gathering of the believing righteous. In one case 'the harvest of the earth is ripe' (v. 15), and in the other 'its grapes are ripe' (v. 18). The two are combined in Joel 3:13.

The first reaper is 'like a son of man', wears a crown of gold and sits on a cloud. He is surely the Lord Christ at his second coming. We need not be offended that he was given a rather peremptory command to take his sickle and reap, for the order was issued by an angel coming out of the temple, that is, with a message from God, who has appointed Jesus to be the Judge (John 5:22; Acts 17:31; Rom. 2:16). He wielded his sickle, 'and the earth was harvested' (v. 16).

The second reaper received a similar command: 'Take your sharp sickle and gather the clusters of grapes from the earth's vine'

(v. 18). The grapes were then thrown 'into the great winepress of God's wrath' and trampled underfoot. The vision of blood rising some four feet and extending 1,600 stadia (more than 180 miles) is horrific, and needs of course to be interpreted, not visualized. G. E. Ladd writes: 'The thought is clear: a radical judgment that crushes every vestige of evil and hostility to the reign of God.'[26] Dr Leon Morris favours a more symbolical understanding of 1,600 stadia:

> Of the explanations suggested perhaps the best is that which sees it as the product of sixteen (the square of four, the number of the earth which is the abode of the wicked) and one hundred (the square of ten, the number of completeness). Blood stretching for 1,600 stadia thus stands for the complete judgment of the whole earth and the destruction of all the wicked.[27]

Once again we cannot fail to be impressed that the incomparable Christ is at the centre of each vision. At the beginning of chapter 14 we see him as the Lamb standing on Mount Zion, while at the end of the chapter we see him sitting on a cloud as the son of man with his sickle. In the former vision he guarantees the security of his redeemed people; in the latter he functions as judge on the last day, separating the wheat from the chaff.

The song of Moses and of the Lamb (15:1–4)

Before John describes the outpouring of the seven bowls of God's wrath, which will be reminiscent of the plagues in Egypt, he draws a striking analogy between Israel's exodus from Egypt and the redemption achieved by Christ. As the Israelites gathered by the Red Sea, victorious over Pharaoh, so John sees a multitude of people, standing by what looked like a sea of glass and fire, victorious over the beast and his image. That is, they had resisted the pressures from their persecutors and had refused to do obeisance to Caesar. As Miriam took her tambourine to celebrate God's triumph, so the victorious people of God celebrate with harps. And as Moses and Miriam sang a song of praise to God (Exod. 15), so the song of Moses (the Old Testament victor) has become the song of the Lamb (the New Testament victor), praising God for the greatness of his deeds and the justice of his ways. Because he alone is holy (unique), it is right to give him glory. Indeed all nations will worship him for his righteous acts which have been revealed.

8. Christ coming like a thief in the night (Rev. 15:5 – 19:10)

The call to be ready

In the middle of chapter 16, suddenly and unexpectedly, detached alike from the verses which precede it and from those which follow it, Jesus interrupts the narrative with words of direct speech. Using the first person singular, and apparently addressing anybody and everybody willing to listen, he cries out: 'Behold, I come like a thief! Blessed is he who stays awake and keeps his clothes with him, so that he may not go naked and be shamefully exposed' (v. 15).

Of course, this is not the first time that the thief simile had been used. Indeed, Jesus had used it himself during his public ministry. He said: 'But understand this: if the owner of the house had known at what time of night the thief was coming, he would have kept watch … So you also must be ready, because the Son of man will come at an hour when you do not expect him'(Matt. 24:43–44).[28]

If only the thief would oblige us by sending us an advance notice (better still, an e-mail), alerting us as to the day and time of his intended visit! Then we would be ready. But no, his coming will be sudden and unexpected, like a thief's in the night.

This surprising intervention by Jesus, in the middle of John's account of the outpouring of the bowls of God's wrath, seems to me to be the intended background to these chapters. Some commentators suggest that Jesus' words to Sardis, 'I will come like a thief' (3:3), were a warning that he was coming to deal with the church's affairs. And this may be so. But in Revelation 16:15 he is surely referring to his second coming on the last day.

In chapter 16 John describes the bowls. In chapters 17 and 18 Babylon is first identified and then destroyed. At the beginning of chapter 19 a huge heavenly choir sings its 'Hallalujah Chorus' (vv. 1–10), and at the end Christ rides out in triumph on a white horse

(vv. 11–18) in power and great glory, followed by the armies of heaven and destined to rule the nations. Then in 19:19–20 first the two beasts, then the dragon are destroyed (Babylon having already met its doom), and all humankind, living and dead, are judged. The dominant theme throughout these chapters is the final judgment by Christ the appointed judge. But when will it happen? The judgment is certain, but the day uncertain. We are kept in suspense, on tenterhooks, remembering Jesus' words: 'Behold, I come like a thief!'

The seven bowls (15:5 – 16:21)

A major clue to the understanding of chapters 15 and 16 is to be found in two expressions. First, according to the opening sentence of chapter 15, John saw 'seven angels with the seven last plagues – last, because with them God's wrath is completed'. Secondly, after the outpouring of the seventh bowl, a loud voice from God's throne cried out 'It is done!' (16:17). Being a single Greek verb in the perfect tense, it indicates that God's work of judgment had been accomplished once and for all. 'Completed' and 'done'. These are the two significant and tell-tale verbs. The previous judgments (the seals and the trumpets) were partial; those of the bowls are final. It could be expressed thus: the eye of faith sees in the breaking of the seals the permissive will of God, in the blowing of the trumpets the reformative purpose of God, and in the pouring out of the bowls the retributive justice of God.

In John's preparatory vision (15:5–8) he saw in heaven that the temple stood open. That is, it was by the direct sanction of God that the seven angels emerged as agents of judgment. Their seven bowls were filled with the wrath of God, and the temple was full of God's glory, so that no-one could enter it until the judgment was over.

The first four bowls, like the first four trumpets (8:6–12), were targeted in the same sequence upon earth, sea, fresh water (rivers and springs) and sun. The main difference is that the trumpets damaged only one third of each aspect of creation, whereas the bowls damaged each completely. On the earth, people suffered from 'ugly and painful sores'; sea and freshwater turned into blood, so that all living things in them died; and the intense heat of the sun caused serious scorching.

Talk about earth, sea, water and sun has a modern sound in our era of environmental sensitivity. We are concerned about the earth's bio-diversity, the plankton of the oceans, the availability of clean water and the preservation of the ozone layer to protect us from radiation and its harmful effects. This priority given to life on planet Earth is also a necessary preparation for the coming renewal of all things. As Bishop Paul Barnett has written, 'the destruction of the "old heavens and earth" is now completed, clearing the way for the new creation of God'.[29]

The pouring out of the fifth bowl plunged the kingdom of the beast into darkness and consequent anarchy, and caused great human suffering. Yet the people still 'refused to repent' (repeated in vv. 9 and 11). Like Pharaoh, who endured five of the plagues described here (boils, blood, darkness, frogs and hail), they had hardened their hearts, and it was now too late. Instead of glorifying God, they cursed him.

The contents of the sixth bowl were poured on the River Euphrates, which we have already understood to be a symbol of anti-God forces on the north-eastern frontier of the Roman Empire. By drying up the river, the way was open for the kings from the east to invade. At this point three evil frog-like spirits appear out of three mouths (of the dragon, the beast and the false prophet). They perhaps represent the lies of propaganda by which the kings of the whole world are persuaded to assemble for the final battle 'on the great day of God Almighty'.

Lest the people of God should be unduly alarmed by the massing of godless armies, it is now that Jesus himself intervenes and cries out 'Behold, I come like a thief!' His people must keep awake, clothed and ready (v. 15).

John returns to the gathering of the kings, and to their *rendez-vous* at a place called in Hebrew 'Armageddon' (v. 16). This is another word which, in spite of its popular use to denote a catastrophic conflict, causes commentators much difficulty. It is uncertain how to spell, locate or interpret it. But many believe it to be derived from Megiddo, a strategic site in northern Palestine and the scene of many ancient battles. It is not literal, however. It symbolizes the final battle between the Lamb and the dragon, between Christ and antichrist. For Christ will come in power and glory to rout and destroy the forces of evil.

As the sequences of both the seals and the trumpets ended in the climactic parousia, so does the sequence of the bowls. A loud voice from the temple cried 'It is done!' And a tremendous physical upheaval (including thunder, lightning and a severe earthquake) signified the end. No earthquake like it has ever occurred. The great city Babylon and many other godless cities collapsed in total ruin. Islands and mountains disappeared, and huge hailstones, each weighing about a hundred pounds, fell, causing humans to curse God.

The identity of Babylon (17:1–18)

So far 'Babylon' has been mentioned twice. In 14:8 the fall of Babylon was suddenly announced, without warning. 'Fallen! Fallen is Babylon the Great.' In 16:19, as a result of the outpouring of the seventh bowl, we read that 'God remembered Babylon', that he gave her the cup of his wrath to drink, and that the great city split into three. Thus both verses refer to her overthrow under the judgment of God, but neither tells us what she symbolizes.

So now two whole chapters are devoted to the phenomenon of 'Babylon'. Chapter 17 identifies her for us, while chapter 18 describes in the most graphic detail her devastation and destruction.

The identification of Babylon we owe to one of the seven angels who volunteered to instruct John. He said to him, 'Come, I will show you the punishment of the great prostitute, who sits on many waters' (v. 1). And later he said, 'I will explain to you the mystery of the woman …' (v. 7). The angel's first promise was fulfilled in verses 1–6, where, as a result of what the angel showed John, he exclaimed three times 'I saw … I saw … I saw …' Then the angel's second promise was fulfilled in verses 7–18, where he said to John five times 'you saw … you saw … you saw …', and went on to explain to him the meaning of what he had seen.

Presumably John accepted the angel's offer, so that the angel carried him away 'in the Spirit' (in a state of inspiration) 'into a desert', no doubt the desert in which the persecuted church has taken refuge (12:14).

First, consider what the angel showed John (vv. 3–6). John says at once 'I saw a woman', very different from the woman persecuted by the dragon (for this woman was the persecutor, not the persecuted). The woman he saw was sitting on a scarlet beast (readily recognizable as the beast from the sea). He was sitting on her because Rome the persecutor and Rome the prostitute (violence and vice) were closely associated with one another. Indeed, 'Roman civilization, as a corrupting influence, rides on the back of Roman military power.'[30] The beast was 'covered with blasphemous names' (deeply compromised with the imperial cult), while its seven heads and ten horns confirmed its identity (13:1).

As for the woman herself, she was dressed in flamboyant royal purple and scarlet, adorned with glittering jewellery, and holding a golden cup filled with the filth of her immorality. A title on her forehead proclaimed her to be 'Babylon the Great, the Mother of Prostitutes and of the Abominations of the Earth.' Now twice more, in rapid succession, John says 'I saw … I saw …' He saw the woman drunk with the blood of martyrs, and what he saw astonished him. So again the angel came to his aid.

Consider, secondly, what the angel explained to John (vv. 7–8). The angel is speaking throughout this section and five times reminds him of what he has seen and interprets it.

'The beast you saw' (v. 8), in addition to being ridden by the woman and having seven heads and ten horns, 'once was, now is not, and will come up out of the Abyss and go to his destruction'. These four stages in the biography of the beast may well be an allusion to Nero *redivivus*, which has already been mentioned (13:3). According to this myth, Nero once was, now is not (he committed suicide), will rise again (either literally at the head of an army or symbolically in the policies of Domitian), but will be destroyed. But this is also the course of evil – active from the beginning, seeming sometimes to die down, reasserting itself, but ultimately to be destroyed.

Next we are presented with a second puzzle, which also 'calls for a mind with wisdom' (v. 9). The beast's seven heads are seven hills (obviously those on which Rome is built). They are also seven kings, five of whom have fallen, one still is, and the seventh has not yet arrived. Commentators are divided as to whether the five are the Roman emperors from Augustus to Nero or (because of the background in the prophecy of Daniel) five kingdoms or empires from Ancient Babylonia (or Egypt), through Assyria, Chaldea, Medo-Persia and Greece to Rome.

The interpreting angel now refers to 'the ten horns you saw' (v. 12). They are said to be 'ten kings'. But, because their authority in each case will last for only one hour (that is, a very short time), the reference may rather be to leaders in general or perhaps Roman governors in particular. Unfortunately, their one and only purpose will be to kowtow to the beast and make war against the Lamb. But the Lamb will overcome them (because he is Lord of lords and King of kings), as will also his followers who are 'called, chosen and faithful' (v. 14).

'The waters you saw', continues the angel (v. 15), over which the prostitute presides, are the peoples of the world. But 'the beast and the ten horns you saw' (v. 16), who have served the woman faithfully, will now turn in revulsion against her, will hate her, strip her, eat her flesh and burn her up. For God has put it into their heart to be the agent of his judgment upon her.

Finally, 'the woman you saw' (v. 18) is the great city that rules over the kings of the earth; Babylon in symbol, Rome in reality, the very essence of hostility to Christ and his church.

The fall of Babylon (18:1–24)

Now that the identity of 'Babylon' has been established as Rome the prostitute, aided and abetted by Rome the persecutor, John goes on at once to describe her overthrow. It would not take place in its finality for more than another 320 years, when in AD 410 Alaric the Goth would sack the city. Yet John used the prophetic past-tense throughout chapter 18, expressing the certainty of God's judgment as if it had already taken place. 'Fallen! Fallen is Babylon the Great!' (v. 2, as in 14:8).

It is truly amazing that John could predict the overthrow of Rome with such assurance. For people spoke of Rome as 'the eternal city', and the empire appeared to be invulnerable. Bishop Paul Barnett has written that at that time,

Rome was at the height of her powers. There was no serious threat to her frontiers, nor any sign of major uprising from her own subject peoples. Pirates had been cleared from the seas and brigands from the countryside. Elegant cities dotted the shores of the Mediterranean and were to be found in many inland regions as well. Soon the tyrant Domitian would fall, and the empire would enter [its] golden year ...[31]

So how can John have been so sure? Partly no doubt because he believed in the just judgment of God upon evil, and partly because the Old Testament prophecies of the fall of Babylon in those days had all been fulfilled (e.g. Is. 13:19 and 21:9). So the angel sent to announce Babylon's fall had great authority and splendour (v. 1). He even declared that already the city's destruction had made it a haunt for evil spirits and unclean birds (v. 2; cf. Is. 13:20–22; Jer. 50:39).

And the reason for the devastation of Babylon was that all the nations, kings and merchants of the earth had become infected by her adulteries and luxuries (v. 3). These groupings recur in the second half of the chapter.

Meanwhile, another voice was heard calling God's people to come out of Babylon, in order to avoid contamination. If they did not share her sins, they would not share her plagues either (cf. Jer. 50:8; 51:6, 45). For God remembered her sins ('piled up to heaven' v. 5) and would render to her what she deserved, and even more because of her total self-absorption and boastfulness. For 'mighty is the Lord God who judges her' (v. 8).

The same voice continues to be heard as it addresses three groups of the godless community in mourning over Babylon's downfall: the kings of the earth (vv. 9–10), the merchants of the earth (vv. 11–17a) and the seafarers of the world (vv. 17b–19). The whole passage is reminiscent of an Old Testament funeral dirge, especially Ezekiel's lament over Tyre and Sidon (Ezek. 26 – 28), and each section is concluded with the words of lamentation 'Woe! Woe, O great city' because 'in one hour' she had been brought to ruin (vv. 10, 16, 19).

The kings of the earth, who were guilty of sharing in Babylon's immorality and luxury, will weep and wail over the destruction of the 'city of power'.

The merchants of the earth will also mourn because they will have no more markets and no-one to buy their cargoes of jewellery, fine clothing, articles of ivory, wood and other materials, spices and food, horses and chariots. They even trafficked in human beings as slaves. The special fruit their customers long for will no longer be available. Their financial capital will have disappeared overnight, never to be recovered. The merchants who have lost everything will stand far off and weep that 'such great wealth' could in one hour have been brought to ruin. It is a picture of economic collapse. So those who mourn the devastation of Babylon are those who have 'benefited from Rome's economic exploitation of her empire'.[32]

The seafarers of the world include not only sea captains and sailors (the ship owners' crews of sea-going vessels), but also those who travel by ship and those who earn their living from the sea (merchants and fishermen). They too will stand at a distance from Babylon and watch her burning. Then they will extol her uniqueness: 'was there ever a city like this great city?' (v. 18). Overwhelmed with sorrow, they will weep that her wealth and their profits will vanish in a single hour.

Chapter 18 concludes with a combination of opposites: a celebration and a lament. Verse 20 calls upon heaven to rejoice, and saints, apostles and prophets to rejoice as well. Why? Because God has judged Babylon for the way she has treated them. It sounds at first hearing like an expression of personal revenge, but there is no reason to interpret it in this way. As throughout Revelation (not least in chapter 19), so here, we are called to celebrate the justice and the judgment of our all-righteous God.

Next, a mighty angel threw a huge boulder into the sea and said that with just such violence Babylon would be irrevocably destroyed. In consequence, even the good things of the city's life would disappear with her – the sound of music, the skill of craftsmen, the familiar domestic routine of preparing food for the family, the light of lamps, and the joyful laughter of bride and bridegroom. Never again would these innocent sounds and sights of human culture gladden the life of the city. Why not? Answer: because of the pride of Babylon's merchants, who boasted of their greatness; because of Babylon's resort to sorcery in order to deceive the nations; and because Babylon had shed the blood of the martyrs. Because of these sins Babylon will be no more, and with her disappearance all that is good, beautiful and true will disappear as well.

In the first century AD Babylon was Rome. But Babylon has

flourished throughout history and throughout the world. Babylon is Vanity Fair, wherever it exists. Its profile can be drawn with ease from these chapters. It seems to have six components: (1) idolatry (spiritual unfaithfulness, even promiscuity); (2) immorality (literal as well as symbolical); (3) extravagance and luxury (18:3, 7–8); (4) the use of sorcery and magic (18:23; cf. Is. 47:1–2); (5) tyranny and oppression, leading to the martyrdom of God's people (17:6; 18:24; cf. Is. 14:4–6); and (6) arrogance, even self-deification (18:7; cf. Is. 14:13–15; 47:7ff.; Jer. 50:31–32; Ezek. 28:2). The urgent call still comes to God's people to come out of her, in order to avoid contamination.

Five hallelujahs (19:1–10)

In contrast to the silence of burned-out Babylon, John now heard what sounded like 'the roar of a great multitude in heaven' shouting 'Hallelujah!', that is, 'Praise the Lord!' Five times the word is repeated, if the invitation to 'praise our God' in verse 5 is included. Moreover, as in the Psalms so here, 'Hallelujah' never stands alone. Always some reasons are added to explain why we should praise God. In general, it is because salvation, glory and power belong to him, and because his judgments are 'true and just'.

In particular, however, our hallelujahs arise because God has 'condemned the great prostitute'. She had corrupted the world both by her adulteries (her multiple unfaithfulness) and by her persecution of God's people even to the point of death. Now God has avenged their blood. It was not their personal revenge which they were celebrating, but the vindication of God's justice. Next, the twenty-four elders and four living creatures fell down and worshipped God, endorsing the acknowledgment of God's justice with their 'Amen, Hallelujah!' (v. 4).

Now John repeats that he heard what sounded like 'a great multitude', although this time he added that the noise reminded him of rushing waters and loud thunder. 'Hallelujah!' was again their first word (v. 7). In general it was because the Lord God Almighty was reigning. But in particular, the summons to worship this time is because 'the wedding of the Lamb has come, and his bride has made herself ready'. The judgment of the prostitute and the preparation of the Lamb's bride are in dramatic antithesis to one another. We remember the gaudy clothing of the prostitute; by contrast, the bride had prepared herself with simple 'fine linen, bright and clean', which had been given her to wear. It stood for 'the righteous acts' of God's people, John added. Without these she would not be fit for her bridegroom.

An angel then instructed John to write that those 'invited to the wedding supper of the Lamb' are truly blessed. Overcome either by the angel's appearance or by his message or both, John inadvisedly fell at his feet to worship him, but the angel stopped him, reminding him that he was only a fellow servant of John himself and of all his brothers who bear witness to Jesus. He must worship God and remember that the essence of true prophecy is testimony to Jesus.

9. Christ riding in triumph on a white horse (Rev. 19:11 – 20:15)

The doom of the beast and of Satan

'I saw heaven standing open', John writes (v. 11). The phrase alerts us to the fact that he is about to be given a special revelation of Christ and is going to share it with us. At first our eye lights upon a white horse. Then our attention is drawn to the rider on the white horse. His names and his description (which follow) leave us in no doubt whatsoever that this is the Lord Jesus Christ in the fullness of his divine majesty. Indeed, this is the ninth and penultimate portrait of him in the Revelation. He is here made known to us as the judge who both judges with perfect justice and is preparing to lead the last battle against the forces of evil.

His description and his names

Consider his description. His eyes blaze like fire and pierce the secrets of human hearts. He is crowned with many crowns, symbolizing his universal authority. His robe is blood-stained, indicating surely that he carries with him the achievement of his sacrificial death. The heavenly armies follow him, and like him ride on white horses and are dressed in fine (though not blood-stained) linen. And then, using three Old Testament symbols of the just judgment of Almighty God, a sharp sword juts out of his mouth, he wields an iron sceptre and he treads the winepress of God's righteous anger. It is almost impossible to visualize this mounted portrait of the Messiah – his eyes on fire, his head with many crowns, his mouth holding a sword, his hand brandishing a sceptre, while his feet are treading out the grapes. Symbolically, however, it is a spectacular picture of the Lord Jesus Christ in majesty, power, authority and justice, coming to destroy the powers of evil.

Now we must consider his four names. First, he is called 'Faithful and True' (v. 11), as in his letter to Laodicea he had announced himself as 'the faithful and true witness' (3:14). That is, he had never compromised his allegiance to God. Moreover, since in Scripture the faithfulness of God relates to his covenant and promises, to call Jesus 'Faithful and True' means that it is through Christ that God's covenant has been established and his praises will be fulfilled. 'For no matter how many promises God has made, they are "Yes" in Christ' (2 Cor. 1:20).

Secondly, the rider on the white horse 'has a name written on him that no-one knows but he himself' (v. 12). Since our name stands for our identity, a hidden name means a hidden identity. Jesus Christ has not revealed all of himself to us. However much we may claim to know him, there is still much we do not know. Only he knows himself in his fullness, and only on the last day will we know him as he knows us (1 Cor. 13:12; 1 John 3:2).

Thirdly, his name is 'the Word of God' (v. 13; John 1:1). Just as we reveal ourselves in our speech, so God has revealed himself in his Word, Jesus Christ, and in the full biblical witness to Christ. It is also important to note that he whose name is 'the Word of God' wears a blood-stained robe. For it is on the cross that he has revealed himself fully in both goodness and severity, in love and justice, demonstrating his justice in judgment and his love in salvation.

Fourthly, on his robe and on his thigh he has this name written: 'King of kings and Lord of lords' (v. 16. Cf. 17:14 and Deut. 10:17). This is the most sensational of all Christ's names, and reminds us inevitably of the climax of Handel's *Messiah*. Earthly kings and queens, emperors, presidents and other rulers easily become intoxicated with their power and fame, and tend to become autocratic. But Jesus Christ cuts them down to size. For he has been exalted to the highest place of honour, far above all human rule and authority, power and dominion, and every title that can be given, with all things placed under his feet (Eph. 1:20–23; Phil. 2:9–11). He is King of kings and Lord of lords.

The two beasts are destroyed

Following this revelation of Christ as the rider on the white horse, one naturally expects him to ride forth to the last battle. In anticipation of it and its casualties, an angel issues a loud and grim invitation to predatory birds to 'gather together for the great supper of God' (v. 17). It is a ghastly alternative to that other supper, already mentioned, 'the wedding supper of the Lamb' (19:9). Guests invited to that supper will be blessed indeed. But the guests at God's 'great supper' will be vultures and other scavenging birds, while the food served will be human flesh – the flesh of kings, generals and mighty men, and of all people small and great, who (it is assumed) have received the mark of the beast (v. 20).

Next, John sees the beast, the kings of the earth and their armies assembled to wage war against the rider on the white horse and his army (v. 19). So the dramatic moment has come. The two armies, divine and demonic, are facing one another. It is the threshold of Armageddon. What happens next? Nothing! 'There is no battle', only 'a complete anticlimax'.[33] For the truth is that the battle has already been fought and won by the cross and resurrection of Jesus.

Instead, the time of judgment has come, and the forces of evil are disposed of in the opposite order to their introduction. Babylon has already been overthrown. Now the two beasts will be destroyed, leaving the dragon's fate until chapter 20. The beast from the sea was captured, and with him the beast from the earth, also known as 'the false prophet', the symbol of false religion, responsible for persuading people to worship the Emperor or his statue (v. 20). Both beasts were thrown alive into the lake of fire and so destroyed. At the same time we must remember that they are not sentient beings but symbols of anti-Christian persecution and ideology. The chapter concludes with two dramatic pictures. First, the rest of the beast's army will be killed by the rider on the white horse, using the sword in his mouth, which means that he will overcome evil by his Word. Secondly, the unpleasant spectacle of vultures gorging themselves on human flesh means that in the end evil will be completely and irrevocably destroyed.

Satan's doom (20:1–15)

Chapter 19 concluded with the vision of the victorious rider on the white horse, in other words, with the end of history. We must not imagine, therefore, that chapter 20 begins where chapter 19 left off. Having a 'parallelist' understanding of the book, I believe that yet again John is recapitulating his story from the beginning. Within the fifteen verses of chapter 20 he retells the outline of church history between the first and second comings of Christ. In doing so, now that Babylon and the two beasts have been destroyed, his emphasis is on the fate of the dragon, the arch enemy of God. The chapter divides naturally into three paragraphs: the thousand years (vv. 1–6); the final battle (vv. 7–10); and the last judgment (vv. 11–15).

Revelation 20 is well known for its reference to a millennium or one thousand year period. I am assuming that, like other enumerations in the book, we should not interpret this literally, but as a very long though unspecified period, in fact the whole gospel age. John tells us that he saw an angel descending from heaven equipped with both the key to the abyss and a great chain. He seized the dragon (identified once more as the devil), chained him, threw him into the abyss, and locked and sealed it over him. The purpose of this was not to punish him but 'to keep him from deceiving the nations any more …' Next, John saw some thrones on which two groups were seated – on the one hand, departed saints 'who had been given authority to judge' (v. 4), and on the other, martyrs 'who had been beheaded because of their testimony for Jesus …' The two groups were united in their refusal either to worship the beast or to be branded with his mark. They came to life (an experience later called 'the first resurrection', vv. 5–6) and reigned with Christ throughout the millennium. They were also pronounced especially blessed because they would never die 'the second death', but would serve as priests to God and Christ.

It is important to note that the expression 'for a thousand years' occurs in these six verses four times, on each occasion with a different reference. Together they tell us what happens during the millennium. First, Satan was bound 'for a thousand years' (v. 2). Secondly, the nations were no longer deceived 'until the thousand years were ended' (v. 3). Thirdly, the resurrected saints and martyrs reigned with Christ 'a thousand years' (v. 4). Fourthly, the same resurrected ones served God and Christ as priests 'for a thousand years' (v. 6).

Once aware of this fourfold repetition, and of the four activities described, I think we should boldly affirm that the millennium symbolizes the whole period between the first and second comings of Christ. First, it was at his first coming, specifically by his death and resurrection, that Jesus 'bound the strong man' (Mark 3:27 = Matt. 12:29). Secondly, it is during the same inter-adventual period that the nations have been 'undeceived', and that millions have been converted, as a result of the preaching of the gospel in the power of the Spirit (e.g. Ps. 2:8; Mark 13:10; Luke 10:18; Acts 1:8). Thirdly, during the same period God's people are risen and reigning with Christ, seated with him on thrones in the heavenly places (Eph. 2:5–6, cf. Rev. 3:21). Fourthly, we are priests as well as kings (Rev. 1:6; 5:10; 1 Pet. 2:5, 9). There is no mention here of a millennium 'on earth'; the millennium is a reign with Christ 'in the heavenlies'.

If it be objected that the devil does not *seem* to be bound, nor do the nations *seem* to have been 'undeceived', we can perhaps reply in two ways. First, the binding of Satan is a problem relating to the whole New Testament, and not only to Revelation 20. Throughout the New Testament it is decisively asserted that on the cross Christ defeated and even 'destroyed' the devil, has dethroned and disarmed him, and that everything has been put under his feet (e.g. Col. 2:15; Eph. 1:22; Heb. 2:14). Secondly, Revelation 20 does not say that the devil is bound in regard to all his activities, but only in regard to his deception of the nations. Looking back over the centuries to the beginning of the gospel, there has certainly been an amazing ingathering of the nations to Christ (cf. Rev. 7:9).

When the inter-adventual or thousand-year period is over, John tells us that Satan will be released from his prison 'for a short time' (vv. 3, 7), and that he will deceive the nations again throughout the world. During this time the missionary outreach of the church will no doubt be opposed and curtailed, and the church will experience persecution and tribulation rather than expansion. Satan will also gather the hostile peoples together for a last assault against the church, including Gog and Magog, symbols in Ezekiel 38 and 39 of godless nations. A huge army will muster and march across the earth, spearheaded by Antichrist or the man of lawlessness (2 Thess. 2:1–12), and will surround the camp of God's people, symbolically Jerusalem, the city he loves. The contours of the story are familiar. Already this army, marching to the battle of Armageddon, has been described three or four times, for John reaches the same climax repeatedly (e.g. 11:18; 16:12ff. and 19:19). Each time, as the two armies face each other, we expect a clash of arms, violence and blood. But each time there is no battle, for God himself intervenes and forestalls the conflict. Christ comes in person, the rider on the white horse, and overthrows the lawless one with the breath of his mouth (2 Thess. 1:7–10; 2:8). Or, as John puts it here, 'fire came down from heaven and devoured them' (v. 9). Then the dragon was thrown into the lake of fire, to meet the two beasts there in a fate which has neither intermission nor end.

Now that the dragon, the two beasts and the harlot have all been destroyed, and so all opposition to God's people (whether physical persecution, false ideology or moral compromise) has disappeared with them, the time has come for the judgment of individuals. John sees a great white throne. It is occupied, but by whom he does not say. It may be God the Father, since he is normally the unnamed throne-occupant. But it is more likely to be Jesus Christ, since it is to him that God has delegated the work of judgment (see e.g. Matt. 25:31; John 5:22; Acts 17:31; Rev. 14:14). Earth and sky vanish, to indicate the end of the old creation. Then John saw the dead, great and small, standing before the throne. 'There are no absentees and there are no exemptions.'[34] Then books were opened, both the many books recording the deeds of the dead, and the single 'book of life' registering those who belong to the Lamb (3:5; 13:8). When John says that 'the dead were judged according to what they had done as recorded in the books' (v. 12), he is not saying that sinners are justified by their good works. No, we sinners are justified by God's grace alone through faith in Christ alone. At the same time, we will be judged by our good works. The reason for this is that the Judgment Day will be a public occasion, and that good works will be the only public and visible evidence which can be produced to attest the authenticity of our faith. 'Faith without works is dead.' Both the sea and hades will give up their dead, as now the general resurrection will take place. And then death and hades will be thrown into the lake of fire, meaning that physical death will itself die. 'There will be no more death' (21: 4). But the lake of fire, which will abolish physical death, is itself a second and spiritual death, eternal separation from God. The awful destiny of anyone whose name is not in the book of life is the second death, the lake of fire.

10. Christ coming as the bridegroom to claim his bride (Rev. 21 – 22)

The new universe, the city and the garden

Chapter 20 ended with the fearful contrast between those who are registered in the book of life and those who experience the second death, and so between life and death as the alternative destinies awaiting humankind. Chapters 21 and 22 also mention the second death (21:8), but their whole focus is on life – the book of life (21:27), the water of life (21:6; 22:1–2; 22:17) and the tree of life (22:2, 14, 19).

Now 'eternal life' means the personal knowledge of God through Jesus Christ (John 17:3), just as the second death means separation from him. Moreover John illustrates this life (the ultimate and glorious destiny of the people of God) by the use of three distinct metaphors. The first is security in the city of God, the new Jerusalem. The second is access to the tree of life in the Garden of Eden restored. The third is the intimate relationship of bride and bridegroom in marriage. John has a remarkable facility for mixing his metaphors. He jumps abruptly from one to another (the city, the garden and the wedding) without any apparent sense of incongruity. Just as the lion of the tribe of Judah turned out to be a Lamb as if it had been slain (5:5), so the Holy City John sees descending out of heaven from God is 'prepared as a bride beautifully dressed for her husband' (21:2). It is as difficult to visualize a city as a bride or a bride as a city, as it is to visualize a lion as a lamb or a lamb as a lion. Nevertheless, it is not difficult to interpret the symbols. All three metaphors (the city, the garden and the wedding) represent our close personal fellowship with God, which begins now, once we have been reconciled to him, and which will be consummated when Christ comes.

All things new (21:1–8)

The first eight verses of chapter 21 seem to celebrate the 'newness' of God's eschatological work. They are variations on the theme of newness. For John saw a new heaven and a new earth (v. 1), to which the new Jerusalem descended (v. 2). As a result, 'the old order of things had passed away' (v. 4) and from his throne God could declare, 'I am making everything new' (v. 5).

The promise of a new heaven and a new earth was first made by God to Isaiah (65:17; 66:22). Jesus himself spoke of it as 'the renewal of all things' (Matt. 19:28, literally 'the new birth'), and Paul wrote of it as the creation's liberation from its bondage to decay (Rom. 8:21). It is important therefore to affirm that our Christian hope looks forward not to an ethereal heaven but to a renewed universe, related to the present world by both continuity and discontinuity. Just as the individual Christian is a 'new creation' in Christ (2 Cor. 5:17), the same person but transformed; and just as the resurrection body will be the same body with its identity intact (NB Jesus' scars), yet invested with new powers; so the new heaven and the new earth will not be a replacement universe (as if created *de novo*), but a regenerated universe, purged of all present imperfection, with no more pain, sin or death (vv. 4, 8). John adds the detail that 'there was no longer any sea' (v. 1). Many who love the sea regret this, but we need to remember that to Israel the sea was a symbol of restlessness (Is. 57:20–21), of separation (Ps. 139:9–10) and of hostility to God, being the environment out of which the beast from the sea emerged (13:1).

Next John hears a loud voice emanating from God's throne, addressing him in direct speech and explaining the meaning of the descent of the new Jerusalem: 'Now the dwelling of God is with men, and he will live with them. They will be his people, and God himself will be with them and be their God' (v. 3). This marvellous declaration is all the more impressive because it incorporates the covenant formula, which occurs again and again throughout Scripture, namely 'I will be your God and you shall be my people.' The result of this living relationship between God and his people is that there will be no more tears, death, mourning, crying or pain. For these things belong to the old fallen world-order which has now passed away. Indeed, as the voice from the throne continued, 'I am making everything new!' And only he can do this, since he is the Alpha and the Omega, the Beginning and the End.

So far, in the early verses of chapter 21 two of the metaphors of eternal life in Christ have been mentioned, namely the city (the new Jerusalem) and the marriage (the bride beautifully dressed for her husband). Now the third is at least hinted at in reference to the thirsty who are invited to drink without cost, since it is in the garden that the spring of the water of life is to be found (v. 6). The overcomers (who have refused to compromise) are referred to alongside the thirsty, and, in contrast, eight categories of evil-doers are listed, who will be excluded from the city, the garden and the wedding, and instead will find their place in the lake of fire.

The rest of chapter 21 and most of chapter 22 are in the main devoted to an elaboration of the three metaphors.

The city (21:9–21)

An angel invites John 'Come, and I will show you the bride', as another angel had invited him earlier 'Come, and I will show you the … great prostitute' (17:1). The bride and the prostitute, Jerusalem and Babylon, are set in antithesis to one another throughout the book. As at the beginning of this chapter John saw the Holy City, the new Jerusalem, coming down beautifully dressed like a bride (v. 2), now he is invited to see the bride but is shown the city (v. 10). It is obvious that the two metaphors illustrate the same truth.

John's angel-guide carried him away, not literally but 'in the Spirit', his imagination controlled by the inspiring Spirit, to a high mountain. From this vantage-point John saw the Holy City, the new Jerusalem, coming down from God. The first thing we are told about it is that 'it shone with the glory of God' (v. 11), since the temple of the old Jerusalem was the dwelling place of God's glory (e.g. Ezek. 1 and 10). The city also flashed with the brilliance of a very precious stone, perhaps a diamond.

John now describes the city's wall, together with the wall's gates and foundations. The wall's twelve gates, guarded by twelve angels, had on them the names of Israel's twelve tribes, there being three gates on the east, three on the north and south and west. The wall's twelve foundations had on them the names of the twelve apostles of the Lamb. So the city represented the completed church of both Old and New Testaments.

John goes on to tell us that his angel-guide had a golden measuring rod with which he measured the city, its gates and its walls. We are first told that the city was square, 12,000 stadia (about 1,500 miles) in length and width, and then given the further information that the height of the city was also the same. So the city was a cube, like the holy of holies in the temple (e.g. 1 Kgs. 6:20), indicating that the whole city resembled the most holy place, and that the presence of God permeated the whole city. The only other measurement we are given is that the city wall was 144 cubits thick (about 216 feet).

We will surely agree with Dr Bruce Metzger that the new Jerusalem is 'architecturally preposterous'.[35] One cannot even conceive an enormous cube stretching from London to Athens or Los Angeles to Dallas. One can understand the symbolism, however. The new Jerusalem is a massive impregnable fortress, symbolizing the security and peace of the people of God. The measuring of her confirmed her stability. 'Walk about Zion ... count her towers, consider well her ramparts ...' (Ps. 48:12–13). 'May there be peace within your walls and security within your citadels!' (Ps. 122:7). 'Those who trust in the LORD are like Mount Zion, which cannot be shaken but endures for ever' (Ps. 125:1).

The city John saw was not only huge and solid, but also beautiful – each of its twelve foundations being decorated with a different jewel, each of its twelve gates being made from a single pearl, and the great street of the city being pure gold.

Having grasped the vast dimensions and colourful magnificence of the new Jerusalem, which is filled with the presence of God, it is not surprising that John noticed certain consequent absences (21:22–27). We have already seen that there will be no more sin, pain, tears or death (21:4); now we are ready for four more.

First, 'I did not see a temple in the city' (v. 22). But of course not! The Lord God Almighty and the Lamb are its temple. Their presence fills the city; there is no need for a special building in which to house them. Ezekiel's prophecy will have come true: 'The Lord is there' (Ezek. 48:35).

Secondly, the city needs neither sun nor moon (v. 23), since the glory of God illumines it, and the Lamb is its light (cf. Is. 60:19). Indeed, its light will be adequate even for the nations, that is, the Gentile multitudes who will be numbered among the redeemed (Rev. 7:9ff.).

At this point we need to consider verses 24 and 26. 'The kings of the earth will bring their splendour into it' and 'the glory and honour of the nations will be brought into it'. We should not hesitate to affirm that the cultural treasures of the world will enrich the new Jerusalem. Nature is what God gives us; culture is what human beings make of it. Since human beings are ambiguous, so is their culture. Some of it is evil and even demonic, but some of it is also beautiful, good and true. It is this that will adorn the Holy City.

Thirdly, there will be no night there. Consequently the city's gates will never be shut. They will be permanently open, permitting continuous access to the city and so to the God who lives there (v. 25).

Fourthly, nothing impure will ever enter the city, nor will anybody enter who is guilty of shameful or deceitful deeds, but only those registered in the Lamb's book (v. 27).

The garden (22:1–6)

In these early verses of chapter 22 we are still in the city, which is mentioned twice. Nevertheless, we have now left the walls, gates and foundations of the city, and the emphasis is on the river of life and the tree of life. These allusions are enough to alert us that John has the Garden of Eden in mind, with its many rivers and its tree of life. Perhaps we should think of the context as a garden-city or an urban park. John refers in turn to the river, the tree and the throne.

First, the angel showed John 'the river of the water of life' (cf. Ezek. 47). The water was crystal-clear, and the river flowed out of the throne of God and the Lamb (issuing from his sovereign grace) and down the middle of the city's main street. Thus the water is available at all times to the thirsty.

Secondly, we are told that the tree of life was growing on each side of the river. Access to it had been forbidden after the fall (Gen. 3:23–24), but now the prohibition is lifted. Perhaps there is only one tree on each side, but I prefer the view of some commentators, already prophesied by Ezekiel (47:7), that many trees of life line both riverbanks along its full length, so that, like the water, their fruit will be readily available to all. Thus the hungry may eat and the thirsty may drink to their heart's content. It needs to be mentioned that the Greek word for 'tree' here is the same one used by the apostles Peter and Paul in reference to the cross (*xylos*: Acts 5:30; 10:39; 13:29; Gal. 3:13; 1 Pet. 2:24). John lays such stress on the saving death of the Lamb that he may well see in the tree of life a symbolic allusion to the cross. At all events, every month fresh fruit from the tree was ripe, while the leaves of the tree were for the healing of the nations, indicating the widespread positive benefits that the gospel brings to the Gentile world.

John adds that there will no longer be any curse (v. 3). It is another clear reference to the Garden of Eden, in which the ground was cursed because of Adam, and produced thorns and thistles (Gen. 3:17). That curse is revoked in the new heaven and the new earth.

Thirdly, John moves on from the river and the tree to the throne of God in the garden-city. Its centrality will be restored as in chapters 4 and 5, and the whole of life will be subservient to the rule of God and of the Lamb. His servants will worship him, and they will see his face. God had told Moses plainly: 'You cannot see my face, for no-one may see me and live' (Exod. 33:20; John 1:18). So all that human beings have seen so far is the glory of God (Exod. 33:18, 22), which has been defined as 'the outward shining of his inward being'. Thus they have seen God in the person and works of his incarnate Son (John 1:14, 18; 2:11; 14:9). Such 'sight' is, however, like the poor reflection of a mirror (1 Cor. 13:12). And so it will remain until the veil is lifted when Christ comes again and we will see him 'as he is' (1 John 3:2), even 'face to face' (1 Cor. 13:12). This beatific vision is an indispensable part of God's ultimate purpose for his people.

In addition, God's name will be branded upon our foreheads

(v. 4), sealing us as belonging to him for ever. One more 'absence' is now repeated: 'There will be no more night' (v. 5, cf. 21:25), for the light which the Lord God sheds abroad will banish the darkness. All this is due to God's sovereignty. He reigns, and his people also 'reign for ever and ever', not in any way rivalling his rule, but sharing it.

Epilogue (Rev. 22:6–21)

The last sixteen verses of the book of Revelation are a kind of appendix or epilogue, containing an assortment of warnings and exhortations. Three main themes, however, stand out.

First, John is concerned to authenticate his book, to demonstrate its authority. It was Jesus himself, he affirms, who sent his angel to give John this testimony for the churches (vv. 6, 16). In consequence, John both 'heard and saw' what he went on to record (v. 8), and his words are 'trustworthy and true' (v. 6). One particular expression, with slight variations, John uses five times, namely 'the words of the prophecy of this book' (vv. 7, 9, 10, 18, 19). His readers' duty towards this revelation is clear. They are to 'keep' it (vv. 7, 9), that is, to believe and obey it. They are not to 'seal' it (v. 10, i.e. conceal it), but to make it known to others. And in doing so they must neither add to it nor subtract from it (vv. 18–19).

Secondly, John issues his appeals and warnings against the background of anticipated judgment. When Christ comes, he will 'give to everyone according to what he has done' (v 12). Then will take place the terrible separation. Those who have washed their robes will be blessed, enjoying access to the tree of life and to the new Jerusalem (v. 14), but unredeemed sinners and liars will be excluded, like pariah dogs outside the city (v. 15).

Thus Jesus Christ, who originated all things as Creator, will consummate all things as Judge. For he is 'the Alpha and the Omega, the First and the Last, the Beginning and the End' (v. 13). These very same titles are attributed both to God (1:8) and to Christ (1:17; 22:13). With these tremendous claims of Christ, John opens and closes his book. Everything is contained within these parameters. More than that, John's perspective is that even before creation and after judgment Jesus remains the same. For he is the living one, the eternal one (1:17). So he challenges us today to repent of our cowardly compromise and instead to be his faithful witnesses, following him if necessary even to a martyr's death.

'I am coming soon!'

The third and most distinctive feature of the book's epilogue, however, is that it is punctuated three times by the grand affirmation of Jesus: *'Behold, I am coming soon!'* (vv. 7, 12, 20).

Does this mean that Jesus and his apostles predicted that his return would take place almost immediately, and that they were mistaken? This is a widely held view, but it is not necessary to reach this conclusion, for a number of reasons.

First, Jesus said that he did not know the time of his coming (Mark 13:32; cf. Acts 1:7; 2 Thess. 2:1ff.); only his Father knew. It is therefore antecedently unlikely that he would pronounce on what he knew he did not know. He was not ignorant of his ignorance.

Secondly, Jesus and his apostles urged his followers in other places to marry and have children (Eph. 5:21ff.), to earn their own living (2 Thess. 3:6–10), and to take the gospel to the ends of the earth (Matt. 24:14 = Mark 13:10; Matt. 28:19; Rom. 11:25). These instructions are hardly compatible with an imminent parousia. Some of the parables also implied delay (e.g. Matt. 25:19).

Thirdly, Jesus did predict the destruction of Jerusalem within the lifetime of his contemporaries, and it is sometimes hard to discern whether he is referring to this or to the end (e.g. Mark 13:30).

Fourthly, 'apocalyptic' is a particular literary genre with its own literary conventions. For example, it expresses what will happen *suddenly* in terms of what will happen *soon*. Some of the prophets of the eighth and seventh centuries BC, for example, regularly announced that 'the day of the Lord is near' (e.g. Joel 2:1), although it did not begin to materialize, with Christ's coming, for several more centuries. In other words, there is often a gap between promise and fulfilment, since it is only 'through faith and patience' that we inherit the promises (Heb. 6:12, cf. Heb. 11:39).

How then should we interpret the adverb 'soon'? We need to remember that, with the great events of Christ's coming, death, resurrection and exaltation, the new age had dawned (e.g. Luke 11:20; Acts 2:17; 1 Cor. 10:11; 2 Tim. 3:1; Heb. 1:2; 1 Pet. 1:20; 2 Pet. 3:3; 1 John 2:18), and that there is now nothing on God's eschatological calendar before the parousia. The parousia is the very next event on his timetable. 'It was, and still is, true to say', wrote Charles Cranfield, 'that the Parousia is at hand'.[36] Thus Christian disciples are characterized by faith, hope and love. Faith apprehends the *already* of Christ's achievement. Hope looks forward to the *not yet* of his salvation. And love characterizes our life *now* in the meanwhile. So 'soon' may be chronologically inexact; but it is theologically correct.

Fifthly, Jesus intended his followers to be both patient and vigilant, like farmers waiting for the rain (Jas. 5:7ff.) and like householders on their guard against thieves (Matt. 24:42–44. Cf. 1 Thess. 5:1–4; Rev. 3:3; 16:15).

In the context of the book of Revelation, Christ's repeated assurance 'Behold, I am coming soon' has a special significance. It indicates that, although he is coming to judge, he is also coming to complete the salvation of his people, coming as the heavenly bridegroom to claim his bride.

The wedding

We have seen that John develops three metaphors of eternal life, each illustrating in a different way the perfect relationship with God which awaits us in the end. The first was an architectural model, namely the gates, walls and foundations of the new Jerusalem, which needs no temple since the whole city is the inner sanctuary of God's presence. Next came the garden, paradise restored, with continuous access to the tree of life and the water of life. Thirdly, and much more personally than the city and the garden, John refers to the eternal union of Christ with his church in terms of the wedding of the bridegroom to his bride.

According to Jewish custom, a marriage took place in two stages, the betrothal and the wedding. The betrothal included an exchange of promises and gifts, and was regarded as being almost as binding as a marriage. The betrothed couple could be called 'husband' and 'wife', and if a separation took place, it would have to be a 'divorce' (see Matt. 1:18–19). The wedding followed some time after the betrothal and was essentially a public social occasion. It began with a festive procession, accompanied with music and dancing, in which the bridegroom and his friends went out to fetch his bride, who will have made herself ready. He would then bring her and her friends and relatives back to his home for the wedding feast, which might last as long as a week. During it the bride and bridegroom would receive a public blessing from their parents, and be escorted to the nuptial chamber where they would consummate their marriage in the intimacy of physical union.

The Bible betrays no embarrassment about sex and marriage. It is uninhibited in its use of the marriage metaphor to depict the covenant between God and Israel. Yahweh's love for Israel is portrayed, especially by Isaiah, Jeremiah, Ezekiel and Hosea, in bluntly physical terms. Speaking through Ezekiel to Israel, God said,

> 'You grew up and developed and became the most beautiful of jewels. Your breasts were formed and your hair grew, you who were naked and bare.
>
> 'Later I passed by, and when I looked at you and saw that you were old enough for love, I spread the corner of my garment over you and covered your nakedness. I gave you my solemn oath and entered into a covenant with you, declares the Sovereign Lord, and you became mine' (Ezek. 16:7b–8).

Jesus himself implied, in a daring statement, that he was his followers' bridegroom, so that while he was still with them it would be inappropriate for them to fast (Mark 2:19–20). Then Paul, though much maligned as a misogenist, developed the metaphor further. He pictured Christ as the bridegroom, who had loved his bride the church and sacrificed himself for her, in order that he might present her to himself unblemished and radiant (Eph. 5:25–27). When Paul added that 'this is a profound mystery', he seems to have meant that the 'one flesh' experience in marriage symbolizes the union of Christ with his church (Eph. 5:31–32).

It is this same vivid imagery that John picks up. He has already declared that 'the wedding of the Lamb has come', that 'his bride has made herself ready' and that 'those who are invited to the wedding supper of the Lamb' are blessed (19:7, 9). Mixing metaphors, John has also described the new Jerusalem as 'coming down out of heaven from God, prepared as a bride beautifully dressed for her husband' (21:2, 9).

But where is he? He is nowhere to be seen! It is not for the bride to fetch the bridegroom, but for the bridegroom to go and fetch his bride! She has made herself ready, beautifully dressed and bejewelled. Now, however, she can do no more than wait – except that she takes the liberty of expressing her longing for him: 'The Spirit and the bride say, "Come!"' (v. 17). For the supreme ministry of the Holy Spirit is to bear witness to Christ, and the supreme desire of the bride is to welcome her bridegroom.

It is thus that the book of Revelation leaves the church – waiting, hoping, expecting, longing, the bride eagerly looking for her bridegroom, clinging to his threefold promise that he is coming soon, and encouraged by others who echo her call 'Amen. Come, Lord Jesus' (v. 20; cf. 1 Cor. 16:22).

Meanwhile she is confident that his grace will be sufficient for her (v. 21), until the eternal wedding feast begins and she is united to her bridegroom for ever.

I think and hope that my readers will have been impressed by the picture of Christ that John has painted in the book of Revelation – the eternal Christ who never changes, but who challenges us to follow him today. We have seen him now supervising his churches on earth, now sharing God's throne in heaven, now controlling the course of history, now calling the world to repentance, now riding on a white horse to judgment, and now promising to come soon to claim and marry his bride.

CONCLUSION

One book in four parts

The four parts of this book are all explorations into the colourful identity of Jesus Christ. In Parts I and IV we have considered the witness of the New Testament to Christ, and in Parts II and III the witness of church history to him.

We have been aware throughout that there is a fundamental difference between these two witnesses, and so between the biblical and the historical parts of our study. For Christians believe that Scripture is the written revelation of God, so that it possesses a unique divine authority, whereas the pronouncements of church leaders are the fallible opinions of human beings, however distinguished they may have been.

This difference is deliberately expressed in the structure of the book. Parts II and III (Christ as interpreted by church history) are firmly held within the parameters of Parts I and IV (Christ as presented in the New Testament).

This same difference I have felt obliged to remember whenever I have submitted the cameos of Parts II and III to critical scrutiny. My evaluation of them has often been appreciative (especially in Part III), but has sometimes been negative (especially in Part II). For example, I have felt free to ask questions about, and even express criticism of, the monastic tradition, Christian mysticism, the feudal categories of Anselm's atonement doctrine, the Enlightenment's portrayal of Jesus as a merely human teacher, the Latin American Roman Catholic image of Jesus as the tragic victim, with no comparable emphasis on his resurrection triumph, the tendency of liberation theologians to confuse liberation with salvation, and the World Council of Churches' loss of the imperatives of the Christian mission.

But how dare I express such unfavourable criticisms? Is it not presumptuous to do so? My answer is that yes it would be insufferably arrogant if it were not that God has graciously given us in Scripture a criterion by which to judge all human movements and traditions. In consequence, we must keep returning humbly to the biblical portraits of Christ, and judge ours by them, since they alone are normative.

Inevitably, I have been selective in my choice of church leaders and their views of Christ. But we have no liberty to be selective in relation to the biblical models of Christ, accepting those we like and rejecting those we dislike. The 'pick and mix' mentality of our post-modern culture is incompatible with the Christian mind's view of Scripture. To be sure, it is legitimate to select biblical topics for specialist study (for example, Paul's view of this or Peter's view of that), but only in order to clarify what these particularities contribute to the total New Testament portrait of Christ. The goal of such studies is not to remain selective, but to become comprehensive.

Church history's extraordinary variety of Jesuses, some of them bearing little resemblance to the authentic Jesus of the apostolic witness, constitutes a healthy warning to us today. By all means let us add to Part III, for there is no limit to the ways in which the New Testament Jesus can influence and inspire us. But let us not add to Part II yet more Jesuses, unless we are confident that they can be justified by reference to the New Testament Jesus himself (Parts I and IV).

But how can we come to know the authentic Jesus for ourselves – this incomparable Christ who has no peers?

I end with a story which the late Donald Coggan, former Archbishop of Canterbury, sometimes told (although he was unable to remember its origin):[37]

> There was a sculptor once, so they say, who sculpted a statue of our Lord. And people came from great distances to see it – Christ in all his strength and tenderness. They would walk all round the statue, trying to grasp its splendour, looking at it now from this angle, now from that. Yet still its grandeur eluded them, until they consulted the sculptor himself. He would invariably reply 'There's only one angle from which this statue can be truly seen. *You must kneel.*'

NOTES

Introduction

[1] J. Pelikan, *Jesus through the Centuries* (Yale University Press, 1985), p. 1.

[2] P. Brierly (ed.), *UK Religious Handbook, Religious Trends* (Christian Research, 1999).

[3] From the prologue to his *Commentary on Isaiah*, quoted in Vatican II's *Dogmatic Constitution on Divine Revelation*, para. 25 *The Documents of Vatican II* (Geoffrey Chapman, 1966).

[4] Introduction to Erasmus' Greek New Testament (1516).

[5] *Lectures on Romans* in vol. 25 of *Luther's Works* (1515; ET Concordia, 1972). Gloss on Rom. 1:5 (p. 4) and Commentary on Rom. 10:6 (p. 405).

[6] S. C. Neill, *Christian Faith and Other Faiths* (OUP, 1961), p. 69.

[7] Sadhu Sundar Singh, *With and Without Christ* (Cassell, 1929), pp. 100–101.

[8] E. Stanley Jones, *The Christ of the Indian Road* (1925; Hodder & Stoughton, 1926), p. 64.

[9] P. W. Barnett, *Jesus and the Logic of History* (Apollos, 1997), p. 163.

[10] ET, 1910.

[11] 'I still believe', N. T. Wright has written, 'that the future of serious Jesus-research lies with what I have called the "Third Quest"'. (*Jesus and the Victory of God*, SPCK, 1996, p. 78.)

[12] R. W. Funk, R. W. Hoover and the Jesus Seminar, *The Five gospels* (Macmillan, 1993), p. 5.

Part I: The original Jesus

[1] O. Cullmann, *The Christology of the New Testament* (SCM, 2nd ed. 1963), p. 160.

[2] W. Barclay, *The Acts of the Apostles* (St Andrew's Press, 1953, 2nd ed. 1955), p. xiv.

[3] S. C. Neill and T. Wright, *The Interpretation of the New Testament 1861–1986* (1964; OUP, 2nd ed. 1988), p. 205.

[4] Tatian's *Diatessaron* may be found in Allan Menzies (ed.), *The Ante-Nicene Fathers* (Eerdmans, 1973), vol. X, pp. 33–138.

[5] Augustine's *Harmony of the gospels* may be found in Philip Schaff (ed.), *The Nicene and Post-Nicene Fathers* (Eerdmans, 1973), vol. VI, pp. 64–236.

[6] R. A. Burridge, *Four gospels, One Jesus?* (SPCK, 1994), p. 166.

[7] A. Schweitzer, *The Quest of the Historical Jesus: a critical study of its progress from Reimarus to Wrede* (1906; ET Adam and Charles Black, 1910).

[8] A. N. Wilson, *Paul: The Mind of the Apostle* (Pimlico, 1998), p. 18.

[9] W. D. Davies, *Paul and Rabbinic Judaism* (SPCK, 1948), p. 140.

[10] J. W. Fraser, *Jesus and Paul* (Marcham Manor Press, 1974), p. 192.

[11] D. Wenham, *Paul: Follower of Jesus or Founder of Christianity?* (Eerdmans, 1995).

[12] Ibid., p. 377.

[13] Ibid., p. 378.

[14] Ibid., p. 33.

[15] See J. Stott, *The Message of 1 Timothy and Titus* in The Bible Speaks Today series (IVP, 1996), pp. 21–34.

[16] This is so long as we may see the *ataktoi* in 2 Thess. 3 as playing truant because of what William Hendriksen has called their 'Parousia hysteria'. W. Hendriksen, *Exposition of I & II Thessalonians* (Baker, 1955), p. 107.

[17] Tertullian, *On the Resurrection of the Flesh,* ch. xxiv.

[18] A. T. Hanson, *Studies in the Pastoral Epistles* (SPCK, 1968), p. 110.

[19] Quoted by Eusebius, *Hist. Eccl.*, 2.23.46.

[20] A. M. Hunter, *The Unity of the New Testament* (SCM, 1943), p. 7.

[21] See also his *Introduction to the New Testament* (SPCK, 1945).

[22] E. Hoskyns and N. Davey, *The Riddle of the New Testament* (Faber & Faber, 1958), p. 12.

[23] Ibid., p. 170.

[24] O. Cullmann, *The Christology of the New Testament* (1957; ET SCM, 1959), p. 68.

[25] James D. G. Dunn, *Unity and Diversity in the New Testament* (SCM/Trinity Press International, 1977; 2nd ed. 1990), p. 32.

[26] Ibid., p. 371.

[27] C. F. D. Moule, *The Birth of the New Testament* (Adam & Charles Black, 1962; 3rd ed. 1981), p. 17.

[28] Neill and Wright, *The Interpretation of the New Testament 1861–1986*, p. 204.

[29] Ibid., p. 312.

[30] Ibid., p. 349.

Part II: The ecclesiastical Jesus

[1] Introductory note to the *First Apology* of Justin Martyr, in A. Roberts and J. Donaldson (eds.), *The Ante-Nicene Fathers* (1885; Eerdmans, n.d.), vol. I, p. 160.

[2] Martyr, *First Apology*, para. 137.

[3] Ibid., para. 44.

[4] Martyr, *Second Apology*, paras. 8, 13.

[5] Ibid., para. 13,

[6] Martyr, *First Apology*, para. 46.

[7] B. B. Warfield, *The Person and Work of Christ* (Presbyterian and Reformed, 1950), p. 215.

[8] W. Carus, *Memoirs of the Life of the Rev. Charles Simeon* (CUP, 1847), p. 600.

[9] J. Pelikan, *Jesus through the Centuries* (Yale University Press, 1985), p. 112.

[10] Dostoyevsky, *The Brothers Karamazov* (1880), Book 6, chapter 3.

[11] J. Denney, *The Atonement and the Modern Mind* (Hodder & Stoughton, 1903), p. 184.

[12] Anselm, *Cur Deus Homo* (1474; Williams & Norgate, 1863), i.xi.

[13] 'The good God will forgive me; that's his job, his speciality'. Quoted by S. C. Neill in *Christian Faith Today* (Penguin, 1955), p. 145.

[14] Anselm, *Cur Deus Homo*, i.xxi.

[15] Ibid., ii.xix.

[16] Ibid., i.xxx.

[17] Ibid., ii.vi.

[18] Ibid., ii.vii.

[19] Ibid., ii.xi.

[20] Quoted by M. H. Pope in *The Song of Songs*, in the Anchor Bible

Commentary (Doubleday, 1977), p. 19.

[21] *St Bernard's Sermons on the Canticle of Canticles* (Browne & Nelson, 1920), translated from the original Latin, in two volumes.

[22] Ibid., vol. I, p. xiv.

[23] Ibid., vol. I, p. 9.

[24] Ibid., vol. I, pp. 1–67.

[25] 'Bernard of Clairvaux' in J. Julian (ed.), *A Dictionary of Hymnology* (John Murray, rev. ed. 1907).

[26] Thomas à Kempis, *The Imitation of Christ*, trans. George F. Maine (1441; Collins, 1957), p. vii.

[27] Ibid., vol. III, p. 21.

[28] Ibid.

[29] Ibid.

[30] Ibid., vol. II, p. 7.

[31] Ibid., vol. II, p. 8.

[32] Ibid., vol. III, p. 5.

[33] Ibid., vol. I, p. 15.

[34] J. Stalker, *Imago Christi: the example of Jesus Christ* (Hodder & Stoughton, 1894), p. 27.

[35] Ibid., p. 24.

[36] Thomas à Kempis, *The Imitation of Christ*, vol. I, p. 8

[37] Ibid., vol. I, p. 10.

[38] Ibid., vol. III, p. 12.

[39] Ibid., vol. I, p. 20.

[40] Quoted in R. H. Bainton, *Here I Stand* (Hodder & Stoughton, 1951), p. 45.

[41] Quoted in J. Atkinson, *The Great Light: Luther and Reformation* (Paternoster, 1968), p. 16.

[42] This was Luther's so-called 'tower experience', because it took place in the tower of Wittenberg's Black Cloister. His account of it appeared first in his introduction to the Latin edition of his *Works* (1545).

[43] Martin Luther, *Commentary on the Epistle to the Galatians* (1535; James Clarke, 1953), p. 10.

[44] Ibid., p. 143.

[45] Ibid., p. 26.

[46] A. Schweitzer, *The Quest of The Historical Jesus: a critical study of its progress from Reimarus to Wrede* (1906; ET Adam & Charles Black, 1910), pp. 4–5.

[47] Ibid., p. 68.

[48] Ernest Renan, *The Life of Jesus* (1863; Watts/Rationalist Press Association, 1904), p. 12.

[49] Ibid., p. 148.

[50] Ibid., p. 144.

[51] Ibid., p. 119.

[52] Ibid., p. 121.

[53] Ibid., p. 141.

[54] Ibid., p. 142.

[55] Ibid., p. 151.

[56] Ibid., p. 148.

[57] Ibid., p. 151.

[58] Ibid.

[59] Dickenson W. Adams (ed.), *The Papers of Thomas Jefferson,* second series, *Jefferson's Extracts from the gospels* (Princeton University Press, 1983), p. 403.

[60] Ibid., p. 388.

[61] John A. Mackay, *The Other Spanish Christ* (SCM, 1932), p. 96.

[62] Ibid., p. 97.

[63] Ibid.

[64] Ibid.

[65] Ibid.

[66] Ibid., p. 102.

[67] Ibid., p. 110.

[68] Henri Nouwen, *Graçias: a Latin American Journal* (Orbis, 1983), p. 105.

[69] Ibid., p. 106.

[70] W. T. A. Barber, *Raymond Lull: the Illuminated Doctor: A study in medieval missions* (1903; Charles H. Kelly, n.d.). See also R. Lull, *The Book of the Lover and the Beloved: Proverbs xii* (Sheldon Press, 1978).

[71] Mackay, *The Other Spanish Christ*, p. 126.

[72] Ibid., p. 147.

[73] D. Martin, *Tongues of Fire: the explosion of Protestantism in Latin America* (Blackwell, 1990), p. 231.

[74] Ibid., p. 155.

[75] O. Costas, *The Church and its Mission: A Shattering Critique from the Third World* (Coverdale, 1974), p. 223.

[76] J. M. Bonino, *Revolutionary Theology Comes of Age* (SPCK,

1975). Its American title is *Doing Theology in a Revolutionary Situation* (Fortress, 1975).

[77] Ibid., p. xxiii.

[78] Ibid., p. 145.

[79] From the eleventh of his *Theses on Feuerbach*, to be found in Marx and Engels, *On Religion* (Schocker, 1964), p. 72.

[80] G. Gutierrez, *A Theology of Liberation: History, politics and salvation* (SCM, 1974), p. 21.

[81] For a survey of these, see C. Rowland (ed.), *The Cambridge Companion to Liberation Theology* (Cambridge University Press, 1999).

[82] Gutierrez, *A Theology of Liberation*, p. 15.

[83] Ibid., p. 13.

[84] J. A. Kirk, *Liberation Theology: an evangelical view from the Third World* (Marshall Morgan and Scott, 1979), p. 95.

[85] Papers by Bishop K. H. Ting, *Love Never Ends* (Yilin Press, 2000), pp. 198–199.

[86] Bonino, *Revolutionary Theology Comes of Age*, p. xv.

[87] J. Stott (ed.), *Making Christ Known: Historic mission documents from the Lausanne movement, 1974–1989* (Paternoster, 1996), pp. 24–27.

[88] H. J. Cadbury, *The Peril of Modernizing Jesus* (Macmillan, 1937), p. 1.

[89] Ibid., p. 48.

[90] Ibid., p. 42.

[91] Ibid.

[92] The Revd Dr N. T. Wright, Canon of Westminster. It was Tom Wright who suggested in the early 1980s that a 'Third Quest' for the historical Jesus had begun. These scholars all went to work as historians and were determined to set Jesus in his Jewish context. Among them were Anthony Harvey, *Jesus and the Constraints of History* (Duckworth, 1982), Marcus J. Borg, *Conflict, Holiness and Politics in the Teachings of Jesus* (Edwin Mellen Press, 1984), E. P. Sanders, *Jesus and Judaism* (SCM, 1985), Gerd Theissen, *The Shadow of the Galilean* (SCM, 1986), and James H. Charlesworth, *Jesus within Judaism* (SCM, 1988).

[93] N. T. Wright, *Jesus and the Victory of God* (SPCK, 1996), p. 609.

[94] N. T. Wright, *The Challenge of Jesus* (SPCK, 2000), p. 90. Cf. also ibid., p. 653.

[95] Wright, *The Challenge of Jesus*, p. 91.

[96] The *Shekinah* was the visible manifestation in the temple of God's immanent presence.

[97] Wright, *The Challenge of Jesus*, p. 84.

[98] Ibid., p. 92; Wright, *Jesus and the Victory of God*, p. 653.

[99] Wright, *Jesus and the Victory of God*, p. 361.

[100] Ibid., p. 151.

[101] J. R. Mott, *The Decisive Hour of Christian Missions* (Student Volunteer Movement, 1910), p. v.

[102] Ibid., p. 94.

[103] Ibid., p. 69.

[104] Ibid., p. 39.

[105] Ibid., p. 69.

[106] Ibid., pp. 100–101.

[107] Ibid., p. 106.

[108] Visser't Hooft, *No Other Name* (SCM, 1963), p. 95.

[109] *The International Bulletin of Missionary Research* (April, 1988). Published by the Overseas Ministries Study Centre, New Haven, Connecticut, USA.

[110] Stott (ed.), *Making Christ Known*, p. 16.

[111] C. S. Lewis, *An Experiment in Criticism* (CUP, 1961), p. 19.

[112] Quoted from 'A Credible Response to Secular Europe' in *The Evangelical Review of Theology*, June 1994.

Part III: The influential Jesus

[1] K. S. Latourette, *The History of the Expansion of Christianity* (Eyre and Spottiswoode, 1938), vol. I, p. 240.

[2] Ibid., vol. I, p. 241.

[3] See, for example, H. R. Niebuhr, *Christ and Culture* (Faber, 1952); P. Brooks, *The Influence of Jesus* (Macmillan, 1903) and W. B. Carpenter, *The Witness to the Influence of Christ* (Archibald Constable, 1905).

[4] Entitled *One Solitary Life*, but anonymous, this eloquent testimony has often been quoted, most recently by George Carey, Archbishop of Canterbury, in his millennium message *Jesus 2000*.

[5] M. A. Habig (ed.), *St Francis of Assisi: Writings and Early Biographies* (Herald, 1972), p. 301.

[6] Ibid., p. 301.

[7] Thomas of Celano, *The Second Life of St Francis* (J. M. Dent & Co., 1904), p. 521.

[8] G. K. Chesterton, *St Francis of Assisi* (1923; Hodder and Stoughton, 23rd ed. 1943).

[9] Ibid., p. 15.

[10] Ibid., p. 17.

[11] Ibid.

[12] Ibid., p. 189.

[13] W. Barclay, *The Gospel of Mark* in *The Daily Study Bible* (St Andrew Press, 2nd ed. 1956), p. 138.

[14] M. Hengel, *Property and Riches in the Early Church* (SCM, 1974), pp. 26–27.

[15] Justin Martyr, *Dialogue with Trypho a Jew*, ch. 88, in Thomas Falls (ed.), *Saint Justin Martyr, The Fathers of the Church* (Catholic Press of America, 1977), vol. 6, p. 290.

[16] A. Edersheim, *The Life and Times of Jesus the Messiah* (Longmans Green, 2nd and 3rd eds. 1886), vol. I, pp. 251–252.

[17] Quoted by Revd I. Boseley, *Christ the Carpenter, his trade and his teaching* (Arthur H. Stockwell, n.d.), pp. 52–53.

[18] Cf. Gal. 6:6; 1 Cor. 9:4ff.; 2 Cor. 11:7ff.; 12:13; 1 Thess. 2:9; 2 Thess. 3:8.

[19] See H. de Borchgrave, *A Journey into Christian Art* (Lion, 1999), pp. 173–174.

[20] F. A. Rees, *The Gospel in Great Pictures* (Arthur H. Stockwell, n.d.), pp. 19–21.

[21] *Jesus the Carpenter and his Teaching* by a Working Man (Mills and Boon, 1921), pp. 68–69.

[22] Boseley, *Christ the Carpenter*, p. 15.

[23] A. J. P. Taylor, *English History 1914–1945* (OUP, 1965), p. 142, n. 3.

[24] B. Holman, *Good Old George: The life of George Lansbury* (Lion, 1990), p. 181.

[25] Quoted in ibid., p. 174.

[26] Ibid., p. 177.

[27] Ibid., p. 18.

[28] Ibid., p. 172.

[29] Ibid., p. 187.

[30] Ibid., p. 177.

[31] J. Stalker, *The Life of Jesus Christ* (1879; T. & T. Clark, rev. ed.

1939), p. 21.

[32] J. Paterson Smyth, *A People's Life of Christ* (1921; Hodder & Stoughton, rev. ed. 1949), p. 59.

[33] Matt. 9:36; 14:14; 15:32; 20:34; Mark 6:34; 8:2; Luke 7:13.

[34] S. G. Browne, T. F. Davey and W. A. R. Thomson (eds.), *Heralds of Health: The saga of Christian medical initiatives* (CMF, 1985), p. 7. See also J. T. Aitken, H. W. C. Fuller and D. Johnson (eds.), *The Influence of Christians in Medicine* (CMF, 1984): 'To the Christians belongs the credit of raising the social status and treatment of sick and handicapped persons in early times', p. 170.

[35] Aitken, et al., *The Influence of Christians in Medicine*, pp. 9–10.

[36] A. D. Miller, *An Inn Called Welcome: The story of the Mission to Lepers, 1874–1917* (The Mission to Lepers, 1965), p. 5. See also M. A. Habig (ed.), 'St Francis of Assisi', in *English Omnibus of the Sources for the Life of St Francis* (SPCK & Herald, 3rd ed., 1972). See also Matt. 10:8 'Heal the sick, raise the dead, cleanse those who have leprosy …'

[37] Father Auguste Pamphile, *Life and Letters of Father Damien* (CTS, 1889). See also Browne, et al., *Heralds of Health*, pp. 156–157.

[38] Miller, *An Inn Called Welcome*, p. 11.

[39] From his introduction to a little pamphlet he wrote entitled *Lepers in India* (1874; John F. Shaw, 1882).

[40] P. Brand and P. Yancey, *The Gift of Pain* (Zondervan, 1993), p. 88.

[41] See D. Clarke Wilson, *Ten Fingers for God: Paul Brand's biography* (Hodder and Stoughton, 1966).

[42] Brand and Yancey, *The Gift of Pain*, p. 323.

[43] Leo Tolstoy, *A Confession, The Gospel in Brief* and *What I Believe*, 1882–4 (World Classics, No. 229, Oxford University Press, new ed. 1940), pp. 315–319.

[44] Ibid., p. 323.

[45] Ibid., p. 406.

[46] Quotations from G. Woodstock, *Gandhi* (Fontana, 1972), pp. 24, 39, 67 and 85–86.

[47] M. K. Gandhi, *What Jesus Means to Me* (Ahmedabad: Navajivan Publishing House, 1959), p. 6.

[48] J. Ellul, *Violence* (SCM, 1970), p. 15.

[49] Martin Luther King, Jr, *Strength to love* (1963; Fontana, 1969), pp. 47–55.

[50] W. B. Ryan, *Infanticide, its law, prevalence, prevention and history* (Churchill, 1862), p. 198. See also Plato's *Republic* (OUP, 1993), V. 460 and Aristotle's teaching about the secret destruction and disposal of weak or deformed babies, as documented by I. Smale in *A History of Children* (Silver Fish Publishing, 1998), vol. I, p. 80.

[51] G. Milligan, *Selections from the Greek Papyri* (Cambridge University Press, 1910), p. 32.

[52] W. H. S. Jones, *The Doctor's Oath: an Essay in the History of Medicine* (Cambridge University Press, 1924), quoted by N. M. de S. Cameron in *The New Medicine: Life and Death after Hippocrates* (Crossway Books, 1991), p. 35.

[53] Tertullian's *Apology*, Chapter IX, in Allan Menzies (ed.), *The Ante-Nicene Fathers* (Eerdmans, 1973), vol. 3, p. 25.

[54] A. E. Williams, *Barnardo of Stepney: the father of nobody's children* (George Allen and Unwin, 1943), p. 7.

[55] Ibid., p. 5.

[56] Ibid., pp. 72–73.

[57] Ibid., p. 106.

[58] Ibid., p. 191.

[59] Mrs Barnardo and J. Marchant, *The Memoirs of the Late Dr Barnardo* (Hodder and Stoughton, 1907), pp. 64–65.

[60] Ibid., p. 273.

[61] E.g. Gen. 18:4; 19:2; 24:32; 43:24; Judg. 19:21 and Luke 7:44.

[62] E.g. 1 Sam. 25:41; John 13:1–17; 1 Tim. 5:10.

[63] See G. A. Frank Knight, 'Feet-washing', in James Hastings (ed.), *Dictionary of Religion and Ethics* (T. & T. Clark, 1904), vol. 5.

[64] B . F. Westcott, *The Gospel According to St John* (Murray, 1892), p. 192.

[65] See P. A. Wright, *The Pictorial History of the Royal Maundy* (Pitkin Pictorials, 1966).

[66] Calvin, *The Gospel according to St John 11–21* (Oliver & Boyd, 1961), p. 60, comment on John 13:14 .

[67] C. W. Hall, *Samuel Logan Brengle: Portrait of a Prophet* (Salvation Army, 1933), p. 89. See also Richard Collier, *The General Next to God* (Collins, 1965), p. 72.

[68] W. Clark, *Samuel Logan Brengle: Teacher of Holiness* (Hodder and Stoughton, 1980), pp. 18, 156.

[69] C. W. Colson, *Born Again* (Hodder and Stoughton, 1976), pp. 278–279.

[70] W. Axling, *Kagawa* (SCM, 1932), p. 51.

[71] C. J. Davey, *Kagawa of Japan* (Epworth, 1960), p. 95.

[72] Ibid., pp. 125–126.

[73] Toyohiko Kagawa, *Meditations on the Cross* (SCM, 1936), p. 44.

[74] Ibid., p. 104.

[75] Ibid., p. 105.

[76] Ibid., p. 90.

[77] Ibid., pp. ix and 15.

[78] Ibid., p. 95.

[79] Toyohiko Kagawa, *Christ and Japan* (SCM, 1934), pp. 99–100, 108, 113.

[80] Kagawa, *Meditations on the Cross*, p. 95.

[81] J. Eareckson Tada, *Joni* (Zondervan, 1976).

[82] Quoted by P. Yancey in *Where is God When it Hurts?* (Zondervan, 1977), p. 120.

[83] J. Eareckson Tada, *Heaven Your Real Home* (Zondervan, 1995), p. 53.

[84] W. Temple, *Nature, Man, and God* (Macmillan, 1934), p. 478.

[85] Eareckson Tada, *Heaven Your Real Home*, p. 70.

[86] Ibid., p. 51.

[87] C. E. Padwick, *Henry Martyn* (IVP, 1922), p. 177.

[88] The narrative of their romance is told by D. Bentley-Taylor in *My Love Must Wait: the story of Henry Martyn* (IVP, 1975).

[89] J. R. C. Martyn, *Henry Martyn (1781–1812), scholar and missionary to India and Persia: a biography*, Studies in the History of Missions, vol. 16 (Edwin Mellen Press, 1999), p. 108.

[90] Padwick, *Henry Martyn*, p. 146.

[91] Martyn, *Henry Martyn*, p. 108.

[92] Padwick, *Henry Martyn*, p. 168.

[93] Martyn, *Henry Martyn*, p. 128.

[94] L. Newbigin, *The Household of God: lectures on the nature of the church* (1953; SCM, 1964), p. 25.

[95] D. M. Paton (ed.), *The Ministry of the Spirit: selected writings of Roland Allen* (World Dominion Press, 1960), p. x.

[96] R. Allen, *Missionary Methods: St Paul's or Ours?* (1912; World Dominion Press, rev. ed., 1927). His other famous book was *The Spontaneous Expansion of the Church, and the causes which hinder it*

(1927; World Dominion Press, 2nd ed., 1949).

[97] Allen, *Missionary Methods*, p. 3.

[98] Ibid., p. 115.

[99] Ibid., p. 109.

[100] Ibid., pp. 184–185.

[101] Ibid., p. 185.

[102] See e.g. Acts 14:22–23.

[103] Allen, *Missionary Methods*, p. 194.

[104] Paton (ed.), *The Ministry of the Spirit*, p. xv.

[105] Ibid., p. xvi.

[106] R. Allen, *Pentecost and the World: the revelation of the Holy Spirit in the Acts of the Apostles* (OUP, 1917), pp. 36, 88.

[107] John Pollock, *Shaftesbury, The Poor Man's Earl* (Hodder and Stoughton, 1986), p. 23.

[108] Edwin Hodder, *The Life and Work of the Seventh Earl of Shaftesbury KG*, 3 vols. (Cassell, 1887), vol. 3, pp. 2–3.

[109] Ibid., p. 8.

[110] Ibid., p. 10.

[111] Ibid., p. 12.

[112] Ibid., p. 10.

[113] Ibid.

[114] Pollock, *Shaftesbury*, p. 172.

[115] Quoted by G. T. Manley, *The Return of Christ* (IVF, 1960), p. 20.

[116] R. Isaac and S. Wilberforce, *The Life of William Wilberforce* (London: John Murray, 1838), vol. 1, p. 149.

[117] W. Wilberforce, *Real Christianity*, abridged and edited by J. M. Houston (1829; Multnomah Press, 1982), p. 89.

[118] Ibid., p. 85.

[119] Ibid., p. 3.

[120] Ibid., p. 103.

[121] G. R. Balleine, *A History of the Evangelical Party in the Church of England* (1908; Church Book Room Press, 1951), p. 118.

[122] J. C. Pollock, *Wilberforce* (Lion, 1977), p. 27.

[123] Ibid., p. 56.

[124] K. Heasman, *Evangelicals in Action: an appraisal of their social work in the Victoria era* (Geoffrey Bles, 1962), p. 285.

[125] R. C. K. Ensor, *England 1870–1914* (OUP, 1936), pp. 137–138.

[126] M. Hennell, *John Venn and the Clapham Sect* (Lutterworth Press,

1958), p. 207.

[127] Ibid.

[128] K. S. Latourette, *A History of the Expansion of Christianity*, 7 vols. (Eyre and Spottiswoode, 1938–47), vol. 7, pp. 503–504.

[129] S. C. Neill and N. T. Wright, *The Interpretation of the New Testament 1861–1986* (1964; OUP, 2nd ed. 1988), p. 19.

Part IV: The eternal Jesus

[1] H. Lindsey, *The 1980s: Countdown to Armageddon* (1981; Marshall Morgan & Scott, 1983), p. 104.

[2] Ibid., p. 8.

[3] R. Bauckham, *The Climax of Prophecy: Studies on the Book of Revelation* (T. & T. Clark, 1993), p. ix.

[4] H. B. Swete, *The Apocalypse of St John* (Macmillan, 1906), p. xcii.

[5] G. K. Beale, *The Book of Revelation*, in *The New International Greek Testament Commentary* (Eerdmans/Paternoster, 1999), p. 108.

[6] 'Death and hades' are frequently bracketed in the book of Revelation, 'death' being the event of dying and 'hades' the abode of the dead.

[7] *The Epistle of Ignatius to the Ephesians*, ch. 6.

[8] *The Martyrdom of Polycarp*, chs. 9–16 from B. J. Kidd (ed.), *Documents Illustrative of the History of the Church* (SPCK, 1938), vol. I, pp. 68–71.

[9] C. J. Hemer, *The Letters to the Seven Churches of Asia in their local setting* (JSOT Press, 1986), p. 87, cf. p. 104.

[10] Beale, *Revelation*, p. 226.

[11] W. M. Ramsay, *The Letters to the Seven Churches of Asia* (Hodder & Stoughton, 1904), pp. 391–392.

[12] Beale lists fourteen resemblances between Dan. 7 and Rev. 4 in *Revelation*, p. 313ff.

[13] Swete, *Apocalypse*, p. 70. Or perhaps they were cherubim. See Ezek. 10:20.

[14] Beale describes it as 'a book containing God's plan of judgment and redemption', in *Revelation*, p. 340.

[15] See for example G. Aulen, *Christus Victor* (1930; SPCK, 1931).

[16] G. E. Ladd, *A Commentary on the Revelation of John* (Eerdmans, 1972), p. 106.

[17] B. M. Metzger, *Breaking the Code: understanding the book of Revelation* (Abingdon, 1993), p. 64.

[18] Exod. 7:14ff. = Rev. 8:8; Exod. 9:13ff. = Rev. 8:7; Exod. 10:1ff. = Rev. 9:1ff.; and Exod. 10:21ff. = Rev. 8:12.

[19] T. F. Torrance, *The Apocalypse Today* (James Clarke, 1960), p. 75.

[20] Bauckham, *Climax of Prophecy*, p. 185.

[21] Beale, *Revelation*, p. 722.

[22] S. R. F. Price, *Rituals and Power: the Roman imperial cult in Asia Minor* (CUP, 1984), pp. 54–58, 197–198.

[23] Dio Cassius, *Roman History*, edited by T. E. Page (William Heinemann Ltd, n.d.), Book 67, section 4.

[24] Suetonius, *Domitian* 13, edited by Brian Jones (Bristol Classical Press, 1995).

[25] Kidd (ed.), *Documents Illustrative of the History of the Church*, vol. I, pp. 38–39.

[26] Ladd, *Commentary on the Revelation of John*, p. 202.

[27] L. Morris, *The Revelation of St John* (Tyndale Press, 1969), p. 186.

[28] = Luke 12:39–40. Paul also used the metaphor (1 Thess. 5:2, 4), and so did Peter (2 Pet. 3:10), so that it seems to have been common currency in the early church.

[29] P. Barnett, *Apocalypse Now and Then* (Anglican Information Ovice, 1989), p. 131.

[30] Bauckham, *Climax of Prophecy*, p. 343.

[31] Barnet, *Apocalypse Now and Then*, p. 138.

[32] Bauckham, *Climax of Prophecy*, p. 371.

[33] Barnett, *Apocalypse Now and Then*, p. 143.

[34] Metzger, *Breaking the Code*, p. 95.

[35] Ibid., p. 101.

[36] C. E. B. Cranfield, *The Gospel According to St Mark: an introduction and commentary* (CUP, 1966), p. 408.

[37] When I wrote to Lord Coggan in October 1999, asking for permission to use this story, he replied that some time back he had had a stroke, which had left him 'staggering, stammering and stuttering'. But his handwriting was perfectly legible, and he sounded in good spirits. He died in June 2000.